Issues in Space

Series Editors

Stacey Henderson, Adelaide Law School, The University of Adelaide,
Adelaide, SA, Australia

Melissa de Zwart, Adelaide Law School, The University of Adelaide,
Adelaide, SA, Australia

The 'Issues in Space' series brings together a broad range of authors and disciplines to promote a diversity of views, perspectives, and critical approaches in the space sector. This series is designed to influence the development of the domestic and global space industry while it is in its formative stage, rather than trying to redress imbalances once they are entrenched in the industry.

This series aims to particularly promote the work of authors from traditionally marginalised groups, including women, early career researchers, and others; voices that are important in discussions of the development of the space industry. The scope of this series covers a broad range of key areas and disciplines that will be explored. Fundamental areas such as: outer space, space law, space policy, space regulation, space archaeology, space ethics, space situational awareness, space traffic management, military activities in space, commercial space, dispute resolution for space activities, space courts, space security, sustained human presence in space, space resource utilisation, space governance, space settlement, armed conflict in space, space resource utilisation, space manufacturing, space tourism, private actors in space, and space mining.

Issues in Space is an interdisciplinary series in that it is devoted to space scholarship but with the added unique focus on the promotion of diversity of authors, disciplines and opinions.

Melissa de Zwart • Stacey Henderson
John Culton • Deborah Turnbull
Amit Srivastava

Editors

Human Uses of Outer Space

Return to the Moon

 Springer

Editors
Melissa de Zwart
College of Business, Government and Law
Flinders University
Bedford Park, SA, Australia

Stacey Henderson
College of Business, Government and Law
Flinders University
Bedford Park, SA, Australia

John Culton
Andy Thomas Centre for Space Resources
University of Adelaide
Adelaide, SA, Australia

Deborah Turnbull
School of Psychology
University of Adelaide
Adelaide, SA, Australia

Amit Srivastava
School of Architecture and Built
Environment
University of Adelaide
Adelaide, SA, Australia

ISSN 2662-902X   ISSN 2662-9038   (electronic)
Issues in Space
ISBN 978-981-19-9464-7   ISBN 978-981-19-9462-3   (eBook)
https://doi.org/10.1007/978-981-19-9462-3

This Springer imprint is published by the registered company Springer Nature Singapore Pte Ltd.
The registered company address is: 152 Beach Road, #21-01/04 Gateway East, Singapore 189721, Singapore

Contents

Contributors

Marco Aliberti European Space Policy Institute, Vienna, Austria

Adam James Carter School of Psychology, The University of Adelaide, Adelaide, SA, Australia

Nigel J. Cook School of Civil, Environmental and Mining Engineering, The University of Adelaide, Adelaide, SA, Australia

John Culton Andy Thomas Centre for Space Resources, The University of Adelaide, Adelaide, SA, Australia

Vinicius Guedes Gonçalves de Oliveira College of Business, Government and Law, Flinders University, Adelaide, SA, Australia

Francesco de Zwart Adelaide Law School, The University of Adelaide, Adelaide, SA, Australia

Melissa de Zwart College of Business, Government and Law, Flinders University, Adelaide, SA, Australia

Anastasia Ejova School of Psychology, Faculty of Health and Medical Sciences, The University of Adelaide, North Terrace Campus, Adelaide, SA, Australia

Justin Fidock Intelligence, Surveillance and Space Division, Defence Science and Technology Group, Department of Defence, Fairbairn, Canberra, Australia

Stacey Henderson College of Business, Government and Law, Flinders University, Adelaide, SA, Australia

Volker Hessel School of Chemical Engineering and Advanced Materials, The University of Adelaide, Adelaide, SA, Australia

Manuel Varon Hoyos School of Chemical Engineering and Advanced Materials, The University of Adelaide, Adelaide, SA, Australia

Heidi Long School of Psychology, The University of Adelaide, Adelaide, SA, Australia

Anna Ma-Wyatt School of Psychology, The University of Adelaide, Adelaide, SA, Australia
CNRS IRL CROSSING, Adelaide, SA, Australia

Rachel Neef Adelaide Law School, The University of Adelaide, Adelaide, SA, Australia

Jessica O'Rielly School of Psychology, The University of Adelaide, Adelaide, SA, Australia

Melissa Oxlad School of Psychology, The University of Adelaide, Adelaide, SA, Australia

Rodrigo Praino College of Business, Government and Law, Flinders University, Adelaide, SA, Australia

Rachel A. Searston School of Psychology, Faculty of Health and Medical Sciences, The University of Adelaide, North Terrace Campus, Adelaide, SA, Australia

Carolyn Semmler School of Psychology, Faculty of Health and Medical Sciences, The University of Adelaide, North Terrace Campus, Adelaide, SA, Australia

Rachel Stephens School of Psychology, Faculty of Health and Medical Sciences, The University of Adelaide, North Terrace Campus, Adelaide, SA, Australia

Sharni Whitburn School of Psychology, The University of Adelaide, Adelaide, SA, Australia

Chapter 1
Returning Humans to the Moon

Stacey Henderson and Melissa de Zwart

Abstract Now that it has become likely that more humans will need to live and work in space for sustained periods of time, it is essential that we consider matters beyond the engineering questions of how we go to space to the broader questions of how we will live when we get there. What will we need? What will the effects of sustained living in space be for us, emotionally, cognitively, physically, and should we consider the impact we will have on the environment to which we are travelling? This chapter introduces the diverse yet complementary set of expertise contained in this book, which mirrors the way we will have to work together as teams of diverse experts in space to maximise mission success.

1.1 Introduction

There are currently multiple space programs around the world aiming to establish permanent human habitats in outer space, including on the Moon. Whilst there has been sustained human presence in space in Low Earth Orbit since 2000, the issues to be encountered by those travelling to the Moon and beyond, will be even more complex. With the Artemis missions, the US and its partners plan to create the Lunar Gateway, to be followed by the landing of the first woman and next man on the Moon (NASA, 2021). The Artemis project will then form the basis of planned, sustained human missions to Mars. Russia and China have also announced their intentions to establish a permanent base on the Moon and have commenced the deployment of modules which will form part of this project (Wall, 2022). Further, commercial operators have also indicated their intentions to create sustained human presence in Low Earth Orbit, on the Moon and even Mars.

The potential for the presence of multiple bases on the Moon, operated by competing or collaborating entities, including state and commercial enterprises, will

S. Henderson (✉) · M. de Zwart
College of Business, Government and Law, Flinders University, Adelaide, SA, Australia
e-mail: stacey.henderson@flinders.edu.au

M. de Zwart et al. (eds.), *Human Uses of Outer Space*, Issues in Space, https://doi.org/10.1007/978-981-19-9462-3_1

1

generate new challenges for human survival and mission success. These challenges go far beyond the technical and require consideration of interdisciplinary perspectives to succeed. It is essential that we consider matters beyond the engineering questions of how we go to space and start considering the broader questions of how we will live there. Who are the best people to live in space and how should they be chosen? What will we need to survive and thrive in space? What will the effects of sustained living in space be for us - emotionally, cognitively, physically? How can law provide protection for humans living in space? Should we consider the impact that we will have on the environment to which we are travelling? The chapters in this book begin to explore some of these questions.

1.2   Returning Humans to the Moon…to Stay

This book contains chapters considering issues relating to the humans involved, commercial actors, and geopolitical challenges and conflict arising in the context of sustained human presence in space.

The characteristics of the individuals chosen to go to space will have a significant impact on mission success, perhaps more so than the technology sending them there. In *Optimising Mission Success: A Holistic Approach to Selecting the Best People to Travel to Space*, Melissa Oxlad, Sharni Whitburn, and Adam Carter consider selection of people with the "right stuff" to be astronauts from the perspective of psychology. They note that views about what constitutes the "right stuff" to be an astronaut have evolved over time, from a focus on purely technical expertise to a broader, holistic approach that considers an individual's technical, physical, psychological, and social characteristics. They describe each of these selection domains and suggest processes to facilitate the evaluation and selection of the best people to travel to space to optimise mission outcomes.

The effect of long-term space habitation on mental processing and cognitive function is a key planning consideration for deep space habitation. In *Clear Thinking in Deep Space: A Guide by Cognitive Scientists*, Anastasia Ejova, Rachel Searston, Rachel Stephens, and Carolyn Semmler expand on the psychological considerations that were raised in the previous chapter. They consider how individuals chosen to go into space can be trained to perform mission critical tasks in space. They then consider ongoing monitoring of cognitive performance during missions and how high-level thinking can be sustained, and errors prevented, over extended durations in space.

In *The Challenges and Opportunities of Human-Robot Interaction for Deep Space Habitation*, Anna Ma-Wyatt, Justin Fidock, Jessica O'Rielly, Heidi Long, and John Culton explore the interactions between humans and robots that will be a key part of activities off-Earth. The interactions between humans and robots in space will be cooperative in complex environments, and will include interactions with robotic vehicles, either remotely operated or supervised by a human. As the authors note, sustained human activity in space will bring with it new challenges for near real-time and delayed supervisory control for complex tasks in the harsh environment of space. Among these challenges are trust and maintaining situational awareness, both of which will be crucial for mission success. Drawing upon recent results from studies of human-robot interaction over extended periods of time for remote teams, including the cognitive implications of human-robot teaming, the chapter discusses the potential implications for crewing for long term deep space habitation.

The risk of both forward and backward contamination has been recognized since the dawn of space exploration. The discovery of bacteria on the International Space Station indicates that life can exist in the harshest of space conditions. In *Legal and Ethical Planetary Protection Frameworks for Crewed Missions*, Melissa de Zwart, Stacey Henderson, and Rachel Neef, explore the potential for humans to contaminate and alter the natural environment of the Moon or Mars, and the potential for return of harmful contamination to Earth. They argue that there is a need to move beyond a simply scientific approach to answering questions about harmful contamination, to a broader ethical consideration about why we are going to space, and what impact sustained human presence in space might have on the Moon, Mars, and humanity.

The next chapter in the book explores commercial and economic activities in cis-lunar space. In *Moon Resources and a Proposition for Supply Chains*, Manuel Varon Hoyos, Nigel Cook, and Volker Hessel, consider trade and commerce in space processing which will require the establishment of a supply chain. The authors discuss the challenges posed by the unique environmental conditions of space to production and supply chains, and the logistical obstacles involved in transporting goods manufactured in space to customers. They note that there is a technological leap needed before a space economy and supply chain can be established and become profitable.

Francesco de Zwart, Stacey Henderson, and John Culton take the consideration of commercial space activities one step further in their chapter, *CSR/ESG in Commercial Space Operations and the Artemis Accords*. They explore whether there is a need for corporate social responsibility in space and what that might mean for large commercial space actors. The authors argue that corporate social responsibility and environment social governance areas, activities, principles, and disclosures risk being displaced in commercial space activities with unintended consequences for the corporate shareholder purpose of corporate actors.

In *Back to the Moon: cooperation and conflict*, Marco Aliberti, Vinicius Guedes Gonçalves de Olivera, and Rodrigo Praino, observe that forthcoming lunar exploration activities appear to feature a competitive approach. This may lead to a progressive polarization of the international space community around two separate, and potentially conflicting, blocs. The authors discuss the growing competition dynamics between different space powers in the context of returning humans to the Moon. This chapter also analyses issues ranging from the creation of safety zones on the surface of the Moon and the protection of cultural sites, to the use and exploitation of its resources, from a policy perspective.

1.3 Conclusions

This book takes a unique interdisciplinary approach to the planned return of humans to the Moon. Bringing together a diverse, yet complementary, set of expertise, the book consciously brings those different experts together in jointly authored chapters, mirroring the way we will have to work together as teams of diverse experts in space. It creates interwoven chapters co-written by various teams of psychologists, lawyers, engineers, and policy experts. In doing so, this book aims to fill a gap in the area of space studies which tends to focus on narrow, discipline specific issues. The book stresses the needs of the human in the hostile environment of space and aims to provide a launchpad for further work in this area.

References

NASA (National Aeronautics and Space Administration). (2021). Artemis. https://www.nasa.gov/specials/artemis/

Wall, M. (2022). Not just Artemis: China and Russia plan to put boots on the Moon, too. Space.com. https://www.space.com/china-russia-moon-base-ilrs

Chapter 2
Optimising Mission Success: A Holistic Approach to Selecting the Best People to Travel to Space

Melissa Oxlad, Sharni Whitburn, and Adam James Carter

Abstract Have you ever wanted to travel to space? How do you know if you have the characteristics needed for personal, crew and mission success? Since the early days of space exploration, space agencies have focused on choosing people with the "right stuff" to be astronauts. Initially, this meant selecting those with the relevant technical expertise. However, over time, especially now, as we embark on longer missions and potential space habitation, views about what constitutes the "right stuff" have broadened. While technical expertise remains important, a holistic approach that considers physical, psychological and social characteristics is needed. People's bodies must be able to endure the rigours of space flight and microgravity-related impacts. People must have suitable personalities and be able to cope with isolation and boredom. Finally, people must be culturally competent and have excellent interpersonal skills to cope with living with a small group of people in a confined space and to fulfil assigned roles and offer or respond to sound leadership. Here we describe each of the four domains – technical expertise and physical, psychological and social characteristics – to select the best people to travel to space to optimise positive outcomes. We also discuss how mission purpose and length influences the importance of each domain; needs differ for space tourists, astronauts and those on deep-space missions or set for space habitation. At the end of this chapter, readers will clearly understand key selection domains and processes and can assess their suitability for space travel.

2.1 Introduction

For many, space is the last frontier to conquer. The stars capture our attention at night and arouse our curiosity about what else may lay beyond our atmosphere. The first space race between the United States (U.S.) and Russia in the early 1960s

M. Oxlad (✉) · S. Whitburn · A. J. Carter
School of Psychology, The University of Adelaide, Adelaide, SA, Australia
e-mail: melissa.oxlad@adelaide.edu.au

© The Author(s), under exclusive license to Springer Nature Singapore Pte Ltd. 2023
M. de Zwart et al. (eds.), *Human Uses of Outer Space*, Issues in Space, https://doi.org/10.1007/978-981-19-9462-3_2

5

captivated the world and saw a whole generation of young people dare to dream about becoming an astronaut. However, while dreams should be nurtured, aside from financial constraints, there are many other reasons why space travel, particularly long-term space travel or habitation, can only be achieved by a select group.

From the commencement of space travel, space agencies sought to choose people who had the "right stuff" for their programs. People with the "right stuff" were those with specific skills and attributes deemed most suitable to manage the demands of such an important role. While the focus has traditionally been on selecting people with the correct technical expertise and abilities, particularly during the early years of space exploration, other factors such as crew compatibility and harmony have long been recognised as necessary for longer space missions (Nicholas & Foushee, 1990). In the past, focusing on technical expertise was a successful strategy, as those selected were a homogenous group of people, often with pilot and/or military experience, who undertook relatively short missions. However, as space exploration continues to evolve, increased crew diversity may impact mission success.

Potential crew will be drawn from a larger pool of applicants. Globally, the number of nations with one or more space agencies or organisations has increased, with many countries currently exploring human-crewed spaceflight and potential space habitation. Despite this increased interest in space exploration, historically, with the exception of the National Aeronautics and Space Administration (NASA), who has selected approximately 22 groups of astronauts (Blodgett, 2022a, January 6), the selection of astronauts has been relatively infrequent. For example, the European Space Agency (ESA) has only called for applications three times since 1978 (ESA, 2021a), and Russia only had its first competitive call for cosmonauts in 2012 (previously, selected cosmonauts were only pilots in peak physical health; Space Safety Magazine, 2016).

As an illustration of the growing interest in space travel, in its most recent call for astronauts, NASA had more than 12,000 applicants between March 2nd and March 31st 2020 (Blodgett, 2022a, January 6). Similarly, in their March 2021 call, the ESA received more than 23,000 applications (ESA, 2022), a substantial increase from their 2008 call, which resulted in 8413 applications (ESA, 2021b). In addition, private companies such as SpaceX offer commercial flights to Earth and Lunar orbit and the International Space Station (ISS), and members of the public are increasingly interested in travelling to space with companies such as Blue Origin and Virgin Galactic.

Additionally, potential crew will come from gender and culturally diverse backgrounds and, as well as astronauts and payload specialists (typically people who travel to space to use their specific expertise to undertake or oversee mission experiments), will increasingly include members of the public with minimal training. Also, people will be in space for varying amounts of time. For example, space tourists (civilians who pay to travel to space for a luxury life experience without the work responsibilities of astronauts) will typically undertake relatively brief journeys, while deep-space travellers (those whose missions are beyond the earth-moon orbit, including travel to Mars) will embark on much longer missions than previously recorded. Therefore, as space travel and habitation expand and more people seek to travel to space, there is a clear need to reassess how to select the best people to achieve safe and optimal outcomes.

Several questions, such as the following, must be considered. First, what should be the selection criteria for space travel? How, if at all, should selection criteria and processes differ for people wanting to be space tourists compared to those taking longer journeys to the ISS, the Moon or Mars? Finally, which people are best suited for successful space habitation?

Many of these questions will take time and further research to answer accurately, but past experience and what we know about people's physical, psychological and social needs and capabilities can inform initial perspectives. Therefore, when making recommendations about the best candidates for selection, it is best to take a holistic approach. First, as a minimum requirement, it is essential that those travelling, including crew and payload specialists, have the necessary technical expertise to accurately and safely perform their duties. The degree of technical expertise required will vary according to the nature and timing of the mission. In addition to their technical expertise, people must possess optimal physical, psychological and social characteristics, capabilities and health.

For example, physically, people's bodies need to successfully endure the rigours of space flight and the changes that occur due to being in a microgravity environment (where people and objects appear to be weightless). Psychologically, people must have the personality characteristics to succeed, be motivated and resilient, and able to cope with isolation, monotony and living in confined space. Socially, people must have effective interpersonal skills to cope with living with a small group of others in a confined space for an extended period. They must also have cultural sensitivity and competence to interact respectfully with diverse crew members from diverse backgrounds, including those with physical disabilities, and be able to fulfil any assigned roles and offer or respond to sound leadership. The best people to travel to space for extended periods must have strengths in all four domains – technical, physical, psychological and social capabilities (Fig. 2.1). Detailed information about each of these domains is provided below. At the same time, it should be acknowledged that, even with the best selection process based on high-quality evidence and past experience, individual differences need to be considered.

The exact steps and time needed for astronaut selection vary by space agency. For NASA, the approximately 18-month process usually involves:

1. call for applications;
2. potential astronauts submit an application;
3. applications reviewed to identify highly-qualified applicants;
4. possibly contacting highly-qualified applicants' referees for more information;
5. reviewing applications of highly-qualified applicants to select possible interviewees;
6. bringing a select group of highly-qualified applicants to the Johnson Space Center to undertake activities and an initial interview;
7. a second round of activities and interview at Johnson Space Center;
8. selection and announcement of astronaut candidates;

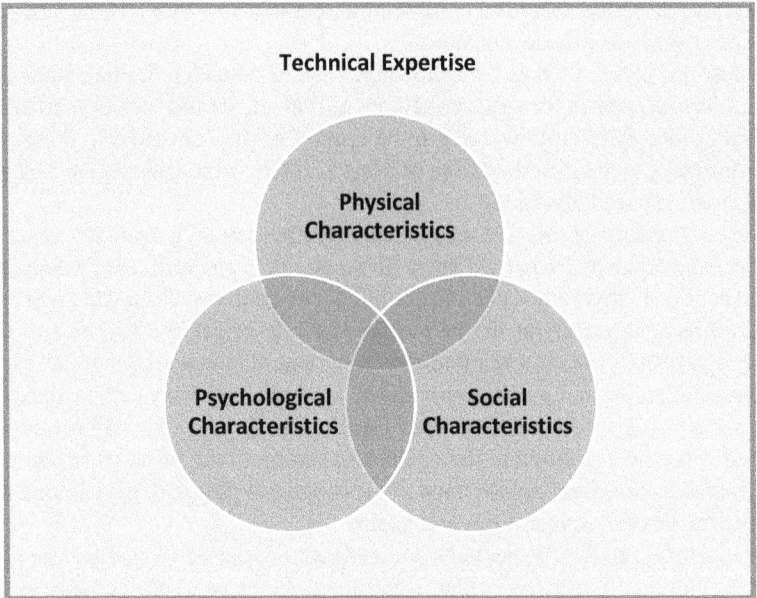

Fig. 2.1 Domains to consider in selecting the best people for space travel

9. finally, the selected candidates report to the Johnson Space Center (Blodgett, 2021, September 24).

Similarly, the ESA process, taking more than a year to complete, involves:

1. call for applications;
2. potential astronauts submitting an application;
3. screening (additional medical screening for applicants with a physical disability);
4. initial testing;
5. assessment center;
6. medical tests (medical review of the disability for applicants with a physical disability);
7. a panel interview;
8. a final interview (ESA, 2021a).

Table 2.1 summarises the key selection criteria applied by different space agencies.

Importantly, initial selection does not guarantee that a person will become an astronaut. Following initial selection, people become 'astronaut candidates' and must undergo further rigorous training and evaluation, which may take years. Successful completion of the training is required to become an astronaut and then astronauts must await assignment to a relevant mission, requiring further formal mission training once assigned.

Table 2.1 Comparisons of space selection requirements

Selection criteria	U.S.[a]	Europe[b]	Russia[c]	China[d]
Citizenship	Must be a U.S. citizen or have U.S. dual citizenship	Any citizen from Austria, Belgium, the Czech Republic, Denmark, Estonia, Finland, France, Germany, Greece, Hungary, Ireland, Italy, Latvia, Lithuania, Luxembourg, the Netherlands, Norway, Poland, Portugal, Romania, Slovenia, Spain, Sweden, Switzerland and the United Kingdom	Russian	Screened for political loyalty
Age	No age restrictions. Ages have ranged from 26–46 (average age, 34 years)	Maximum age of 50 years	Under 33 years	25–30 years
Technical	Appropriate degree and 2 years of professional related experience or 1000 h as pilot-in-command in jet aircraft		Degree-level education At least 5 years work experiences (with at least 3 years for one company)	Degree-level education
Pilot licence	Pilot licence and flying experience is beneficial but not required	Not required to be a licenced pilot but must be medically fit enough to undertake the responsibilities of a pilot		Active-service military pilots only; at least 800 flying h; successful management of emergencies during flight seen as advantageous

(continued)

Table 2.1 (continued)

Selection criteria	U.S.[a]	Europe[b]	Russia[c]	China[d]
Physical health	Must pass a swimming test during the first month of training and gain SCUBA diving licence in preparation for spacewalk training	Willing and able to perform strenuous physical activities; proficient swimmers; be willing to spend extended time underwater simulating microgravity	Fitness: Run 60 m: 8.5 sec Shuttle run 10 × 10 m: 26 secs Run 1 km: 3 min, 35 secs Ski race 5 km: 21 min Long jump standing: 230 cm Pull-ups: 14 times Static arms flexing on bars: 20 times Static angle position on bars: 15 secs Swimming 25 m: 19 secs Swimming freestyle 200 m: 19 min	Outstanding physical health
Physical health: eyesight	Must have 20/20 vision in both eyes; eye-surgery and glasses can be used to improve vision	Must meet the requirements to be a private pilot		
Physical health: hearing		25 dB or better in each ear		
Physical – body size requirements	Must meet appropriate measurements for spacesuits and spacecraft	Must meet body size requirements of space vehicles Height: 150–190 cms Body Mass Index (BMI): normal	Height: 150 – 190 cm Height seated: 80–99 cm Weight: 50–90 kg Max. shoulder breadth: 52 cm Max. width between armpit angles: 45 cm Max. hip width seated: 41 cm Max. foot length: 29.5 cm	Height: 160 – 172 cm Weight: 50–70 kg

(continued)

Table 2.1 (continued)

Selection criteria	U.S.[a]	Europe[b]	Russia[c]	China[d]
Psychological		Seen as paramount – must be willing to undergo psychometric testing	Screen for personality, temperament, values, motivation, intelligence, memory, attention, perception, stress resistance, ability to work under pressure and time deadlines	Outstanding mental health
Social	Willingness to achieve competence in Russian language	It is paramount that astronauts work well in a team, in confined spaces and under stressful conditions. Experience in working as part of a team to achieve challenging objectives is an asset	Screen for attitudes towards people, tolerance, interpersonal cooperation, conflict management	

[a]Blodgett (2022b);
[b]European Space Agency (2021a);
[c]Space Safety Magazine (2016);
[d]China Space Report (2016)

2.2 Technical Expertise

Technical expertise is an obvious prerequisite for a person to travel to space, particularly for longer-term missions. Indeed, early on, technical expertise was NASA's main selection focus. While exact requirements may vary according to the space program or agency, commonly, astronauts require university qualifications in science, technology, engineering or mathematics (STEM). For NASA, applicants must have a minimum of a Masters degree in science (biological, physical or computer), technology, engineering, or mathematics and at least 2 years of relevant professional experience or a minimum of 1000 h as the pilot in command flying jet aircraft (Blodgett, 2022b, February 8). If a person does not have a Masters degree, they can still be considered provided they have completed at least 2 years towards a Doctorate in Philosophy in STEM, completed a doctoral degree in medicine or a nationally recognised pilot training program, or have a qualification and experience in teaching (as long as their degree is in science, engineering or mathematics) (Blodgett, 2022b, February 8). Similarly, NASA will also consider degrees in Clinical, Physiological or Experimental Psychology (Blodgett, 2022b, February 8).

With a focus on ensuring the necessary technical expertise, although appearing to offer knowledge beneficial for space travel, degrees in multiple areas, including some areas of technology, social science, psychology, nursing, exercise physiology and aviation, are not deemed sufficient by NASA for astronaut selection (Blodgett, 2022b, February 8). While NASA seeks people with STEM-related qualifications, the organisation encourages people to study fields of personal interest and does not recommend one area of study over another.

Technical knowledge and skill have always been central to astronaut selection. Indeed, in the early days, recruiters focused almost exclusively on astronauts' technical abilities as the "best and the brightest" in their fields and gave little thought to crew behaviour or compatibility (Nicholas, 1990). Moreover, among the highly-motivated early astronauts themselves, the prize of travelling to space was so highly valued that they were not concerned with who the other crew members were or their compatibility (Nicholas, 1990). As early as 1990, researchers questioned whether such an approach would continue to yield the best outcomes when mission length increased and noted that experienced Russian cosmonauts who had travelled for longer periods had spoken of the importance of crew behaviour and compatibility (Nicholas, 1990).

At the same time, researchers stated that technical skills alone would be insufficient for successful missions (Nicholas & Foushee, 1990). Despite being a successful approach in the past, they identified a range of factors that would likely render such an approach obsolete. For example, it was suggested that a combination of larger crews, increased time in space (from a small number of days to months and years), need for crew to be more autonomous and take increased responsibility for their safety, increased automation and greater crew diversity, would raise a range of potential difficulties including increased tension between crew members (Nicholas & Foushee, 1990). These researchers recognised that it was no longer sufficient to dismiss astronaut behaviour; including psychological and social characteristics and capabilities in astronaut selection was essential as these factors could adversely impact the success of future missions. They noted that "despite high technical qualification, a crew's performance will slip if there is interpersonal strife. In other words, selection and training must go beyond the technical skills emphasis of the past" (Nicholas & Foushee, 1990 p454). Over the years, these insights have proven to be highly relevant and underline the need to consider technical skills in combination with physical, psychological and social characteristics and capabilities during astronaut selection processes.

2.3   Physical Characteristics

Astronauts must be in peak physical health to safely undertake their strenuous duties. Indeed, NASA requires all potential astronauts to meet medical requirements, which cannot be waived. For the safety of the individual and the whole crew and mission success, astronauts must not have any medical condition that could prevent them from completing all required tasks or which may worsen due to training and spaceflight. The exact nature of the medical screening will vary according to mission length. Screening involves identifying obvious and asymptomatic disease and risk for disease that would impact missions (Gray et al., 2019). NASA medical specialists consider an astronaut's ability to undertake normal duties and what would be needed if a serious health issue should develop while in space.

Given the requirement for optimal health, strict criteria exist to ensure an astronaut's health does not compromise mission success. Potential astronauts must have good vision; 20/20 vision in both eyes or the ability to attain this via surgery or glasses and some programs also specify hearing requirements. Other health conditions that are likely to prevent an individual from becoming an astronaut include cardiovascular diseases, ear, nose and throat issues, renal issues including kidney stones, thyroid problems, headaches/migraine and psychiatric and behavioural disorders (Gray et al., 2019; Johnston et al., 2014).

Additionally, astronauts are typically required to meet anthropometric (body size) requirements. People must be of a height and weight and proportion that enables them to fit in space suits and all space vehicles safely. The exact standards may vary by space agency, but typically people must be within "normal" height and weight specifications. Sometimes due to anthropometric characteristics and possible health differences debate has existed about whether sex should play a role in selection for space. For example, it has been argued that females are a more logical choice as astronauts and that an all-female crew would be beneficial due to women typically being smaller than males (smaller mass and require less space), using less oxygen, producing less carbon dioxide and using less consumables and allowing for a smaller spacecraft (Landis, 2000). Such an argument has particularly been made for an all-female crew to travel to Mars (Landis, 2000).

While space agencies must consider pre-existing medical conditions, they must also weigh the effects of space on the human body. When astronauts enter space, they experience microgravity, the near-weightless environment associated with space flight. The immediate effect of such an environment is Space Adaption Syndrome, a type of motion sickness that can involve nausea, vomiting, dizziness, headaches, fatigue, diarrhea and loss of appetite (Hodkinson et al., 2017; Kornilova & Kozlovskaya, 2003). It usually occurs over the first few days as astronauts adjust their spatial orientation to their surroundings (Hodkinson et al., 2017). Astronauts are suspended upright within the space shuttle; however, the surroundings outside the space shuttle move and change (De la Torre, 2014). Astronauts who are more dependent on visual cues are more likely to experience Space Adaption Syndrome because their visual cues are not aligned with the orientation of their body (Chen et al., 2015).

The most visible symptom of microgravity is the redistribution of body fluid from the lower to the upper part of the body resulting in facial swelling and puffiness and the legs having reduced volume, appearing to shrink (Costa et al., 2021; Hodkinson et al., 2017). In addition, the redistribution of body fluid decreases blood pressure, therefore reducing the heart's workload, and as a result, the heart experiences cardiac atrophy and becomes a more spherical shape (May et al., 2014). This physiological change does not seem to compromise cardiovascular function or cause cardiac dysrhythmia; however, some astronauts may be at an increased risk of cardiovascular disease dependent on their pre-flight health condition (Sides et al., 2005).

Visual functioning is also important before and during spaceflight and, like cardiovascular functioning, can be affected by microgravity. For example, during flight, astronauts are at risk of Visual Impairment Intracranial Pressure Syndrome (VIIP), recently renamed Spaceflight-Associated Neuroocular Syndrome (SANS) (Hodkinson et al., 2017). Microgravity redistributes body fluids and changes the intracranial pressure of the eye, which appears to impact vision; optic nerve sheath distension, optic disc swelling, globe flattening and cotton wool spots have been noted (Khossravi & Hargens, 2021; Mader et al., 2011). Further knowledge about SANS prevention and countermeasures is needed, especially for longer missions to the moon and Mars (Khossravi & Hargens, 2021).

Other health effects also arise during spaceflight. For example, the constant temperature and humidity onboard the spaceflight can affect astronauts' skin with many astronauts reporting experiencing rashes, acne, reddening, dryness, itchiness, bruising and peeling of the skin and slow healing after cuts (Braun et al., 2019). Most commonly, they experienced rashes on their scalp, face, neck, torso, arms and hands (Braun et al., 2019). These skin conditions resulted from the space environment and hygiene practices. Over-washing and space suits were implicated in skin peeling, while acne and redness were associated with poor hygiene (Braun et al., 2019). Astronauts have reported a lack of hygiene products, and some have reported having reactions to the products provided. In some instances, astronauts can use skin care products, but many do not maintain a consistent skin regime due to work demands (Braun et al., 2019).

Skin rashes in space can also indicate inflammation due to immune system dysregulation (Crucian et al., 2015, 2016). Microgravity, radiation exposure, stress, changed circadian rhythms and nutrition, and prolonged isolation and confinement can adversely affect various body systems, including the immune system (Crucian et al., 2018; Ponomarev et al., 2021). Generally, females typically have a stronger immune response than males and are more susceptible to autoimmune disorders (Klein and Flanagan 2016; Ponomarev et al., 2021). However, while anticipated, sex-related differences in immune system functioning have yet to be tested in space (Ponomarev et al., 2021). Despite this, given potential challenges with immune functioning, countermeasures to assist both sexes regulate their immune system are important. These countermeasures may involve pre-flight immune screening, vaccination and quarantine, exercise, adequate sleep, stress management skills, medications, functional foods and nutritional supplements such as probiotics and vitamins (Crucian et al., 2018; Ponomarev et al., 2021). Vitamin D supplements are particularly important due to microgravity-induced bone loss during space missions and its possible impact on immune system functioning (Costa et al., 2021; Crucian et al., 2018).

Microgravity also effects the bones due to reduced weight bearing. Changes include reduced osteoblast activity (cells involved in formation and mineralisation of bones) and increased osteoclast activity (cells involved in breakdown and resorption of bones) (Costa et al., 2021), resulting in bone loss (Stavnichuk et al., 2020). Astronauts typically lose 1–2% of their calcium each month in space, although the rate of calcium loss tends to reduce over time (Landis, 2000). The decrease in calcium increases the risk of osteoporosis and fractures, and as a result, some commentators have argued that an all-female astronaut crew would be unsuitable for long space missions as females are typically at an increased risk of developing osteoporosis (Landis, 2000). This position has been countered with the argument that it is not known whether bone calcium loss from osteoporosis and microgravity are similar and that data have not confirmed differences in bone loss between male and female astronauts (Landis, 2000). Additionally, exercise and medications used to mitigate post-menopausal osteoporosis on Earth taken in space could minimise bone loss (Landis, 2000).

Another significant health risk to astronauts is the impact of space travel on sleep. Astronauts are often required to remain awake for extended periods of time (Pandi-Perumal & Gonfalone, 2016) and many environmental factors, such as microgravity, temperature, noise, vibration, workload, stress, isolation and monotony can negatively affect the quality and quantity of sleep, resulting in sleep deprivation (De la Torre, 2014; Wu et al., 2018). Sleep deprivation, sleepiness and fatigue can impair thinking, memory and judgement, increasing the likelihood of mistakes or accidents risking the health and safety of the crew and the mission (Pandi-Perumal & Gonfalone, 2016; Wu et al., 2018). In longer missions, efforts to improve environmental conditions such as addressing wind speed, noise, carbon dioxide, and temperature as well as providing private sleep areas, restraints and comfortable sleeping bags appear beneficial (Wu et al., 2018). Work-rest schedules and sleep medications are also suggested to assist with astronaut sleep (Wu et al., 2018). However, responses to sleep deprivation tests and genotype screening can also be used in crew selection to select those less likely to be affected by sleep deprivation (Wu et al., 2018).

In addition to the health risks discussed, astronauts must also contend with radiation exposure, which can cause cellular damage to DNA and increase the risk of certain cancers (Hodkinson et al., 2017). However, the astronaut selection process may assist in minimising such potential damage. People on Earth living in areas exposed to highly natural radiation have developed a high adaptive response to external radiation (Ghiassi-nejad et al., 2002; Mortazavi et al., 2003). Therefore, testing could be included in astronaut selection to choose people who are less susceptible to radiation or radioresistent (Cortese et al., 2018; Mortazavi et al., 2003). Also, exposure to high LET radiation may possibly offer a way to elicit a radioadaptive response (Cortese et al., 2018) and vitamin C supplementation may reduce the adverse effects of ionizing radiation exposure (Mortazavi et al., 2015).

Astronauts must also know about space medicine, given the need to manage medical events without returning to Earth. For example, during an emergency medical event such as cardiac arrest, various cardiopulmonary resuscitation methods have been adapted to microgravity conditions. While this is beneficial, necessary post-care is unlikely to be available in a space environment, and therefore, it is essential to minimise the risk of cardiac events via rigorous selection processes

(Hodkinson et al., 2017). Additional challenges occur regarding medical diagnosis, with imaging currently limited to ultrasound on the ISS (Hodkinson et al., 2017) and medications being negatively influenced by being in space; radiation exposure and excessive vibration may degrade some medications, and therefore, medications must have a long expiration date and remain stable after their expiration date (Du et al., 2011). In addition, microgravity-related physiological changes can also impact the body's response to medication. For example, changes to the cardiovascular system may alter the body's response to medications that regulate blood pressure and heart rate (Hodkinson et al., 2017).

It is clear that astronauts are exposed to many health risks and must be in peak physical condition before flight. Although they must meet physical health requirements for their safety and that of their fellow crew, there is also increasing recognition that diversity and inclusivity are important values that may also benefit space exploration. As a result, in its most recent call for astronauts, the ESA called for astronauts with a physical disability to become part of the 'Parastronaut Fly! Feasibility Project', exploring the feasibility of astronauts with a physical disability travelling into space (ESA, 2021a). In this world-first call for applications, 287 people applied, with 29 people advancing to the next stage of selection (ESA, 2022). In this initiative, people who would meet all technical and psychological requirements to be an astronaut but would typically be excluded due to physical disability can apply to join the ESA astronaut reserve. After selection, they will assist in identifying and developing solutions to barriers to sending people with a physical disability to space, including adaptions needed to training, spacecraft and the impact on their health.

The ESA has specific criteria about which physical disabilities make people eligible to apply. They developed the criteria after considering the abilities needed to safely perform the role of an astronaut, referring to the categories used by the Paralympic Committee, and deciding what adjustments could realistically be made given current technology (ESA, 2021a). As a result, the eligible physical disabilities are lower limb deficiency (congenital or due to amputation), including single or double foot deficiency through the ankle and single or double leg deficiency below the knee; leg length difference (shortened limbs at birth or as a result of trauma); and short stature (less than 130 cm tall) (ESA, 2021a). Additionally, people with a physical disability must be able to read with minimal assistance from visual aids; understand safety and emergency instructions and follow verbal instructions; communicate with space and ground crew; move autonomously to ensure appropriate self-care in orbit; remain calm under pressure; operate, maintain and repair systems; and work in confined space with a small group of people for long periods (ESA, 2021a). As with astronauts without a physical disability deployed to the astronaut reserves, astronauts with a physical disability will be trained for specific space missions when needed.

While requirements for astronaut selection must be holistic, it is clear that physical characteristics and health remain essential components in astronaut selection. Astronauts must possess sufficient health to use all equipment safely, endure the strains on their body, minimise the possibility of deteriorating health while in space, and understand space medicine to assist themselves or fellow crew as needed. In addition, astronauts must possess appropriate psychological and social characteristics.

2.4 Psychological Characteristics

Astronauts need to be in good psychological health as they will face several individual and team-based challenges during space exploration and habitation. Pre-flight psychological selection aims to identify people high in logical reasoning, attentional abilities, and visual and auditory perception (Manzey et al., 1995). In addition, people who manage stress well, are work orientated, loyal, have high empathy and low aggression, and a good sense of humour are sought after (Manzey et al., 1995).

Indeed, selection processes have often considered key aspects of personality, such as the Big Five Personality Traits (openness, conscientiousness, extraversion, agreeableness and neuroticism), to identify people best suited to be an astronaut. While certain personality traits may be valued more than others and confer benefits, flexibility and balance are also needed. The ideal astronaut should exhibit low levels of neuroticism, facilitating team cohesion and allowing them to maintain harmony during a long space mission, and lower levels of extraversion (the tendency to be outgoing, socially confident)/higher levels of introversion (the tendency to be shy, quiet, reserved), allowing them to adapt to the limited social interaction within the isolated space environment (Bartone et al., 2018; Landon et al., 2017). At the same time, having some astronauts who exhibit some aspects of extraversion, particularly warmth and sociability, can boost crew morale and be beneficial in team environments (Bartone et al., 2018; Landon et al., 2017). Therefore, a crew comprising a mix of introverted and extraverted astronauts may be worth further exploration (Bartone et al., 2018). In addition, astronauts should exhibit moderate openness to aid team communication and adaptability and high levels of agreeableness to contribute to team cooperation (Bartone et al., 2018; Landon et al., 2017). Conscientiousness, the tendency to be organised, thorough, diligent and goal-directed, is generally a strong predictor of individual and team performance and adaptability, but its role in space is debated. It may be that achievement aspects are beneficial for adaptability but dependability aspects are not relevant or negatively related to adaptability (Bartone et al., 2018). Astronauts tend to score higher on conscientious than the general population but highly conscientious people may become frustrated by difficulties such as delays, equipment failure and restricted social interaction (Landon et al., 2017). Conscientiousness may be important for self-care and living in small groups but further research is needed to truly understand its role in crew performance (Landon et al., 2017). Overall, no one perfect personality profile for astronauts exists (Landon et al., 2018) but to maximise effective team-work the following profile has been offered; a minimum level of conscientiousness, low to moderately high extraversion, moderate openness, moderately high to high agreeableness and high emotional stability (Landon et al., 2017).

Resilience, the ability to adapt during challenging situations, and hardiness, the ability to cope with the stress of challenging situations, are other important personality traits to consider. Given the many challenges encountered during space travel, resilience is imperative. Similarly, three components of hardiness – commitment, control and challenge – are also key. Commitment, a person's capacity to see purpose and meaning in their work (Bartone et al., 2018), is especially relevant to astronauts who sacrifice time with their family and friends to explore the unknown. Control, a person's belief that they have the skills and resources to complete a task (Bartone et al., 2018), is also needed with astronauts requiring confidence in their abilities and those of their team. Finally, challenge, a person's openness to new experiences and ability to see challenges as opportunities for learning and growth (Bartone et al., 2018) may assist astronauts to embrace new experiences and learn from problems to avoid repeating them.

In addition to personality characteristics, astronauts must be highly motivated, with motivation a key factor in team and mission success. Motivation may take the form of own gain, relative gain, and joint gain motivation (Collins, 2003). Own gain motivation involves being motivated to gain a reward for oneself, relative gain motivation is the motivation to compete with others to gain a reward, and joint gain motivation is the motivation to collaborate with others for a shared reward (Collins, 2003). People who exhibit joint gain motivation are well suited to being part of a space crew due to their tendency to collaborate with others, which is valuable given the importance of teamwork to mission success (Collins, 2003).

When considering the psychological characteristics of people most suited to be astronauts, people's ability to tolerate isolation is also central. Being so far from home with only a small number of others may result in feelings of isolation (Landon et al., 2017; Szocik et al., 2018). In trying to understand the impact of isolation, researchers have conducted experiments on Earth where they try to simulate life in space. These experiments, called Earth-based analog studies (observational studies where an environment is created to simulate space conditions and produce similar physical, psychological and social effects on the body), have shown that isolation can lead to an increase in anxiety, difficulty sleeping and irritability, and that as the isolation continues, an increase in depression (Collins, 2003). When considering the ability to tolerate isolation, personality may be important. More introverted (shy, quiet) people may cope better with isolated environments, particularly during longer missions, due to their lower need for social interaction (Bartone et al., 2018).

Astronauts viewing the Earth as a distant dot, highlighting that their loved ones are far-beyond reach, may markedly increase the sense of isolation and contribute to poor psychological wellbeing (Kanas, 2014). This experience, termed the "Earth-out-of-view" phenomenon, may result in homesickness, depression, psychosis and suicidal thinking (Kanas, 2014). Therefore, it is important to assess a person's ability to cope with isolation and consider ways to support astronauts' mental health. As people are predisposed to experience positive psychological wellbeing when in habitats that match their evolutionary environments (Szocik et al., 2018), using images, plants, or virtual reality to connect astronauts to Earth may help counter some potentially adverse effects of isolation and Earth-out-of-view.

When considering psychological wellbeing in space, astronauts must also be able to cope with living in confined spaces for extended periods. This ability is important as confinement has been associated with increased hostility and irritability, decreased positive mood (Collins, 2003), and over time with physical and cognitive exhaustion (Basner et al., 2014). Furthermore, the limited space can force people to become overly familiar with others, resulting in increased annoyance from even the most minute behaviours of others (Peldszus et al., 2014). Therefore, it is essential that astronauts are emotionally stable, that crew members are compatible (Collins, 2003) and that astronauts can personalise the spacecraft environment to minimise the adverse effects of confinement (Peldszus et al., 2014).

While astronauts have key tasks to achieve during missions, monotony and boredom can also arise, posing significant psychological stressors (Peldszus et al., 2014) and potentially increasing the adverse impacts of confinement. Extroverted people are at higher risk of boredom which may be problematic as, in what has been referred to as a "personality paradox" (Suedfeld & Steel, 2000), extraverted people who seek new, thrilling experiences and adventure, are the people most likely to volunteer for something like space travel (Suedfeld & Steel, 2000). When faced with repetitive tasks and monotony, among a small group of people in confined space, such people are likely to experience adverse effects of boredom (Peldszus et al., 2014; Suedfeld & Steel, 2000). Increased variability in crew backgrounds and experiences may reduce some aspects of monotony and boredom, by providing novelty and stimulation, especially later in a mission when people seek new and interesting things with which to engage (Kanas, 2014). Also, providing entertainment and coordinating crew leisure activities during flight may provide time for informal communication between the crew and may combat monotony (Manzey et al., 1995).

Difficulties with psychological wellbeing may arise while in space, particularly on longer-term missions, reinforcing the importance of careful crew selection and psychological monitoring throughout the mission. For deep-space missions and habitation, ground-based monitoring and two-way communication will be limited, and there will be no visiting crews or re-supply flights (Manzey, 2004), further highlighting the crucial importance of careful crew selection and training. Being mindful of the potential for even small mistakes to have disastrous effects and relying on technology for survival can result in high levels of stress and fear. After the initial euphoria of being in space declines, anxiety, depression, sleep disturbances, and inter- and intra-crew conflicts may arise, and can contribute to operational mistakes and impact crew safety (Kass et al., 1995).

Psychological difficulties are more likely in longer missions. For example, in missions longer than 6 weeks, astronauts have been found to experience significant interpersonal and psychological difficulties after the half way point of their missions (Kanas, 2014), with social monotony and boredom, as well as isolation and confinement beginning to take their toll (Manzey, 2004). Such psychological difficulties may differ in their presentation, with culture potentially impacting the manifestation and identification of psychological health difficulties. For example, multiple studies have documented Russian cosmonauts experiencing a condition known as asthenia or asthenisation, which may present as dizziness, weakness, sleep and appetite disturbances, fatigue, restlessness, attention and concentration problems, headache, irritability, fluctuating emotions (De la Torre, 2014; Kanas, 2014). It is important to be aware of differing presentations and, where possible, people with optimal psychological health should be selected as astronauts to minimise deterioration in psychological health while in space, and training should include strategies to manage stress and enhance wellbeing.

Space travel requires people to be in optimal psychological health. Astronauts must possess desirable personality characteristics, be appropriately motivated, and able to tolerate isolation, monotony and boredom and living in confined space. They must also be able to manage any anxiety and, as discussed below, have the necessary social characteristics to be successful.

2.5   Social Characteristics

As well as possessing the necessary physical and psychological characteristics, astronauts must have the requisite social skills such as high-level interpersonal skills and cultural sensitivity and competence. They must also be able to assume one or more roles within the team, and leaders must possess appropriate highly-developed leadership skills.

Astronauts must possess high-level interpersonal skills to be able to live and work harmoniously with a small group of others, in confined space for varying amounts of time. While it may not be possible to avoid all interpersonal conflict, good interpersonal skills will help to minimise such conflict and contribute to mission success. Part of having well-developed interpersonal skills requires being culturally competent and sensitive to reduce the possibility of crew miscommunication and adverse impacts on team performance (Landon et al., 2017).

Those selecting astronauts and astronauts themselves must be aware of the central role of culture, particularly as crews become increasingly diverse and countries cooperate in their space endeavours. Often questionnaires are used in the recruitment process. While they offer valuable information, language-dependent questionnaires may negatively affect selection due to language effects when recruiting astronauts from different countries (Goeters & Fassbender, 1992). Therefore, language and cultural differences among a multi-cultural crew must be considered at the beginning of the recruitment process to ensure a psychologically valid and equitable selection process.

Language differences must be considered in terms of how they may affect interactions between astronauts. A multi-cultural crew may encounter challenges communicating with each other, and miscommunication could lead to mistakes during routine activities (Landon et al., 2017). It has been argued that Russians typically have greater language abilities than Americans (Ritsher, 2005) and Russian cosmonauts have been found to demonstrate greater flexibility than American astronauts concerning working in bilingual teams (Kanas et al., 2000). However, language differences are not insurmountable. For example, in another isolated environment (an arctic mission), people from Greenland, Denmark, the United Kingdom and Russia successfully navigated communication difficulties using body language (Leon & Sandal, 2003). Indeed, one person articulated that, "lack of common language did not cause real communication problems. With body and eye language we were able to understand each other pretty well" (Leon & Sandal, 2003 p263).

Language is not the only cultural difference to consider. Cultural norms such as privacy are crucial considerations when selecting astronauts who will share a confined spacecraft. In a multi-cultural team, cultures accustomed to living in small spaces and close proximity may adjust faster to the spacecraft but may also be unaware of other crew members' need for privacy. For example, in Russia, there is not a word for privacy; the closest words translate to aloneness, seclusion, and keeping secrets (Ritsher, 2005). As a result, Russian crew members may perceive other astronauts who express a need for privacy as unfriendly or offended (Ritsher, 2005).

Other less obvious cultural differences must also be considered during astronaut selection. For example, 'Eastern' countries such as China and Russia tend to display high collectivism, with people more likely to have an interdependent sense of self and a strong motivation to contribute to the team (Arieli & Sagiv, 2018; Ritsher, 2005). In comparison, 'Western' countries such as the U.S. tend to display high individualism, with people more likely to have an independent sense of self and a preference to work alone (Arieli & Sagiv, 2018). In addition, people from Russia tend to be more emotionally expressive in public and private and feel equally comfortable displaying positive feelings such as joy and excitement and negative feelings such as frustration and anger (Ritsher, 2005). Astronauts from other cultures that tend to suppress their emotions may struggle to accommodate other very emotionally expressive astronauts. Therefore, cultural sensitivity and competence and opportunities for astronauts to become well acquainted with one another before their mission are essential to foster understanding of each other's cultural norms, emotional expression, and personalities.

When selecting astronauts, recruiters look for people to fulfil very specific roles. The key roles include the Commander, who assumes responsibility for crew activity and mission completion; the Co-pilot, who assists the Commander and is responsible for vehicle and life support systems; and the Flight Engineer, who maintains communication systems with ground control. Multiple people can fulfil these roles depending on the type of mission (Groemer et al., 2020). Aside from fulfilling their specific job title, people may also assume different broad team roles, i.e., organiser, doer, challenger, innovator, team builder and connector (Mathieu et al., 2015). Such team roles have been associated with the Big Five Personality Traits noted earlier as important psychological characteristics for astronauts. For example, the team builder is often associated with agreeableness as they can cooperate with others, whereas the innovator is associated with openness because they consider different ideas and perspectives (Mathieu et al., 2015). Just as individuals may hold multiple space-specific roles, they may fill one or more team roles; as long as all roles are filled, the team will likely be successful (Anania et al., 2017).

Another key to mission success is leadership. The crew are likely to perceive the Commander as the leader, and as such, Commanders require high-level leadership skills. Varying leadership styles exist, with some styles better suited to space than others. Additionally, mission length may also require variations in leadership style (Palinkas, 2001). For instance, an authoritarian leadership style can be beneficial when urgent decisions are required, but a more participative leadership style allows the crew to collaborate on decisions and is likely to sustain crew morale (Nicholas & Foushee, 1990). In longer missions, greater flexibility is required to accommodate the impacts of isolation, confinement and more unstructured time, with the Commander needing to employ task-focused and support-focused leadership (Palinkas, 2001). Successful leaders are often responsible, emotionally stable, and effective communicators, whereas followers need to be adaptable, active listeners and willing to put the team's needs above their own (Landon et al., 2017). Astronauts need to have both leader and follower traits because they have different specialities and will be assigned differing roles (Landon et al., 2017).

Astronauts' social characteristics are pivotal for space mission success. High-level interpersonal skills and cultural sensitivity and competence are necessary. Additionally, people must know and accept their designated role and leaders must possess and demonstrate excellent leadership skills.

Reader Activity 1: Space Checklist – Do You Have What It Takes to Be an Astronaut?

Characteristics of an astronaut	Answer: select Yes for those you meet
Technical skills:	
Appropriate qualifications in STEM	YES/NO
Required level of experience	YES/NO
Pilot qualifications and experience	YES/NO
Physical characteristics:	
Vision	YES/NO
Hearing	YES/NO
Body size	YES/NO
Psychological characteristics:	
Personality – openness, conscientiousness, extraversion, agreeableness, neuroticism.	YES/NO
Ability to tolerate uncertainty	YES/NO
Motivation – own gain motivation, relative gain motivation, joint gain motivation. Joint gain motivation results in better outcomes.	YES/NO
Social characteristics:	
Team characteristics – organiser, doer, challenger, innovator, team builder or connector. Need someone for each role.	YES/NO

(continued)

Characteristics of an astronaut	Answer: select Yes for those you meet
Leadership – leadership and follower traits – a good astronaut should have both.	YES/NO
Orientation – work orientation, mastery orientation and competition orientation. Work and mastery orientation results in better outcomes.	YES/NO
Cultural characteristics:	
Collectivist vs Individualist cultures – collectivist cultures may contribute better to the team.	YES/NO
Privacy and personal space – some cultures have already adapted to living in close proximity with one another.	YES/NO
Foreign language competence – those who can communicate via verbal or body language will contribute better to the team.	YES/NO

2.6   Considerations of Missions Length

Taking a holistic approach to selecting people for space travel, considering technical expertise, and physical, psychological and social characteristics is essential to maximise positive outcomes. However, the importance of each domain (and elements within it) will vary depending on the length of the mission (See Fig. 2.2).

With Dennis Tito's trip to the ISS in 2001, the realm of space tourism officially began. Tito, who paid $20 million, became the first person to privately fund space travel, spending 6 days on board the ISS (Britannica, 2021). At a similar time, private companies such as SpaceX, Blue Origin and Virgin Galactic entered the market, offering everyday people the opportunity to undertake space travel. While the amount of time in space can vary considerably with these companies, space tourists typically spend shorter periods in space than astronauts and substantially less time than those who will undertake deep-space travel and habitation.

For people seeking to be space tourists, taking to the skies for relatively short periods, technical expertise, and physical characteristics are the most pertinent domains. While space tourists will not require specific technical qualifications or extensive knowledge and skills, for their safety and that of the others travelling with them, they must be able to participate in relevant training and execute all relevant instructions as required. They must also be of sufficient health and must meet body size measurements to ensure they can safely travel. In contrast, psychological and social characteristics are less relevant, given their brief time away from Earth. Also, given that their travel is so brief, factors such as isolation, boredom, confinement, interpersonal skills, culture and leadership are unlikely to affect mission success.

While some selection domains appear of less relevance and importance for space tourism, all domains are pivotal when selecting people for deep-space travel and habitation. Indeed, they are all potentially of greater importance than for shorter

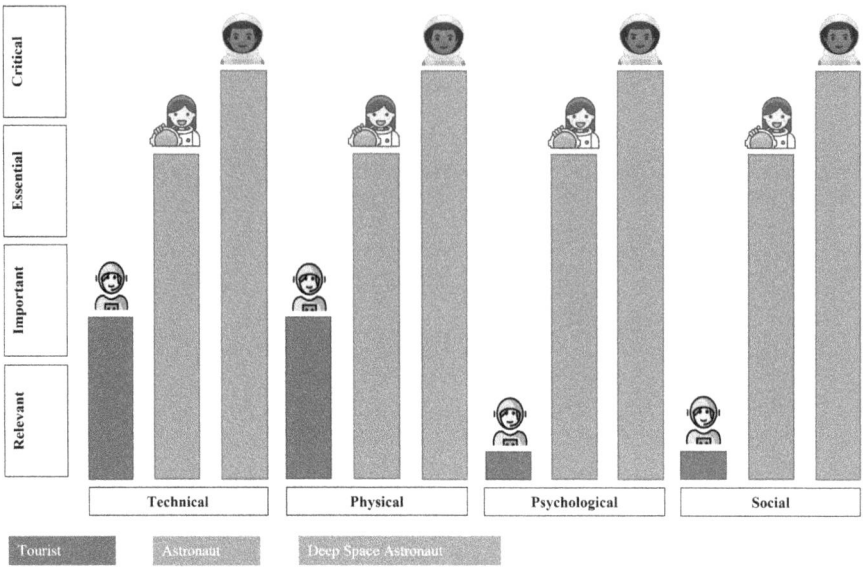

Fig. 2.2 Relative importance of selection domains

space missions undertaken by astronauts. This is due to the additional stressors deep-space astronauts will encounter. These include long-term exposure to microgravity and radiation, increased autonomy, increased reliance on machines for survival, extreme isolation and loneliness, limited social interaction and reduced novelty and contact with families, cultural issues and Earth-out-of-view phenomenon (Kanas, 2014). Additionally, deep-space astronauts will contend with limited ground-based monitoring and two-way communication, with communication delays when seeking to contact mission control. With space travel to the ISS and the Moon, communication largely occurs in real-time, taking only seconds between the communication and receipt of information (Marquez et al., 2019). In contrast, with deep-space travel, communication delays will increase the further astronauts travel from Earth; when on Mars' surface, astronauts' communication will take 4–40 min to reach mission control on Earth (Keebler et al., 2015; Marquez et al., 2019), meaning real-time mission monitoring or seeking guidance quickly in the case of problems or crises is not possible. Additionally, there will be no visiting crews or re-supply flights (Manzey, 2004). As a result, deep-space astronauts will need to be more autonomous, self-reliant and able to manage physical and psychological health problems (Keebler et al., 2015).

Those seeking to participate in deep-space exploration must not only have sufficient technical skills to execute their roles but must also be able to troubleshoot and problem solve any difficulties that arise, given the delay in communication with ground control and the time it would take to send any assistance (e.g., travel time to Mars is approximately 7–9 months, with astronauts remaining on Mars for

17–20 months waiting for the optimal conditions to return to Earth; Genta & Maffione, 2019). Additionally, such astronauts must also be in optimal physical health to face additional health challenges due to longer exposure to microgravity and radiation. Furthermore, astronauts must be more autonomous and will find it extremely challenging to receive medical care due to long communication delays and the inability to return to Earth early (Robertson et al., 2020). Recently, it has been identified that the most survivable medical events would be shoulder dislocation, skin laceration and upper body fracture, while sudden cardiac arrest, sepsis and cardiogenic shock are most likely to adversely impact mission success (Robertson et al., 2020).

Extended missions will also mean that psychological and social characteristics become increasingly important. Astronauts will experience increased isolation, with limited communication with ground control and astronauts' families and will spend extended time (7–9 month travelling in each direction as well as 17–20 months awaiting the optimal conditions to return to Earth; Genta & Maffione, 2019) with their crew mates in confined environments. In these cases, emotional stability, interpersonal and conflict management skills and cultural competence will be essential for individual and crew wellbeing and mission success.

Reader Activity 2: Space Checklist – Do You Have What It Takes to Be an Space Tourist?

Characteristics of a space tourist	Answer: select Yes for those you meet
Technical skills:	
Willing to do training: 2–5 days	YES/NO
Physical characteristics:	
Medical checks: pre-flight medical screening and last-minute medical check	YES/NO
Able-bodied	YES/NO
Height: 5′0″ – 6′4″	YES/NO
Weight: 50 kgs – 100 kgs	YES/NO
Climb 7 flights of stairs in under 90 s	YES/NO
Social characteristics:	
Comfortable with no pilot/fully automated spacecraft: 6 passengers	YES/NO
Comfortable with piloted spacecraft: 4 passengers	YES/NO
Travel time:	
Can travel for 11 min	YES/NO
Can travel for 90 min minimum	YES/NO

2.7 Summary/Conclusion

As space exploration expands, more people seek to travel to the last frontier. Given the inherent risks and the need to optimise safety and mission outcomes, we must establish ways to select the best people for such exploration. Traditionally, selection processes relied upon selecting small numbers of largely homogenous crews, often with aviation and/or military backgrounds, and focused on technical expertise. As the nature of space travel is evolving, including greater crew diversity, varying reasons for travel (from space tourists to those who will undertake deep-space travel and habitation) and for varying lengths of time (from minutes to years) it is time to reassess selection processes. Given these changes, to maximise mission success, selection processes must be more holistic and comprehensive. Selection processes must consider four domains – technical knowledge and skills and physical, psychological and social characteristics. The relative importance of each of these domains varies depending on mission length and purpose (i.e., brief space tourism versus deep-space habitation). Each domain has recommended characteristics and we have provided an overview of the evidence to offer guidance about selecting for such qualities. At the same time, we have noted that there is no one profile of the optimal space traveller and individual differences must always be considered. Additionally, wider factors such as crew size and composition (sex balance, culture) and mission length must be weighed in decision making. Finally, in addition to careful selection processes, adequate training is also essential, especially as we embark on deep-space exploration and habitation.

References

Anania, E. C., Disher, T., Anglin, K. M., & Kring, J. P. (2017). Selecting for long-duration space exploration: Implications of personality. *IEEE Aerospace Conference, 2017*, 1–8. https://doi.org/10.1109/AERO.2017.7943814

Arieli, S., & Sagiv, L. (2018). Culture and problem-solving: Congruency between the cultural mindset of individualism versus collectivism and problem type. *Journal of Experimental Psychology. General, 147*(6), 789–814. https://doi.org/10.1037/xge0000444

Bartone, P. T., Krueger, G. P., & Bartone, J. V. (2018). Individual differences in adaptability to isolated, confined, and extreme environments. *Aerospace Medicine and Human Performance, 89*(6), 536–546. https://doi.org/10.3357/AMHP.4951.2018

Basner, M., Dinges, D. F., Mollicone, D. J., Savelev, I., Ecker, A. J., Di Antonio, A., Jones, C. W., Hyder, E. C., Kan, K., & Morukov, B. V. (2014). Psychological and behavioral changes during confinement in a 520-day simulated interplanetary mission to mars. *PLoS One, 9*(3), e93298. https://doi.org/10.1371/journal.pone.0093298

Blodgett, R. (2021, September 24). Astronaut selection timeline. Astronaut Selection Timeline I NASA.

Blodgett, R. (2022a, January 6). Astronaut selection. https://www.nasa.gov/feature/astronaut-selection

Blodgett, R. (2022b, February 8). Frequently asked questions. Frequently Asked Questions I NASA.

Braun, N., Thomas, S., Tronnier, H., & Heinrich, U. (2019). Self-reported skin changes by a selected number of astronauts after long-duration mission on ISS as part of the skin B project. *Skin Pharmacology and Physiology, 32*(1), 52–57. https://doi.org/10.1159/000494689

Britannica, T. (Editors of Encyclopaedia). (2021, August 4). Dennis Tito. Encyclopedia Britannica. https://www.britannica.com/biography/Dennis-Tito

Chen, W., Chao, J.-G., Chen, X. W., Wang, J. K., & Tan, C. (2015). Quantitative orientation preference and susceptibility to space motion sickness simulated in a virtual reality environment. *Brain Research Bulletin, 113*, 17–26. https://doi.org/10.1016/j.brainresbull.2015.01.007

China Space Report. (2016). Astronaut selection and training – China space report (wordpress. com). Accessed 2022, April 19th.

Collins, D. L. (2003). Psychological issues relevant to astronaut selection for long-duration space flight: A review of the literature. *Journal of Human Performance in Extreme Environments, 7*(1), 43–67. https://doi.org/10.7771/2327-2937.1021

Cortese, F., Klokov, D., Osipov, A., et al. (2018). Vive la radiorésistance!: Converging research in radiobiology and biogerontology to enhance human radioresistance for deep space exploration and colonization. *Oncotarget, 9*(18), 14692–14722. https://doi.org/10.18632/oncotarget.24461

Costa, F., Ambesi-Impiombato, F. S., Beccari, T., Conte, C., Cataldi, S., Curcio, F., & Albi, E. (2021). Spaceflight Induced Disorders: Potential Nutritional Countermeasures. *Frontiers in Bioengineering and Biotechnology, 9*, 666683. https://doi.org/10.3389/fbioe.2021.666683

Crucian, B., Stowe, R. P., Mehta, S., Quiriarte, H., Pierson, D., & Sams, C. (2015). Alterations in adaptive immunity persist during long-duration spaceflight. *NPJ Microgravity, 1*(1), 15013–15013. https://doi.org/10.1038/npjmgrav.2015.13

Crucian, B., Babiak-Vazquez, A., Johnston, S., Pierson, D. L., Ott, C. M., & Sams, C. (2016). Incidence of clinical symptoms during long-duration orbital spaceflight. *International Journal of General Medicine, 9*, 383–391. https://doi.org/10.2147/IJGM.S114188

Crucian, B. E., Choukèr, A., Simpson, R. J., Mehta, S., Marshall, G., Smith, S. M., Zwart, S. R., Heer, M., Ponomarev, S., Whitmire, A., Frippiat, J. P., Douglas, G. L., Lorenzi, H., Buchheim, J. I., Makedonas, G., Ginsburg, G. S., Ott, C. M., Pierson, D. L., Krieger, S. S., Baecker, N., et al. (2018). Immune system dysregulation during spaceflight: Potential countermeasures for deep space exploration missions. *Frontiers in Immunology, 9*, 1437. https://doi.org/10.3389/fimmu.2018.01437

De la Torre, G. G. (2014). Cognitive neuroscience in space. *Life (Basel, Switzerland), 4*(3), 281–294. https://doi.org/10.3390/life4030281

Du, B., Daniels, V. R., Vaksman, Z., Boyd, J. L., Crady, C., & Putcha, L. (2011). Evaluation of physical and chemical changes in pharmaceuticals flown on space missions. *The AAPS Journal, 13*(2), 299–308. https://doi.org/10.1208/s12248-011-9270-0

European Space Agency. (2021a). Astronaut applicant handbook. ESA_Astrosel_Handbook.pdf.

European Space Agency. (2021b, June 23). Wide range of applications for ESA's astronaut selection. ESA – Wide range of applications for ESA's astronaut selection.

European Space Agency. (2022, January 18). Astronaut selection: stage one complete. ESA – Astronaut selection: stage one complete.

Genta, G., & Maffione, P. F. (2019). A graphical tool to design too-ways human Mars missions. *Acta Astronautica, 154*, 301–310. https://doi.org/10.1016/j.actaastro.2018.03.035

Ghiassi-nejad, M., Mortazavi, S. M. J., Cameron, J. R., Niroomand-rad, A., & Karam, P. A. (2002). Very high background radiation areas of Ramsar, Iran: Preliminary biological studies. *Health Physics, 82*(1), 87–93. https://doi.org/10.1097/00004032-200201000-00011

Goeters, K. M., & Fassbender, C. (1992). Results of the ESA study on psychological selection of astronaut candidates for Columbus missions II: Personality assessment. *Acta Astronautica, 27*, 139–145. https://doi.org/10.1016/0094-5765(92)90190-t

Gray, G. W., Johnston, S. L., Saary, J., & Cook, T. (2019). Medical Evaluation and Standards. In M. Barratt, E. Baker, & S. Pool (Eds.), *Principles of clinical medicine for space flight*. Springer. https://doi.org/10.1007/978-1-4939-9889-0_11

Groemer, G., Gruber, S., Uebermasser, S., Soucek, A., Lalla, E. A., Lousada, J., Sams, S., Sejkora, N., Garnitschnig, S., Sattler, B., & Such, P. (2020). The AMADEE-18 Mars analog expedition in the Dhofar region of Oman. *Astrobiology, 20*(11), 1276–1286. https://doi.org/10.1089/ast.2019.2031

Hodkinson, P. D., Anderton, R., Posselt, B., & Fong, K. (2017). An overview of space medicine. *British Journal of Anaesthesia, 1*, 143–153. https://doi.org/10.1093/bja/aex336

Johnston, S. L., Blue, R. S., Jennings, R. T., Tarver, W. J., Gray, G. W. (2014). Astronaut medical selection during the shuttle era: 1981–2011. Aviation Space and Environmental Medicine, 85, 823–827. https://doi.org/10.3357/ASEM.3968.2014.

Kanas, N. (2014). Psychosocial issues during an expedition to Mars. Acta Astronautica, 103, 73–80. https://doi.org/10.1016/j.actaastro.2014.06.026

Kanas, N., Salnitskiy, V., Grund, E. M., Gushin, V., Weiss, O., Kozerenko, O., Sled, A., & Marmar, C. (2000). Interpersonal and cultural issues involving crews and ground personnel during Shuttle/Mir space missions. Aviation Space and Environmental Medicine, 71, A11–A16.

Kass, J., Kass, R., & Samaltedinov, I. (1995). Psychological considerations of man in space: Problems & solutions. Acta Astronautica, 36(8–12), 657–660. https://doi.org/10.1016/0094-5765(95)00155-7

Keebler, J. R., Dietz, A. S., & Baker, A. L. (2015). Effects of Communication Lag in Long Duration Space Flight Missions: Potential Mitigation Strategies. Proceedings of the Human Factors and Ergonomics Society 59th Annual Meeting, 59(1), 6–10. https://doi.org/10.1177/1541931215591002

Khossravi, E. A., & Hargens, A. R. (2021). Visual disturbances during prolonged space missions. Current Opinion in Ophthalmology, 32(1), 69–73. https://doi.org/10.1097/ICU.0000000000000724

Klein, S. L., & Flanagan, K. L. (2016). Sex differences in immune responses. Nature reviews. Immunology, 16(10), 626–638. https://doi.org/10.1038/nri.2016.90

Kornilova, L. N., & Kozlovskaya, I. B. (2003). Neurosensory mechanisms of space adaptation syndrome. Human Physiology, 29, 527–538. https://doi.org/10.1023/A:1025899413655

Landis, G. (2000). An all-woman crew to Mars: A radical proposal. Space Policy, 16(3), 167–179. https://doi.org/10.1016/s0265-9646(00)00020-5

Landon, L. B., Rokholt, C., Slack, K. J., & Pecena, Y. (2017). Selecting astronauts for long-duration exploration missions: Considerations for team performance and functioning. REACH – Reviews in Human Space Exploration, 5, 33–56. https://doi.org/10.1016/j.reach.2017.03.002

Landon, L. B., Slack, K. J., & Barrett, J. D. (2018). Teamwork and collaboration in long-duration space missions: Going to extremes. The American Psychologist, 73(4), 563–575. https://doi.org/10.1037/amp0000260

Leon, G. R., & Sandal, G. M. (2003). Women and couples in isolated extreme environments: Applications for long-duration missions. Acta Astronautica, 53(4), 259–267. https://doi.org/10.1016/S0094-5765(03)80003-6

Mader, T. H., Gibson, C. R., Pass, A. F., Kramer, L. A., Lee, A. G., Fogarty, J., Tarver, W. J., Dervay, J. P., Hamilton, D. R., Sargsyan, A., Phillips, J. L., Tran, D., Lipsky, W., Choi, J., Stern, C., Kuyumjian, R., & Polk, J. D. (2011). Optic disc edema, globe flattening, choroidal folds, and hyperopic shifts observed in astronauts after long-duration space flight. Ophthalmology, 118(10), 2058–2069. https://doi.org/10.1016/j.ophtha.2011.06.021

Manzey, D. (2004). Human missions to Mars: New psychological challenges and research issues. Acta Astronautica, 55(3–9), 781–790. https://doi.org/10.1016/j.actaastra.2004.05.013

Manzey, D., Schiewe, A., & Fassbender, C. (1995). Psychological countermeasures for extended manned spaceflights. Acta Astronautica, 35(4–5), 339–361. https://doi.org/10.1016/0094-5765(95)98736-S

Marquez, J. J., Hillenius, S., Deliz, I., Zheng, J., Kanefsky, B., & Gale, J. (2019). Enabling communication between astronauts and ground teams for space exploration missions. IEEE Aerospace Conference, 2019, 1–10. https://doi.org/10.1109/AERO.2019.8741593

Mathieu, J. E., Tannenbaum, S. I., Kukenberger, M. R., Donsbach, J. S., & Alliger, G. M. (2015). Team role experience and orientation: A measure and tests of construct validity. Group & Organization Management, 40(1), 6–34. https://doi.org/10.1177/1059601114562000

May, C., Borowski, A., Martin, D., Popovic, Z., Negishi, K., Hussan, J. R., Gladding, P., Hunter, P., Iskovitz, I., Kassemi, M., Bungo, M., Levine, B., & Thomas, J. (2014). Affect of microgravity on cardia shape: Comparison of pre- and in-flight data to mathematical modeling. Journal of the American College of Cardiology, 63(12), A1096–A1096. https://doi.org/10.1016/S0735-1097(14)61096-2

Mortazavi, S. M., Cameron, J. R., & Niroomand-rad, A. (2003). Adaptive response studies may help choose astronauts for long-term space travel. *Advances in Space Research, 31*(6), 1543–1551. https://doi.org/10.1016/s0273-1177(03)00089-9

Mortazavi, S. M. J., Foadi, M., Mozdarani, H., Haghani, M., Mosleh-Shirazi, M. A., Abolghasemi, P., Nematollahi, S., & Sharifzadeh, S. (2015). Future role of vitamin C in radiation mitigation and its possible applications in manned deep space missions: survival study and the measurement of cell viability. *International Journal of Radiation Research, 13*(1), 55–60. https://doi.org/10.7508/IJRR.2015.01.007

Nicholas, J. (1990). Human duration in long-duration spaceflight: Introduction. *Journal of Spacecraft and Rockets, 27*(5), 449–450. https://doi.org/10.2514/3.55614

Nicholas, J., & Foushee, C. H. (1990). Organization, selection, and training of crews for extended spaceflight: Findings from analogs and implications. *Journal of Spacecraft and Rockets, 27*(5), 451–456. https://doi.org/10.2514/3.26164

Palinkas, L. A. (2001). Psychosocial issues in long-term space flight: Overview. *Gravitational and Space Biology Bulletin, 14*(2), 25–33.

Pandi-Perumal, S. R., & Gonfalone, A. A. (2016). Sleep in space as a new medical frontier: the challenge of preserving normal sleep in the abnormal environment of space missions. *Sleep Science, 9*(1), 1–4. https://doi.org/10.1016/j.slsci.2016.01.003

Peldszus, R., Dalke, H., Pretlove, S., & Welch, C. (2014). The perfect boring situation—Addressing the experience of monotony during crewed deep space missions through habitability design. *Acta Astronautica, 94*(1), 262–276. https://doi.org/10.1016/j.actaastro.2013.04.024

Ponomarev, S., Kalinin, S., Sadova, A., Rykova, M., Orlova, K., & Crucian, B. (2021). Immunological Aspects of Isolation and Confinement. *Frontiers in Immunology, 12*, 697435–697435. https://doi.org/10.3389/fimmu.2021.697435

Ritsher, J. B. (2005). Cultural factors and the international space station. *Aviation Space and Environmental Medicine, 76*(6 Suppl), B135–B144.

Robertson, J. M., Dias, R. D., Gupta, A., Marshburn, T., Lipsitz, S. R., Pozner, C. N., Doyle, T. E., Smink, D. S., Musson, D. M., & Yule, S. (2020). Medical event management for future deep space exploration missions to Mars. *The Journal of Surgical Research, 246*, 305–314. https://doi.org/10.1016/j.jss.2019.09.065

Sides, M., Vernikos, J., Convertino, V., Stepanek, J., Tripp, L., Draeger, J., Hargens, A., Kourtidou-Papadeli, C., Pavy-LeTraon, A., Russomano, T., Wong, J., Buccello, R., Lee, P., Nagalia, V., & Saary, J. (2005). The Bellagio report: Cardiovascular risk of spaceflight: Implications for the future of space travel. *Aviation, Space and Environmental Medicine, 76*(9), 877–895.

Space Safety Magazine. (2016). Historical evolution of Russian cosmonauts selection criteria. Historical evolution of Russian cosmonauts selection criteria – (spacesafetymagazine.com).

Stavnichuk, M., Mikolajewicz, N., Corlett, T., Morris, M., & Komarova, S. V. (2020). A systematic review and meta-analysis of bone loss in space travelers. *NPJ Microgravity, 6*, 13. https://doi.org/10.1038/s41526-020-0103-2

Suedfeld, P., & Steel, G. D. (2000). The environmental psychology of capsule habitats. *Annual Review of Psychology, 51*(1), 227–253.

Szocik, K., Abood, S., & Shelhamer, M. (2018). Psychological and biological challenges of the Mars mission viewed through the construct of the evolution of fundamental human needs. *Acta Astronautica, 152*, 793–799. https://doi.org/10.1016/j.actaastro.2018.10.008

Wu, B., Wang, Y., Wu, X., Liu, D., Xu, D., & Wang, F. (2018). On-orbit sleep problems of astronauts and countermeasures. *Military Medical Research, 5*, 17. https://doi.org/10.1186/s40779-018-0165-6

Chapter 3
Clear Thinking in Deep Space: A Guide by Cognitive Scientists

Anastasia Ejova, Rachel A. Searston, Rachel Stephens, and Carolyn Semmler

Abstract The effects of long-term space habitation on mental processing have been explored both on Earth and in space. This chapter highlights the key topics of study within the discipline of cognitive science that will help to plan for deep space habitation and ultimately further develop the scientific knowledge required to sustain and enhance human cognitive functioning in space. We illustrate how cognitive scientists study human cognition and the unexplored questions that will need to be answered as this knowledge is extended into new environments. We first focus on the selection of individuals into training for deep space habitation – what key cognitive characteristics will these individuals need? How might we enhance current efforts in defining valid measurements to decide who should go into space for very long missions? The next challenge is training these individuals to perform mission critical tasks in space – how might we design training programs that promote durable yet flexible cognitive structures, allowing efficient adaptation to the inherent unpredictability of space? Finally, we look toward monitoring of cognitive performance from within the individual and by external devices – how we can sustain high-level thinking and prevent errors over extended durations in space? Being able to adapt to unfamiliar and extreme environments requires insight into cognitive structures and yet we do not have clear evidence for how the physical and physiological challenges of space impact upon this key aspect of cognitive functioning.

3.1 Introduction

Clear thinking will be critical to successful human exploration of deep space, including the Moon and Mars. NASA has big plans for humans outside of low Earth orbit, including lunar surface operations and a lunar orbital outpost that will be a

A. Ejova (✉) · R. A. Searston · R. Stephens · C. Semmler
School of Psychology, Faculty of Health and Medical Sciences,
The University of Adelaide, North Terrace Campus, Adelaide, SA, Australia
e-mail: anastasia.ejova@adelaide.edu.au

M. de Zwart et al. (eds.), *Human Uses of Outer Space*, Issues in Space,
https://doi.org/10.1007/978-981-19-9462-3_3

launch point to Mars (Cassell, 2019; Patel et al., 2020). Within the coming decades, humans will be experiencing lengthy spaceflights and living for extended periods on the Moon or even Mars. Rather than relying solely on robots, human crewmembers will be essential to these deep space missions because of their unique problem solving skills and flexibility in performance.

To illustrate what deep space life might be like and some of the challenges to be faced by human explorers, see the description of Astronaut Athena in Box 3.1. As acknowledged by NASA's Human Research Program, there is an important question to be addressed before people like Athena venture onto the Moon and beyond: what cognitive abilities – or what aspects of thinking – will be needed for humans to successfully complete deep space missions and stay safe? What aspects of clear thinking should be examined to select the right people and train them for their mission? During a mission, how should cognitive performance be monitored and maintained, and what environmental and psychological risks need to be mitigated?

Box 3.1: Astronaut Athena on the Moon

Image reproduced (Le Moign, 2018)

Imagine Astronaut Athena is stationed at a lunar outpost. She spends most of her days underground – the outpost is based inside a lunar lava tube, which offers protection from radiation, extreme temperature shifts, meteorites, and micrometeorites. As a botanist, Athena's primary role is to study the growth of plants on the moon, including bamboo, which will hopefully be useful as a sustainable material for construction, furniture, cloth and so on. She has a high workload and often feels stressed from the great responsibility she carries and the riskiness of lunar life. The stress affects her sleep. Sometimes Athena feels like she has difficulty concentrating and is forgetful, but according to the regular testing she must do to monitor her performance, she's fine – perhaps she is able to compensate when she has to. Athena misses sunshine, fresh fruit and vegetables, hearing birds sing, taking a bath, and snuggling up in bed, firmly held down by Earth's gravity. Of course, she mostly misses her loved ones back home. However, Athena has formed wonderful new friendships with her lunar team and is so thrilled to be on this adventure – she still has to pinch herself each day to make sure she is not dreaming! Although it took some adjusting, Athena loves the experience of feeling so light – the moon's gravity is 1/6 that of Earth. She will forever treasure the memory of seeing her beautiful blue home planet from afar.

The question of how to ensure clear thinking in deep space for people like Astronaut Athena fits squarely within the remit of cognitive science. Cognitive science is an interdisciplinary field that cuts across psychology, neuroscience, philosophy, linguistics, artificial intelligence and other disciplines. In applying cognitive science to the problem of clear thinking in deep space, basic science approaches will be essential in addressing theories of various cognitive abilities and how best to measure them, and understanding how cognition is impacted by risks in deep space, such as radiation, chronic stress, and weightlessness, which affects the distribution of fluid around the brain and body. Applied science approaches will also be critical, to assess how theories and measures will translate to mission outcomes. Although scientists cannot yet directly study humans in deep space, they can draw on data from other relevant groups of people (see Patel et al., 2020; Strangman et al., 2014). One obvious option is to study humans in spaceflight, such as on the International Space Station (ISS). Another option is to study people in isolated, confined, and extreme (ICE) environments, as analogue environments that capture some elements of deep space or spaceflight. ICE environments can include Antarctic bases, isolation chambers or simulated space camps, submarines, and other extreme environments such as mountaineering expeditions.

Within the field of cognitive science, many types of cognitive abilities have been identified and studied (see e.g., Goldstein, 2018; Quinlan & Dyson, 2008). Several of these abilities are presented below in Fig. 3.1, with typical descriptions. Each of these abilities will be important for clear thinking in deep space, but vary in the degree to which they have been studied in space and space analogue environments (e.g., see Strangman et al., 2014). One can imagine how each of these abilities will be put to the test during deep space missions. For example, considering Astronaut Athena:

- Athena will need to adapt quickly to her new and risky environment, including the procedures to keep the team safe, complex technology and team social dynamics. This will rely on her abilities for **learning** and organising new information in **long-term memory**, and effectively retrieving this information when required.
- With complex duties and risks to manage, Athena will need to be able to focus her **attention** on the most critical information, and be able to effectively process that information in **working memory**.
- With low gravity on the Moon, Athena will need to adapt her skills in **perceiving** the relative position and movement of objects around her, and responsively controlling the **actions** of her body.
- Unexpected events will happen (e.g. micrometeorite damage to equipment), so Athena will need to be able to **reason** effectively, applying existing knowledge to novel situations, plus solve new problems in creative ways and make quick and optimal **decisions**.
- In order to perform a given task in a way that reflects its importance and current difficulty for Athena, she will need to have a strong insight into her own cognitive abilities. That is, Athena will need sound **metacognition** to self-monitor and control all the other abilities in Fig. 3.1.

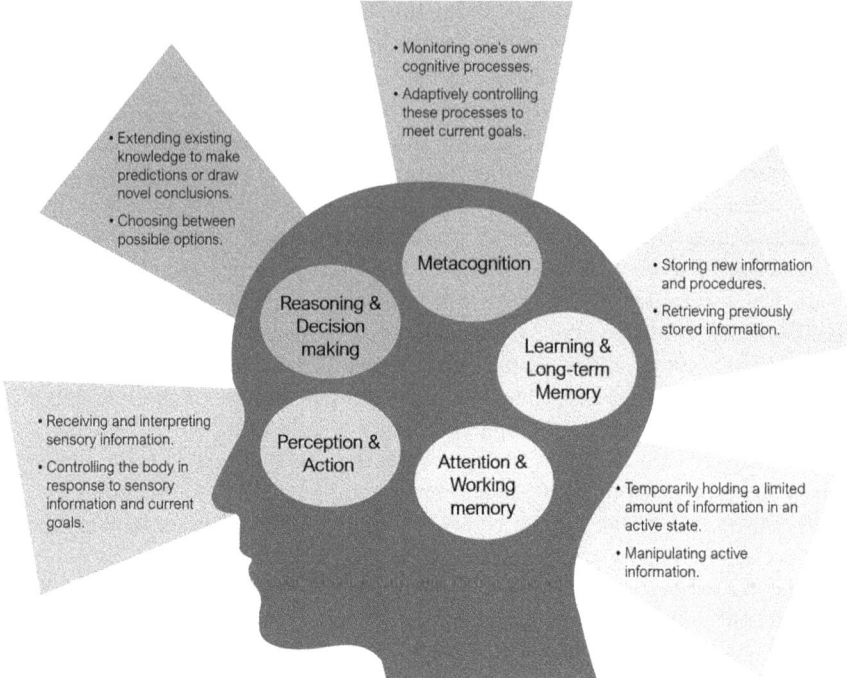

Fig. 3.1 Some of the key types of cognitive abilities that need to be considered for successful human exploration of deep space

In this chapter, we review cognitive science research on how best to select, train and support people for deep space exploration, based on these various kinds of key cognitive abilities.

3.2 How Do We Select the Best People for Deep Space Habitation?

Like current NASA astronauts, Athena needs to pass through a rigorous selection process before completing at least two years of full-time training within the Astronaut Candidate training program. As a part of this program, Athena will be evaluated to determine her suitability for specific missions, such as 1–3 year lunar exploration missions. Her initial selection process will likely consist of the following tests:

- *self-report surveys on personality, teamwork and motivation*
- *evaluation of resumes and other biographical information*
- *face-to-face interviews involving the assessment of mental aptitude (Fig. 3.2), symptoms of mental disorders, basic personality tendencies, applied social skills, interests and preferences, and physical attributes* (Sgobba et al., 2018)

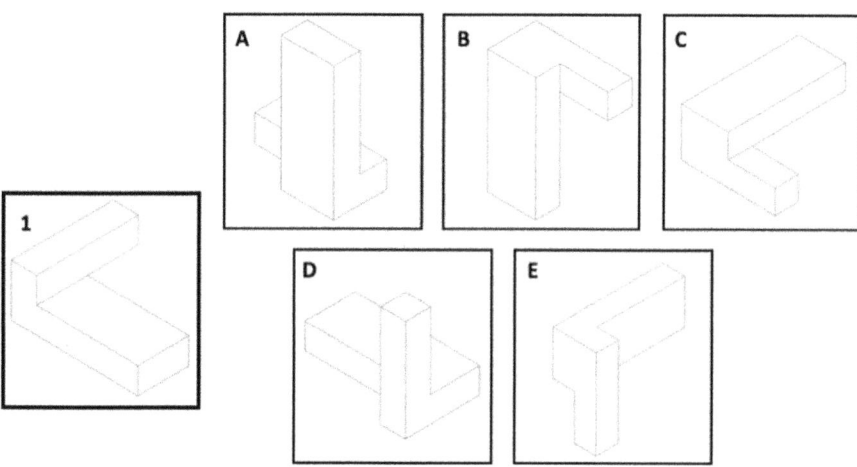

Fig. 3.2 A question similar to the ones featured in one mental aptitude test used in the selection of US Airforce officers: Rotated Blocks (Carretta & Ree, 1996). The test requires the test-taker to identify, for each question like this, which shape (labelled A–E) is the rotated version of the first shape (labelled with a number)

Self-report surveys, mental aptitude tests, and assessments of personality and mental disorders are 'tools of the trade' for psychologists. They take decades to develop through research that tracks their ability to predict performance in different environments, from schools to workplaces. As a consequence, they tend to be available only at substantial cost, and only to approved users – mental health practitioners and researchers (Miller & Lovler, 2019).

NASA does not reveal the combination of surveys and tests that it uses during selection. This is because purchasing and practising an aptitude test can improve performance, and NASA does not wish to give applicants the opportunity to practice (Sgobba et al., 2018).

For future long-duration exploration missions (1–3 years), NASA has identified the following competencies as required, in order of criticality: (1) mental/emotional stability, (2) performance under stressful conditions, (3) group living skills, (4) teamwork skills, (5) appropriate family circumstances, (6) motivation, (7) reasoning and decision-making skills, (8) conscientiousness, (9) communication skills, and (10) leadership capability (Galarza & Holland, 1999). The first four skills support self-care abilities, which are crucial when living and working with others in close quarters and completing team-based mission-critical tasks. Neglecting self-care practices such as exercise, nutrition, sleep, relationship management, and stress management can leave an individual unprepared for critical team or individual tasks (Sgobba et al., 2018, see also Oxlad et al., Chap. 2, this volume).

How can cognitive scientists assist with the selection of individuals with knowledge, skills, abilities, and attitudes that stand up to the stressors of long-duration exploration missions? Cognitive scientists and neuroscientists at the National Institute of Mental Health in the US are currently working on mapping aspects of human functioning to the best available tests, be those objective tests or tests involving self-report. In their project, titled the Research Domain Criteria Initiative (RDoC; Morris & Cuthbert, 2012), these scientists hypothesise that human functioning engages the following systems: negative mood and emotion, positive mood and emotion, cognitive systems, systems for social processes, systems for adaptive arousal and inhibition, and so-called 'sensorimotor' systems for planning and executing actions based on sensory input. All systems are further subdivided, with 'cognitive systems', for example, consisting of attention, perception, declarative memory (consolidated facts and concepts in long-term memory), language, cognitive control (integration of emotional and cognitive systems), and working memory. (Notably, the RDoC model includes all of the cognitive abilities in Fig. 3.1, although in a slightly different configuration). The tests they have developed for selecting astronauts assess the functioning of specific aspects of these sub-systems. For example, the Behavior Rating Inventory of Executive Function (Roth et al., 2013) is recommended as a self-report-based test of the 'goal selection' aspect of cognitive control. The inventory consists of 75 questions, each requiring the respondent to indicate whether a behaviour, such as "trouble making decisions" is "never a problem", "sometimes a problem", or "often a problem". The RDoC scientists also recommend a mental rotation task similar to the example in Fig. 3.2 (along with other 'change detection' tasks) as one of 13 valid objective tests of the ability to actively maintain new information in memory.

NASA and researchers in ICE environments could collaborate with the RDoC scientists in developing a test battery spanning all domains of human functioning. The battery can be administered to all personnel selected for long-term missions in ICE environments – missions such as the 7-to-8-month Antarctic winter-over. Individual and team performance is often assessed during long-term ICE missions, and, so, there is an opportunity to gather a large dataset on how aspects of human functioning at the selection stage predict aspects of performance during the mission.

As this collaborative research initiative progresses, cognitive scientists can help with defining and measuring different aspects of performance in different environments. In particular, cognitive scientists have experience developing:

- measures that capture persistence and learning over time, rather than in pass/fail format (e.g., Luster & Pitts, 2021; Rasmussen & Eliasmith, 2013)
- more stable and theory-based grading criteria for tests that involve an observer's judgement (Roth & Mavin, 2015)
- procedures for combining results for multiple tests into an index of some aspect of performance (e.g, Mani et al., 1999)

Findings connecting pre-mission functioning and long-term mission performance should assist with resolving a lingering question – the question of whether attentional and sensorimotor skills should be assessed as part of the selection process for astronauts. The NASA's selection system is known to place less emphasis on these than the Russian system (Sgobba et al., 2018). Yet, high levels of these abilities are likely to be essential for establishing a mental map of a new environment in the early – adaptational – stages of space habitation (Manzey & Lorenz, 1998).

The RDoC mapping project has the additional advantage that its overarching goal is to determine how aspects of human functioning are altered in people with mental disorders, such as depression, borderline personality disorder, and schizophrenia. As discussed above in the description of Athena's selection process, applicants for NASA's Astronaut Candidate training program are screened for symptoms of mental disorders to ensure that the selected candidates are resilient in the face of stress, isolation, and high-pressure team-work. Working with the RDoC team could enable NASA to improve integration between its protocols for aptitude-related and psychiatric testing. More specifically, the RDoC framework defines human functioning as something that lies along a continuum from highly functional to indicative of mental illness. It is, therefore, possible that the RDoC framework can be used to pinpoint which minor deficits in functioning in a highly competent crew member can, over time, have implications for emotional stability, and, with that, team performance.

Looking even more broadly, developing selection procedures grounded in a theory of human cognitive and emotional functioning would represent a scientific breakthrough that harnesses multiple sub-disciplines of psychology. The development of aptitude and personality tests for use in personnel selection has typically been the remit of the sub-discipline of 'individual differences'. Assessment of emotional stability and instability has typically been the remit of 'clinical psychology'. Meanwhile, cognitive science has sought to develop and test theories about how the brain and mind are structured to enable humans to function quite effectively on a day-to-day basis. Consequently, cognitive scientists have expertise in measuring mental abilities at any given point in time, rather than in terms of stable individual differences (Lee & Webb, 2005). The unique personnel selection requirements of space habitation missions create an opportunity for cross-pollination across these sub-fields to develop more robust selection processes.

3.3 Can We Effectively Train People for Deep Space Habitation?

Now adopting the perspective of our fictional botanist, Astronaut Athena, consider what it might be like to take your first steps on a lunar outpost more than 300 kilometres from the earth's surface. You've spent years studying plant science, horticulture and biotechnology on earth. You've undergone rigorous physical and cognitive testing, including numerous mental aptitude tests like the mental rotation task illustrated in Fig. 3.2 above. You've logged countless hours of zero-g simulation time preparing your mind and body to function, move, and operate in microgravity. Despite all of this careful planning and preparation, with each step you take you encounter new smells, sights, sounds, and problems. On top of the novelty of your surroundings, your body is now beginning to undergo cardiovascular, muscular, bone, and neurovestibular changes resulting from the change in gravity. Should your mission go awry, aid is a long way away, and the comforts of home are well out of reach...

When learning to ride a bicycle we can safely practise the requisite motor patterns and coordination of movements by attaching a set of training wheels, or by starting out with a balance bike. Likewise, when learning new surgical techniques medical students can safely practise in haptic simulators or on cadavers to develop sufficient competency before attempting surgery on their first patients. Looking to domains more analogous to deep space, submariners typically practise tactical and command operations in onshore simulators before progressing to aided training conditions at sea and eventually unaided warlike training operations. Even aviators practise learning to pilot jet and rocket aircraft in immersive flight simulators before undertaking part-task training mission flights and full solo flights at more advanced levels of competency. In each of these domains, the training environments have been carefully constructed to support the gradual development of competency in scenarios that closely resemble the ultimate environment of operation. By contrast, astronauts do not have the luxury of such a gradual familiarisation to their operational environment – space. There are no training wheels for living off-earth for months or even years at a time because such endeavours are pushing the boundaries of human experience, where much of the environment remains unknown and unfamiliar (Dietlein & Pestov, 2004). How then might we train astronauts like Athena to function optimally, and think clearly, on her long-haul mission to the lunar surface?

To answer this question we need to understand how people adapt prior knowledge to new and analogous contexts – a topic that has puzzled educators and psychologists for over a century. For example, the widespread instruction of formal disciplines such as grammar, logic, memory, and even Latin in the nineteenth century was largely driven by the belief that general knowledge can be adapted to any specific situation (Nisbett et al., 1987). Indeed, most modern training programs aim to equip people with knowledge that is durable enough so as not to be immediately forgotten and skills that are flexible enough to be used in a variety of contexts. While long-term retention of knowledge and the ability to transfer skills to novel situations are key indicators of any successful training program, they can be difficult to assess (Soderstrom & Bjork, 2015). In contrast to measures of performance, which are commonly taken during or immediately after a training program, measures of long-term learning and transfer are best taken after a deliberate and extended period of delay using assessments that incorporate analogous but different problems to those encountered during training scenarios. This distinction between the assessment of learning versus performance is critical to designing an effective training intervention for astronauts like Athena because, paradoxically, long-term retention of skills can occur in the absence of performance improvements. For example, Army reservists who continued to practise assembling and disassembling an M60 machine gun even after reaching proficiency in the task were faster to regain proficiency after a delay compared with participants who did not overtrain (Schendel & Hagman, 1982). Likewise, long-term learning outcomes are not guaranteed on the basis of performance improvements observed during training or study. For example, the commonly used study tactic of 'cramming' for an exam is an effective strategy for improving initial exam results but terrible for long-term retention of information and transfer of learning to novel problems and situations – outcomes that are particularly important for training astronauts (Bjork et al., 2013).

We don't want to make the mistake of designing a training program that our astronauts can cram for without the retention of lasting mission-critical competencies. So to prepare our botanist for long-term habitation on the lunar surface, our training program needs to promote long-term gains in competency over short-term gains in performance. But can we design a training intervention that effectively aids transfer of learning to an environment as unfamiliar as the moon or even Mars in the future? A great deal of cognitive science evidence demonstrates that transfer of learning to novel situations is incredibly difficult to facilitate. In fact, learning tends to be bound to the problems, materials and contexts within which the learning occurred. For example, Thorndike (1906) tested the nineteenth century notion described earlier that the study of formal disciplines like logic and Latin can confer more general skills of reasoning and problem-solving. He found that training the rules of one discipline did not, in fact, produce spontaneous generalisation to other disciplines (e.g., studying mathematics is not going to improve language acquisition; Thorndike, 1906). In more recent times, an extensive review of the effects of popular brain training interventions, purpose built to improve general cognitive functioning and stave off cognitive decline, found no lasting benefits (Simons et al., 2016). Brain training applications commonly incorporate tasks aimed at improving some general aspect of cognition, similar to the mental rotation task illustrated above. While there are considerable performance benefits for the trained tasks (e.g., training mental rotation improves mental rotation), there is little evidence of performance improvements for closely or distantly related tasks (e.g., training mental rotation will not make you a better Tetris player let alone better at recognising faces; Sims & Mayer, 2002). The highly specific nature of skill and knowledge acquisition has been demonstrated time and again in areas as diverse as chess, law, medicine, psychology, chemistry, and forensic science. This literature would suggest that subjecting Athena to repeated mental aptitude testing or training that does not closely resemble the kinds of problems she will encounter will do little to improve her reasoning or thinking in space.

The problem of learning and skills transfer presents a real challenge for astronauts preparing to undertake long-haul missions in space, but not an insurmountable one. If the goal is to promote the development of durable competencies that can be applied to a raft of problems that might arise in deep space habitats, like Athena's lava tube outpost, cognitive science and educational psychology research provides some clues as to how best to design more effective training programs. Cognitive Load Theory, for example, is an established framework for designing educational interventions that carefully manage working memory load for optimal development of long-term memory and learning transfer to novel problems (Sweller et al., 1998). Working memory refers to our capacity to consciously hold information in mind and it is easily overloaded (Miller, 1956). Long-term memory, by contrast, refers to our capacity to store information for extended periods of time and is thought to be unlimited. Long-term memory can be viewed as the seat of human skill and expertise as the knowledge structures we store in long-term memory allow us to rapidly recognise and resolve familiar situations and problems. For example, chess grandmasters are able to make more optimal moves in any given game by virtue of their superior long-term memory for chess board configurations (Chase & Simon, 1973). New or unfamiliar problems – commonly encountered when learning a new skill or training for a new endeavour like space flight – are more taxing on working memory because the contents of our long-term memory does not offer an immediate solution to them. Thus, the challenge for any educational or training program is to support the development of relevant knowledge structures in long-term memory with finite working memory resources.

How can we best prepare Athena for the situations and problems she might encounter in a lunar lava tube more than 300 kilometres away from Earth? According to Cognitive Load Theory, a well-designed training program minimises effort expended on extrinsic elements of the training environment and maximises efforts expended on tasks and processes that are intrinsic or most relevant to the goal at hand. Thus, if our goal was to build a simulated training environment to help Athena learn how to operate a rover on the lunar surface, we might start by familiarising her with the basic operational mechanics of the vehicle without other immersive elements like artificial zero-g that may overload her working memory. The increased cognitive load generated from more immersive simulations can result in adverse training outcomes (e.g., see Frederiksen et al., 2020 for an example in surgical skills training). The challenge, then, is to gradually increase Athena's exposure to more and more immersive lunar rover simulations as her competency level increases and she has greater access to long-term memory structures that support more automatic problem-solving. Existing space analogue facilities, such as the Human Exploration Research Analog (HERA) based at NASA Johnson Space Centre (Patel et al., 2020) offer promising training grounds for astronauts preparing for long-duration missions. Advances in immersive virtual reality technology also offer new opportunities to construct controlled training scenarios for astronauts that optimally balance working memory load while facilitating the development of long-term memory structures that support mission-critical competencies.

3.4   How Do We Preserve Optimal Cognitive Functioning for Deep Space Habitation?

Astronaut Athena has been in long-duration spaceflight for 7 months. She notices that a number of routine maintenance tasks are required on various systems within the module she inhabits. She is now outside of normal range for communication with Earth and must carry out these tasks without any instruction or support from ground crew. She has trained for this and thinks that she remembers all of the steps in the process – she has some manuals for reminders, and support from her cohabitants, however, she has been noticing that she is experiencing "space fog" – difficulty in paying attention and in memory…

We humans have always pushed ourselves to extremes – surviving in inhospitable and difficult environments. The ability to have insight into our own cognition and control our behaviour as a function of these insights has been critical to survival. This ability is broadly termed 'metacognition' and can be defined as knowledge concerning one's own cognitive processes and products, or anything related to them. For example, metacognition is involved in learning relevant properties of information or data and then actively monitoring and regulating these processes in relation to relevant cognitive objects or data usually to fulfil an objective or goal (Tarricone, 2011). This broad definition is not very useful unless it is related to measurable behaviour. In our example above Athena is engaging in metacognition when she "thinks she remembers" the steps in the maintenance process and notices that she is "experiencing…difficulty in paying attention". These insights are measurable reports that Athena can make and her performance on tests of cognition or upon the tasks that engage this knowledge and skill can be quantified to either confirm or disconfirm her insights. Critically, if Athena is right and her ability to remember and focus her attention is impaired then she should not carry out these tasks and should use countermeasures to mitigate the decline in performance – in the hope that they recalibrate her metacognitions and do not result in misalignment between her performance and her beliefs about capacity.

Cognitive scientists identified metacognition as a distinct subfield of research in the 1960s. Particular types of metacognition, such as confidence in the accuracy of a perception, has an even longer history, beginning with the very first psychophysical experiments carried out in the 1880s (Peirce & Jastrow, 1884). The two key ingredients to any experiment examining metacognition are (1) measurement of performance on a task (memory, attention, reasoning, detection, inference, etc.) and (2) measurement of the individuals' perception of their own performance (in a trial-by-trial manner). The list of possible questions that can be defined as measures of metacognitive monitoring is extensive, but some of the most studied are confidence, feeling-of-knowing and judgments of learning. These three judgments are mostly related to memory performance but have also been used to assess metacognition in reasoning (Thompson et al., 2011) and problem solving tasks. Characterising metacognitive performance involves contrasting objective performance against subjective judgments. In studies using confidence as a measure, the relationship is characterised by drawing calibration curves that plot percentage of correct decisions against estimated certainty (usually elicited on a 0–100% scale). Further calibration metrics can be calculated to determine whether participants in a study are over or under confident, along with scores representing the degree to which their confidence discriminates correct from incorrect decisions (aka resolution).

3.5 What Does the Basic Science Say About the Types of Challenges That Long Duration Space Habitation Might Present to Human Metacognition?

Sleep deprivation, radiation bursts and exposure to CO_2 spikes have been identified as possible threats to human cognitive performance in spaceflight (Strangman et al., 2014) and they also represent threats to those involved in deep space habitation. But how aware are individuals of these impacts? Fortunately there are some meta-analyses that have characterised the literature regarding the impact of each of these environmental threats on metacognitive performance too; they are however, limited to the terrestrial domain. First, the impact of sleep deprivation on metacognitive performance was reviewed recently by Aidman et al. (2019). They found 10 studies to review that examined metacognitive performance under sleep deprivation proto-cols of up to 63 h. The review considered three descriptors of metacognitive perfor-mance; confidence, bias (over/under confidence) and discrimination (resolution). The overall finding was that although cognitive performance declined on most tasks, participants in these studies were aware of this decline, adjusting their monitoring judgements accordingly. However, the methodological quality of these studies was poor and the samples were limited in terms of age and gender. There has also been some evidence that countermeasures such as caffeine and modafinil given to sleep deprived participants can produce overconfidence (Kilpeläinen et al., 2010). The risk of overconfidence to survival could be greatly amplified in space. In summary, the limited data suggest there is reasonable preservation of metacognitive ability under sleep deprived conditions on Earth at least.

Another potential threat to metacognitive performance in space is the impact of elevated CO_2. An extensive review by Beard (2020) identified no less than 14 sepa-rate effects of elevated CO_2 on perception and cognition. These studies included effects on rapid decision making (as measured by simple and choice reaction time tests), sustained attention and information seeking, and visual perception (including line orientation, stereoacuity, colour sensitivity, depth perception, and coherent motion). None of the studies investigated the impact of CO_2 on metacognitive per-formance. Once again, performance deficits can only be mitigated if they are recog-nised by the human and counter measures are available.

What do we know about the impact of long duration space flight or analogue environments upon metacognitive processes? Do the risks posed to the cognitive capacity of humans in these settings also show up in their ability to have insight into their capacities? Beginning first with analogue environments, there are very few studies that have documented metacognitive performance. A study by Nelson et al. (1990) conducted during a climb to the summit of Mount Everest, was focussed on recall and recognition memory performance. Climbers (12 in total) tested one another in experimenter-participant roles – swapping on each of the 6 testing ses-sions. They found that the feeling-of-knowing was negatively impacted by the extreme environment but memory performance itself was not impacted. This small study indicates that metacognition could be sensitive to the conditions of extreme altitude – however, given the size of the sample and the necessary pragmatic aspects of recording the test results at that time, the findings need to be replicated. In addition to this, recent broad criticism of confounding in studies of metacognition (Paulewicz et al., 2020) have highlighted the need for careful causal analysis of the factors that are thought to influence metacognitive monitoring and control. In sum, again, the evidence is limited that metacognition is impacted by the extreme environment of Mount Everest and there is a clear research gap in understanding the impact of Isolated, Confined, and Extreme environments on metacognitive performance.

3.6   How Do We Monitor and Preserve Metacognitive Functioning in Deep Space Environments?

If we widely accept that cognitive performance will be impacted by deep space habitation, the question is how will we know? Self-reports of "space fog" are one source of evidence, however, what if metacognition is also impaired and our space inhabitants have no insight into the dangers that their impaired cognition might present? The process of actually monitoring cognition in space has been an ongoing challenge that has spurred the development of a number of very quick and simple measurement tasks. One of the most well studied and deployed in crew performance is the Psychomotor Vigilance Test (Basner & Dinges, 2011). This test involves responding as quickly as possible to a count-down clock that appears at randomly defined intermittent intervals on a screen. If the person responds before the timer appears, a false start is recorded. In addition to this, self-report measures that assess stress and fatigue levels can be administered. They simply involve asking the individual a series of questions; for example, asking them to complete a sleep diary, and 11-point rating scales on tiredness, mental fatigue, physical exhaustion, and stress, and sleepiness. The content of a final rating would depend on the time of day, involving a rating of workload in the evening, and sleep quality in the morning. These self-reports are not really classified as metacognitive measures because they do not relate to specific cognitive functions or tasks. They do, however, give some notion of whether or not individuals are aware of their potential for decline in performance in a very general sense. A recent report by Tu et al. (2021) documents an individual level ensemble modelling approach (a machine learning technique that allows prediction of human cognitive performance) that allows astronauts to understand their current performance on the Psychomotor Vigilance Test (defined as their LRM-50 score) as a function of individual history and environmental variables such as CO_2 levels, temperature and radiation. This approach was developed using the data from astronauts before and during space-flight on the ISS. While impressive in terms of its ability to predict cognitive functioning – in practice the value of this information is limited because the environmental conditions in deep space are inherently unpredictable, and so cannot be modelled. Other methods for monitoring occur via wearable physiological sensors that can determine heart-rate and the various metrics that are thought to correspond with the degree of stress being experienced by an individual (Kim et al., 2018), but again these metrics are proxies for metacognitive monitoring by the individual. Cognitive tests and self-report measures take time to complete – when faced with an emergency situation, it is difficult to see how they might be practically deployed to allow a deep space inhabitant to adjust their metacognitive monitoring, detect any misalignment and thus stop themselves from committing a fatal error.

Perhaps one of the most hopeful areas for preventing metacognitive error comes from the development and use of technology that adapts to human functioning. The possibility of machines that can sense and compensate for the cognitive failings of their human crew is not far away (Tu et al., 2021). For example, a brain-computer interface that can determine lapses of attention or dominance of particular neural signals can warn the individual or team mates that it is time to rest. For a full array of the possibilities see Cinel et al. (2019). It may be in these advances that the best solution is found.

3.7 Conclusions

We have followed the travails of Athena, seeing how she might be selected and trained, and how she might then adapt to deep space habitation. In this process we have highlighted the many research gaps that exist in our current understanding of human cognition in deep space. There is much basic science that we can draw upon, which has sometimes been extended into understanding cognition in extreme environments. However, less work is evident in understanding cognition in space for long periods of time and so we must build upon this work to ensure that astronauts sent into these environments can survive and indeed thrive for the long term.

The stressors of the long-duration space exploration missions create a need for selecting crew members with high levels of mental aptitude and sustained positive attitudes towards self-care and teamwork. NASA does not reveal its selection test batteries to reduce the possibility of practice by applicants. However, there would be many benefits to NASA funding further research in Isolated, Confined, and Extreme environments, which tracks the performance implications of a systematic set of tests. These tests should be chosen in collaboration with cognitive scientists, including those behind the RDoC project. The RDoC project seeks to define the components of human functioning and identify the most robust tests of various aspects of cognition. It additionally seeks to identify how deficits in functioning map on to mental illness. Collaboratively, NASA, cognitive scientists, and leaders of research in various ICE environments could examine the impacts of minor deficits in functioning on performance over time in long-term missions in ICE environments. Given their expertise in designing moment-to-moment measures of performance, cognitive scientists could additionally contribute to developing new indices of performance in these complex environments.

Training for deep space habitation involves recognising a key challenge: skills and competencies developed in one context do not easily transfer to another context. Training programs that gradually expose astronauts to varied instances of scenarios they might encounter in space, while minimising extraneous sources of cognitive load, are likely to be more successful at promoting the development of relevant competencies. Indeed, at the heart of this challenge is a need for specific understanding and definition of deep space cognitive expertise. At present, this is an important area for future research that must involve realistic and incremental challenges to elicit the cognitive architecture needed for adaptation in space.

Having insight into our own cognition and being able to adapt as a function of this insight is a core feature of what has made humans able to survive and thrive on Earth over millennia. Humans can be seen as dynamic systems (van Gelder, 1999). This implies that we need to measure functioning over time to capture this adaptation. Adaptation also assumes that people are aware of when their performance is drifting away from optimal and how to bring it back (implying metacognitive awareness) and this becomes much more important as a function of the time delay in communication with deep space; that is, people need to be able to correct their own performance or put measures in place to meet current demands. However, the unique physical and physiological challenges of space might mean a complete adjustment to metacognitive processes and calibration of behaviour. As yet, the evidence on how metacognition is impacted by even long term space flight is limited. Perhaps the best hope we have in assisting in training and adaptation is the use of technology.

Many humans have already successfully completed missions in challenging space and ICE environments. Likewise, we envisage that people like Astronaut Athena will triumph in their pioneering expeditions on the Moon and Mars. With the appropriate processes and training in place, backed by cognitive science, humans will be able to think clearly and excel in the next frontier of deep space habitation.

Contributions

Authors who contributed substantially to each section of this chapter. Abstract: Semmler. Introduction: Stephens. Selecting astronauts: Ejova. Training astronauts: Searston. Preserving astronauts' cognitive functioning: Semmler. Conclusion: Semmler.

References

Aidman, E., Jackson, S. A., & Kleitman, S. (2019). Effects of sleep deprivation on executive functioning, cognitive abilities, metacognitive confidence, and decision making. *Applied Cognitive Psychology, 33*(2), 188–200.

Basner, M., & Dinges, D. F. (2011). Maximizing sensitivity of the psychomotor vigilance test (PVT) to sleep loss. *Sleep, 34*(5), 581–591. https://doi.org/10.1093/sleep/34.5.581

Beard, B. (2020). Characterization of how CO_2 level may impact crew performance related to the HSIA risk. *NASA technical memorandum series*. NASA/TM – 20205011433.

Bjork, R. A., Dunlosky, J., & Kornell, N. (2013). Self-regulated learning: Beliefs, techniques, and illusions. *Annual Review of Psychology, 64*, 417–444. https://doi.org/10.1146/annurev-psych-113011-143823

Carretta, T. R., & Ree, M. J. (1996). Factor structure of the air force officer qualifying test: Analysis and comparison. *Military Psychology: The Official Journal of the Division of Military Psychology, 8*(1), 29–42. https://doi.org/10.1207/s15327876mp0801_3

Cassell, A. M. (2019). Forward to the moon: NASA's strategic plan for human exploration. *NASA Ames Research Center ARC-E-DAA-TN73512.*

Chase, W. G., & Simon, H. A. (1973). Perception in chess. *Cognitive Psychology, 4*, 55-81. https://doi.org/10.1016/0010-0285(73)90004-2

Cinel, C., Valeriani, D., & Poli, R. (2019). Neurotechnologies for human cognitive augmentation: Current state of the art and future prospects. *Frontiers in Human Neuroscience, 13*. https://doi.org/10.3389/fnhum.2019.00013

Dietlein, L. F., & Pestov, I. D. (Eds.). (2004). *Space biology and medicine: Volume IV. Health, performance, and safety of space crews.* American Institute of Aeronautics and Astronautics.

Galarza, L., & Holland, A. W. (1999). Critical astronaut proficiencies required for long duration space flight. *SAE Technical Paper 1999-01-2096.*

Frederiksen, J. G., Sørensen, S. M. D., Konge, L., Svendsen, M. B. S., Nobel-Jørgensen, M., Bjerrum, F., & Andersen, S. A. W. (2020). Cognitive load and performance in immersive virtual reality versus conventional virtual reality simulation training of laparoscopic surgery: a randomized trial. *Surgical endoscopy, 34*(3), 1244–1252. https://doi.org/10.1007/s00464-019-06887-8

Goldstein, E. B. (2018). *Cognitive psychology: Connecting mind, research, and everyday experience* (5th ed.). Cengage.

Kilpeläinen, A. A., Huttunen, K. H., Lohi, J. J., & Lyytinen, H. (2010). Effect of caffeine on vigilance and cognitive performance during extended wakefulness. *The International Journal of Aviation Psychology, 20*(2), 144–159.

Kim, H. G., Cheon, E. J., Bai, D. S., Lee, Y. H., & Koo, B. H. (2018). Stress and heart rate variability: A meta-analysis and review of the literature. *Psychiatry Investigation, 15*(3), 235–245.

Le Moign, V. (2018). Woman Astronaut Image available at https://commons.wikimedia.org/wiki/File:179-woman-astronaut-1.svg

Lee, M. D., & Webb, M. R. (2005). Modelling individual differences in cognition. *Psychonomic Bulletin & Review, 12*(4), 605–621.

Luster, M. S., & Pitts, B. J. (2021). A preliminary investigation into learning behaviors in complex environments for human-in-the-loop cyber-physical systems. *Proceedings of the Human Factors and Ergonomics Society Annual Meeting, 65*(1), 42–46.

Mani, S., Shankle, W. R., Dick, M. B., & Pazzani, M. J. (1999). Two-stage machine learning model for guideline development. *Artificial Intelligence in Medicine, 16*(1), 51–71.

Manzey, D., & Lorenz, B. (1998). Mental performance during short-term and long-term spaceflight. *Brain Research Reviews, 28*(1–2), 215–221.

Miller, G. A. (1956). The magical number seven, plus or minus two: Some limits on our capacity for processing information. *Psychological Review, 63*, 81–97.

Miller, L. A., & Lovler, R. L. (2019). *Foundations of psychological testing.* SAGE Publications.

Morris, S. E., & Cuthbert, B. N. (2012). Research domain criteria: Cognitive systems, neural circuits, and dimensions of behavior. *Dialogues in Clinical Neuroscience, 14*(1), 29–37.

Nelson, T. O., Dunlosky, J., White, D. M., Steinburg, J., Townes, B. D., & Anderson, D. (1990). Cognition and metacognition at extreme altitudes on Mount Everest. *Journal of Experimental Psychology, 119*(4), 367–374.

Nisbett, R., Fong, G., Lehman, D., & Cheng, P. (1987). Teaching Reasoning. *Science (New York, N.Y.), 238*, 625–631. https://doi.org/10.1126/science.3672116

Patel, Z. S., Brunstetter, T. J., Tarver, W. J., Whitmire, A. M., Zwart, S. R., Smith, S. M., & Huff, J. L. (2020). Red risks for a journey to the red planet: The highest priority human health risks for a mission to Mars. *Nature Partner Journals: Microgravity, 6*, 1–13.

Paulewicz, B., Siedlecka, M., & Koculak, M. (2020). Confounding in studies on metacognition: A preliminary causal analysis framework. *Frontiers in Psychology, 11*. https://doi.org/10.3389/fpsyg.2020.01933

Quinlan, P., & Dyson, B. (2008). *Cognitive psychology.* Pearson.

Rasmussen, D., & Eliasmith, C. (2013). A neural reinforcement learning model for tasks with unknown time delays. *Proceedings of the Annual Meeting of the Cognitive Science Society, 35*(35). https://escholarship.org/uc/item/5qb1w7nx

Roth, W.-M., & Mavin, T. J. (2015). Peer assessment of aviation performance: Inconsistent for good reasons. *Cognitive Science, 39*(2), 405–433.

Roth, R. M., Lance, C. E., Isquith, P. K., Fischer, A. S., & Giancola, P. R. (2013). Confirmatory factor analysis of the behavior rating inventory of executive function-adult version in healthy adults and application to attention-deficit/hyperactivity disorder. *Archives of Clinical Neuropsychology, 28*(5), 425–434.

Schendel, J. D., & Hagman, J. D. (1982). On sustaining procedural skills over a prolonged retention interval. *Journal of Applied Psychology, 67*(5), 605–610. https://doi.org/10.1037/0021-9010.67.5.605

Sgobba, T., Landon, L. B., Marciacq, J.-B., Groen, E., Tikhonov, N., & Torchia, F. (2018). Chapter 16 – Selection and training. In T. Sgobba, B. Kanki, J.-F. Clervoy, & G. M. Sandal (Eds.), *Space safety and human performance* (pp. 721–793). Butterworth-Heinemann.

Simons, D. J., Boot, W. R., Charness, N., Gathercole, S. E., Chabris, C. F., Hambrick, D. Z., & Stine-Morrow, E. A. L. (2016). Do "brain-training" programs work? *Psychological Science in the Public Interest, 17*(3), 103–186.

Sims, V. K., & Mayer, R. E. (2002). Domain specificity of spatial expertise: The case of video game players. *Applied Cognitive Psychology, 16*, 97–115.

Soderstrom, N. C., & Bjork, R. A. (2015). Learning versus performance: An integrative review. *Perspectives on Psychological Science: A Journal of the Association for Psychological Science, 10*(2), 176–199. https://doi.org/10.1177/1745691615569000

Strangman, G. E., Sipes, W., & Beven, G. (2014). Human cognitive performance in spaceflight and analogue environments. *Aviation, Space, and Environmental Medicine, 85*(10), 1033–1048.

Sweller, J., van Merrienboer, J. J. G. & Paas, F. G. W. C. (1998). Cognitive architecture and instructional design. *Educational Psychology Review, 10*, 251–296. https://doi.org/10.1023/A:1022193728205

Tarricone, P. (2011). *The taxonomy of metacognition*. Psychology Press.

Thompson, V. A., Prowse Turner, J. A., & Pennycook, G. (2011). Intuition, reasoning and metacognition. *Cognitive Psychology, 63*(3), 107–140.

Thorndike, E. L. (1906). *The principles of teaching based on psychology*. A G Seiler. https://doi.org/10.1037/11487-000

Tu, D., Basner, M., Smith, M. G., Williams, E. S., Ryder, V. E., Rosmoser, A. A., Ecker, A., Acschbach, D., Stahn, A. C., Jones, C., Howard, K., Kaizi-Lutu, M., Dinges, D. F., & Shou, H. (2021). *Dynamic ensemble prediction of cognitive performance in space* (NASA STI program technical publication series, NASA/TP-20210022966).

van Gelder, T. J. (1999). Dynamic approaches to cognition. In R. Wilson & F. Keil (Eds.), *The MIT Encyclopaedia of cognitive sciences* (pp. 244–246). MIT Press.

Chapter 4
The Challenges and Opportunities of Human-Robot Interaction for Deep Space Habitation

Anna Ma-Wyatt, Justin Fidock, Jessica O'Rielly, Heidi Long, and John Culton

Abstract Deep space habitation for long periods of time will generate exciting challenges for human-robot interaction and human-machine teaming more broadly. Human-robot interactions on Earth can take place in the form of a robotic vehicle that is remotely operated by a human (teleoperation), or supervised by a human (supervisory control). In these scenarios, the human plays a critical role in the success of the robot's activity and they work cooperatively in complex environments. In space, there will be new challenges for both near real time and delayed supervisory control for complex tasks in a harsh environment, in terms of maintaining situational awareness and trust. Human-robot interaction will be a key part of a higher proportion of activities off Earth, due to the harsh environment. We therefore also consider challenges associated with human-robot interaction over extended periods of time for remote teams. We review recent results relevant to these problems, including the cognitive implications of human-robot teaming, and discuss the potential implications for crewing for long term deep space habitation.

A. Ma-Wyatt (✉)
School of Psychology, The University of Adelaide, Adelaide, SA, Australia

CNRS IRL CROSSING, Adelaide, SA, Australia
e-mail: anna.mawyatt@adelaide.edu.au

J. Fidock
Intelligence, Surveillance and Space Division, Defence Science and Technology Group, Department of Defence, Fairbairn, Canberra, Australia

J. O'Rielly · H. Long
School of Psychology, The University of Adelaide, Adelaide, SA, Australia

J. Culton
Andy Thomas Centre for Space Resources, The University of Adelaide, Adelaide, SA, Australia

M. de Zwart et al. (eds.), *Human Uses of Outer Space*, Issues in Space, https://doi.org/10.1007/978-981-19-9462-3_4

49

4.1 Introduction

Humans regularly work with automated or semi-autonomous systems. There are some applications already in place within both the transportation and resource sectors. Development of autonomy in cars is also progressing, albeit within certain bounds. With the rise of autonomous and semi-autonomous systems it is important to understand how human performance changes while interacting with these autonomous and semi-autonomous systems, and how these performance changes can be measured. This area of research can be referred to as human-autonomy teaming or human-machine teaming. The benefits of human-autonomy teaming can be considerable. For example, semi-autonomous trains are used in both metropolitan settings but also in remote settings like mines. However, human-autonomy teaming does not eradicate the possibility of a negative outcome. In recent times, and with errors associated with the functioning of autonomous systems and with human error in using autonomous systems leading to catastrophic outcomes, there has been a focus on understanding how we build systems that support human-autonomy teaming more generally. Deep space habitation provides an especially interesting use case when considering the problems and opportunities associated with long term human-robot teaming. Crusan et al., (2017) describe the complexity of establishing long term deep space habitation and identify that integrated human and robot missions will be a necessary component of this work.

Several scenarios are possible for human-machine teaming. The human could be on the loop (through supervisory control) or in the loop (through teleoperation). In situations where robotic vehicles are optionally crewed, human operators may be required to transition between teleoperation and supervisory control. Several studies have shown that there is a cognitive burden associated with supervisory control and teleoperation, and transitions between the two states. It does not seem to be the case that interaction with an automated or semi-autonomous system is less taxing for a human participant. For example, driving with supervisory control has been shown to increase subjective fatigue for human drivers (Neubauer et al., 2012; Schmidt et al., 2018), an effect possibly due to passive fatigue which is the result of monotony or boredom (Matthews et al., 2019). It is worth noting that in this context supervisory control is required for functions that are semi-autonomous or automated for a car. Perception of external hazards also decline (Shen & Neyens, 2017), and there is evidence that driver awareness of the surrounding environment declines (de Winter et al., 2014). There is also the complex question of what should be measured as a change in performance during teleoperation or supervisory control. The dispersion of saccade endpoints can change significantly between periods of teleoperation and supervisory control (e.g. Ma-Wyatt et al., 2018b; 2019). These authors interpreted these data as suggesting that participants were less actively exploring their environment during periods of supervisory control, consistent with other reports that attentional deployment decreases under automated driving conditions (Solís-Marcos et al., 2017).

These studies highlight two key problems in human-machine teaming research. The first is to understand how to quantify and understand human performance in a real environment, and the second is to understand how that is related to the performance and presence of the autonomous or semi-autonomous system. That is, what is due to changes in the complexity of the environment, and how much is related to the interaction with the autonomous or semi-autonomous system. There are numerous approaches to this problem. Ma-Wyatt et al. (2018a) outlined key criteria to assess the suitability of methods for this problem:

1. They should not interfere directly with the performance of the operator on the task
2. They need to offer a continuous stream of information to allow continuous monitoring of the operator's performance. Continuity needs to occur on a time resolution that is sufficient for automation to intervene with the system if a negative risk arises.
3. They need to be sensitive enough to detect changes in those humans' cognitive states that are relevant to the context and the task at hand.
4. They need to have high time resolution to detect a change quickly.
5. They need to be body posture and orientation invariant to allow the human to move freely without losing data.

These criteria are aspirational, although significant progress has been made towards them.

One of the key challenges is to clarify how to meaningfully quantify and characterise human performance in a real environment that does not interfere with the performance of the operator. For this we can seek guidance from fields of study that are relevant to off-Earth scenarios. We are hopeful that learnings from these areas can be easily extended to situations like those we may face during human-machine teaming off-Earth. Indeed, much insight can be found in methodologies used to unobtrusively characterise and monitor human performance currently used in operational environments. While there is diversity in the approach, we consider one example which has delivered promising results for on-Earth environments to illustrate the challenges and opportunities around monitoring human performance.

Eye tracking is a technique whereby an individual's eye movements, or gaze direction, are recorded. Current eye tracking systems are minimally invasive to the user and can be integrated into existing work patterns. Existing implementation has seen this technique employed across many domains including, human-computer interaction (Poole & Ball, 2006), high risk operational environments and pilot cockpits (Ulutas et al., 2020; Scannella et al., 2018). Models based on eye-tracking behaviour have been used to study human-machine teaming and interaction (Dehais et al., 2015). The benefit of this approach is that it satisfies our first criteria, as eye tracking technologies do not interfere directly with the performance of the operator on the task.

Eye tracking techniques provide knowledge into where a person is looking in the environment (Poole & Ball, 2006). This metric may be useful as research has shown that where and when a person chooses to direct the focus of their gaze can provide insight into the kind of information available to the individual at the time and how this information was used to complete the observer's objectives. For example, Dehais et al. (2015) used eye-tracking technologies to understand behaviour of pilots during an unexpected flight event. In another example, the sequences and patterns of eye movements when coupled with an understanding of individual work patterns of an operator were shown to be indicative of operator tasking within an air traffic control setting (Svensson, n.d.). They showed that specific tasking was associated with unique patterns of eye movements with relevant areas of the user interface that was looked at different times depending on the specific tasking in which the operator engaged.

These results, and others like it (e.g. Diez et al., 2001; Regis et al., 2012) provide examples to demonstrate the utility of eye tracking technologies in complex, high risk operational environments. While we have discussed just one exemplar measure used to unobtrusively monitor human performance, currently employed in operational environments, we anticipate that this technique may be easily extended to aspects of human-machine teaming during off-Earth scenarios. But to see this to fruition, there are some considerable challenges that must be addressed. The following section will discuss some of these challenges in turn, and while not exhaustive, we hope that it will provide some insight into the challenges facing many aspects of human-machine teaming (and research investigating this space) in off-Earth environments.

4.2   Key Challenges for Human-Machine Teaming Research: Real Time Utility of Measures and Prediction

We can learn much from methodologies currently used to monitor human operators in operational environments, especially those akin to scenarios which may be faced by those in off-Earth environments. However, one aspect that will impact the usability of this knowledge is how quickly these data can be processed in a deep space environment to be of use operationally. Human-machine interaction and human machine teaming, especially in a deep space environment, is and will continue to be a dynamic process. Real time quantification of this interaction, with the ability to assess quickly and effectively, and make key changes based on the information, will be a necessary aspect of this teaming process and critical to the success of the interaction. Therefore, it is highly important that any measurement of this process be available for use in close to real time. We continue with the running example of using eye tracking technologies and draw on examples from adjacent fields as ways of providing insight into operator performance in an operational environment. We also consider how useful such metrics may be in a real time context.

Signals derived from eye movement behaviours are continuously sampled and thus they provide a means of generating a constant stream of information that can be leveraged to provide insight into behaviour in real time. If we consider an example from the aviation industry, patterns of eye movements have been shown to be useful for the real time assessment of workload. As pilot workload can fluctuate rapidly depending on the flying environment, Di Nocera et al. (2007) assessed the utility of eye movement measures to provide insight into workload in real time. They utilised a measure of spatial gaze dispersion that can be derived from the continuous gaze position record. They showed that measurements of the gaze dispersion were sensitive to variations in mental workload of pilots during the simulated flights. Because gaze dispersion measures can be derived from the continuous eye position signal with a low data processing overhead, the authors argued that metrics based on this may be uniquely suited to inform real time technologies such as those found necessary in human-machine teaming scenarios.

Other work has also shown eye-movement based metrics may be useful in real time adaptive interfaces for the purpose of optimizing a user's tasking. Wilson et al. (2010) used a measurement of a user's mental workload to implement an adaptive aiding system. The authors recorded physiological information from 7 participants that included a combination of eye tracking, electrocardiographic and respiration inputs while they completed the NASA Multiple Attribute Test Battery (MATB, Comstock & Amegard, 1992). Wilson et al. (2010) used this information to train a classifying algorithm based on 5 min of participant practice data under three workload conditions of the MATB, including resting, low workload and high workload. Workload conditions were manipulated according to the number of visual and auditory secondary subtasks required alongside the main task. Participants then completed a round of testing where their mental workload was assessed online using the physiological measures of their internal state. When participants workload was detected to be in the high category, the adaptive system responded by reducing the number of subtasks required by the participant. The results showed the workload classification algorithm had a high classification accuracy with an overall range between 69–97% across all participants. The adaptive aiding also significantly improved participant task performance as task error was reduced by 44% and resource management error was reduced by 33%.

Taken together, these studies highlight the possibility of using measures of human performance to monitor and even modify operator and automation behaviour in real time to support the human-machine working relationship. While the examples highlighted above do focus heavily on just one means of obtaining this information, e.g., eye tracking, it is easy to see how these examples can extend to operations in adjacent fields of interest such as off Earth environments.

4.3 Complexity of the Off-Earth Environment and the Relation to Human-Robot Interaction and Human-Machine Teaming

However, it must be noted that these criteria assume that the environment is well characterised and instrumentation is possible. These assumptions may not apply in deep space, and these problems are writ large. It's a challenging and extreme environment. There is no return to Earth possible with short notice. There will be increased latency lags compared to operations on Earth, so there are challenges around using automated and semi-autonomous vehicles that can tolerate a significant time lag for new instructions in a complex environment. Robots are therefore likely to require greater proportions of teleoperation and the human operator will be required to have longer and more vigilant periods of supervisory control than on Earth. People will spend more of their day reliant on human autonomy teaming for their survival as well as work. Because of the harsh external environment, it is likely that there will be a greater potential requirement for interaction with robots as part of daily life.

An additional key issue is around habitation. Unlike on Earth, humans will necessarily have to interact with technology simply to survive. In a remote mining site on Earth, people may interact with automated or semi-autonomous systems during their shifts, but they are free to walk around outside or pursue their usual leisure activities in their downtime. For example, they may work with robots on a production line or in a mining environment. Human-robot interaction would therefore ordinarily only be a small proportion of their waking hours. For an extended mission in deep space, human-robot interaction or human-machine teaming would be a necessary requirement for all activities outside (even if it is only embedded in the suit itself).

People regularly work in remote environments for extended periods of time. We can look to analogues in submarines and mines but there are key differences: off-Earth environments are hostile, and because of their remote location the timeframe for a return to "normal" conditions is extreme. Because of the hostility of the environment, people will be critically dependent on interaction with technology. They will therefore rely on interaction and integration of their daily lives with robots and automated systems for their entire stay in an off-Earth environment.

On Earth, human robot interaction today is usually carried out in an environment that is constrained and has been characterised ahead of time using extensive training sets. This characterisation of the environment is usually energy and time intensive. In the space environment, the limitations of not being able to build or bring energy sources from Earth will mean that these robots and autonomous systems must also be energy efficient. There are many ways in which one can consider energy efficiency in such problems – for example, in terms of the communications, in terms of the chips used on board the robots or the types of sensors used. One example is to consider power optimisation techniques for mobile edge computing. For example, in a space application, batteries could be supported by energy harvesting through solar panels. A detailed discussion of these issues is beyond the scope of this chapter, but the interested reader might consider a recent review relevant to this particular example (Cong et al., 2020).

The questions around extended human-robot interaction and human-machine teaming in extreme environments such as those experienced in space are complex. How humans cope will necessarily also be affected by how they eat, how they rest, how they work and how they interact with other humans. To understand how to build better hybrid teams, we need collaboration across disciplines with expertise in each of these areas. In the absence of a common language, we can develop a community with respect and openness. We note that our focus is to consider the cognitive burden associated with human-robot interaction and human-machine teaming. To facilitate these interactions, we must establish processes and protocols to enable interaction between disciplines to formulate responses to these complex questions. In the spirit of NASA's paper (Howard, 2018), we propose some principles for thinking about human-robot interaction:

4.3.1   What Proportion of the Day Is Spent on Human-Machine Teaming?

Instead of thinking about the sheer amount of time that is spent on task, we believe it is important also to think about what happens during that refractory period when people are away from work. As a related question, how do people maintain "normal" information processing and wellbeing in a heavily automated environment? Do systems need to be designed differently depending on how long they are used for? While analogues of these problems have been addressed for current space travel, and for on Earth situations like submarines, we believe the key difference here is the duration of the deployment and the harsh external environment. We know that using information displays in VR can lead to simulator sickness and latencies associated with information systems can impact sensorimotor and motor performance (e.g. Allison et al., 2001; Waltemate et al., 2016). Humans operating in this deep space environment could be exposed to variable delays in latencies while using information systems, and this could lead to errors in performance. It is also well documented that there are cognitive effects of human-autonomy teaming that change the way humans gather information in a scene. These questions have typically been addressed over shorter time frames, under situations in which the vast majority of the human's experience is outside of this simulation. What happens to the way humans process information when that proportion is flipped? How do we design information systems to support prolonged interaction? We believe teams addressing these questions should come from behavioural science and engineering and would benefit from feedback from experts in design and architecture as well.

4.3.2   How Can Trust Be Maintained and Built in an Extreme Environment?

A key problem is how to measure effective human-robot interaction? What does success look like in this kind of challenging environment? How do we think about teleoperation and supervisory control in such a hostile environment? Does it become a continuum? Who monitors that it is effective or that it is changing and becoming less effective? How does trust impact on the way the human moves between modes of supervisory control and teleoperation? In a challenging environment, there are interesting questions around how trust is calibrated over time and how it impacts human-machine teaming. A recent meta-analysis identified that there are several factors that seem to drive trust in automation for human-AI interaction, and these include environment factors, human related and robot related (Schaefer et al., 2016). The robot related factors referred to the reliability of the robot. In a challenging environment, it remains unknown how these factors will contribute to trust and trust calibration. Again, we believe the long duration and the criticality of this aspect of human-machine teaming mean more new work is required in this area. We believe human factors, behavioural science and computer scientists would provide useful contributions in this area.

4.3.3 How Can Situational Awareness Be Maintained and Built in an Extreme Environment?

In an extreme environment, it will not be possible to rely on human sensory systems to gain additional situational awareness. There will be no opportunity to "pop one's head outside" to gain an overview of what's going on. In this respect, working in this environment will be more like working in a control room without windows or access to the external environment and there are analogues of these situations on Earth. Operations rooms are typically removed from the real environment being monitored and are reliant on information collected by remote sensors. This information is usually pre-processed before it is considered by human analysts, who integrate multiple sources of information accumulated over different timescales. In a deep space environment, there will be several key differences. The types of sensors providing information will combine local information as well as receive information from Earth. Humans will be very reliant on these sensors but, as for on Earth operations, will also need to be able to make inferences and potentially intervene on that basis. This is a challenging problem on Earth, and already researchers have suggested frameworks to tackle this complex problem (see Endsley, 2017 for discussion).

An additional complexity here though will be that there will be very limited communications with Earth, and long latencies for new information. These latencies could also be variable due to atmospheric conditions, and as equipment degrades over time. It is possible that if sensors go down, it may take more time than on Earth to repair them. The role of explainable AI could be quite relevant to these problems, and any AI used with these sensors must be robust to varying amounts of sensor data. New presentation systems that can present these changes in the information systems so that human analysts can take this variability into account for their inferences could also be very helpful in these types of scenarios. Work in this area would be completed by behavioural scientists as well as simulation experts, computer scientists and experts in AI and sensing.

4.3.4 How Do We Build Models that Account for the Interaction Between Physiological Changes, Teaming Challenges and Technical Challenges?

This is another complex, multidisciplinary question that will require coordination between physiologist, behavioural scientists, engineers, roboticists and AI experts. We believe a key part of this problem will be to develop a cognitive architecture that can support longer term interactions between team members (whether they are humans or robots). This architecture could also be used for dynamic task allocation. There are promising models in this area for adaptive human machine interfaces (HMIs) (e.g. Abbass et al., 2014) but given the likely physiological changes induced by the harsh environment, it will be important to expand the framework to encompass these factors. We believe it would be necessary to have people from cognitive science, behavioural science, as well as AI, engineering and physiology.

4.3.5 How Do We Prepare People to Transition Back to Life on Earth, Away from Intensive Human-Robot Interaction?

What will be the most effective way to support people when they get back - how do you pivot away from living with such reliance on human-autonomy teaming? Should there be a cognitive rest period and if so, what should these look like? What does resilience look like in terms of long-term human machine teaming? It is well documented that astronauts need to re-train their muscles when they return to Earth. If leg muscles can atrophy, will the brain be impacted in the long term? This could be a question again for multidisciplinary teams from medicine, physiology and psychology as well as design and engineering.

4.3.6 How Do You Set Standards for Crewing and Shift Length in an Off-Earth Environment?

Shift length and crew size will necessarily be constrained by the duration and expense of flights, and the amount of cargo that can be transported and stored. Within those constraints, how do you set standards for crewing and shift length? Should you optimise for productivity or wellbeing of the crew? In such an extreme environment, we suggest a fine balance must be made and this could be a question for operations researchers, experts in scheduling, as well as psychology and fatigue.

4.3.7 What "Relaxation" Environment Is Effective in a Heavily Automated Environment?

For "downtime", can architects and behavioural neuroscientists and behavioural scientists work together to establish a way of constructing a built environment that is conducive to "resting" the mind after an effortful day of HRI? Will relaxation bleed into human-machine teaming (e.g. use of video games in leisure time)? Will humans need to do exercises or tasks to retain normal visual functions (if using AR/VR environments for extended periods of time), or normal information processing (if having to adapt to sparse information and long latencies)?

What are the long-term risks of this kind of artificial interaction? This is again a multidisciplinary problem, likely to require coordination between behavioural scientists, physiologists, AI/ML and robotics and potentially embedded systems.

4.4 Summary

As environmental conditions on Earth become more extreme, these questions around human-machine teaming and human-robot interaction may become relevant to the development of new working conditions. If energy efficient approaches to computing fulfill their potential, it may be likely that much of our immediate environment could rely in part if not in whole on autonomous and semi-autonomous systems. Already, AI enabled devices are part of our everyday lives and guide many decisions. Automation and human-machine teaming is already here, albeit in a more subtle way. Could this be the way forward for deep space?

The challenge though is that on Earth people still have a direct experience of the environment around them that can help them to re-calibrate their perception of the world, and also provides valuable stimulation (think sunlight, circadian rhythms, fresh air). In addition to these vital aspects of life on Earth, humans have evolved to use information about their environment to navigate and interact with it. We know how the world feels, looks, smells and sounds. This information is critical to our survival, but the sensory and sensorimotor systems that we use have evolved over many years to optimise our ability to respond to these external cues, and to use them for human interaction.

A shift to a more heavily automated environment (or heavier interaction with a semi-autonomous system) relies on a facsimile of this information, but facsimiles have traditionally involved additional information processing by the human. This creates greater strain on a human's ability to process information, and the "rub" of this sub-optimal process will impact a human's ability to interact with the environment. A key challenge of this interaction with the world is that we will no longer have a direct representation of reality, and yet we will be critically reliant on human-machine teaming for survival. While parts of this problem exist on Earth, the duration and scale of the problem is unprecedented. We don't yet know what it could do to humans, or how to re-acclimatise them to life on Earth.

There will be long latencies for communications with Earth. With limited packets of information able to be transmitted, AI agents (embodied in robots or information systems) will have to be highly resilient in a communications limited environment. There may also be limited opportunities for training the AI agents on Earth before departure to a deep space environment, due to the lack of training sets appropriate for these environments. It is likely therefore that to carry out complex tasks like construct a built environment or mine minerals, humans will have to rely on local teleoperation and supervisory control. Then, there are significant problems of a ground truth and how to work out if there is an error that needs to be addressed, as discussed above. There is therefore a need to think about how to set up low energy sensory systems that can work in these challenging environments. These could help support the human's situational awareness, which in turn supports the human's ability to rapidly respond to a changing environment and to take decisions that help.

These attributes of flexibility and agility have real world implications. Crawford (2012) reviews work that shows humans are several orders of magnitude more efficient than semi-autonomous robots, and at least 1–2 orders of magnitude more efficient than tele-operated robots. For example, Snook (2007, cited in Crawford, 2012) concluded that exploration time could be 1–2 orders of magnitude more productive per unit time if humans were involved compared to terrestrially controlled robots. Crawford also uses results from Garvin (2004, cited in Crawford, 2012) that compare the efficiencies of robotic, telerobotic and human exploration to argue that if humans are 1–2 orders of magnitude more efficient than tele-operated robots then they will be even more efficient when compared with robotic vehicles like MERs or MSL. These results, together with results on the cognitive implications of teleoperation and supervisory control, suggest that the most efficient exploration strategies are likely to be those consisting of human-robotic partnerships.

There are also several open questions around communications that are relevant to these issues. Are latencies between Earth and deep space robotics going to increase or decrease over time? That is, as systems degrade, will the latencies increase? If so, how do we provide training to help people adapt or do we change the crewing schedules? How can these systems be built to adapt to degradation over time?

We believe these extended periods of time in a harsh remote environment where humans are critically dependent on interaction with robots and autonomous systems also raises other more structural questions. How does one standardise modes of interaction across multiple devices within a setting? What's our system of systems approach for thinking about multiple HRI interactions across different tasks and different time scales? Human-robot interaction is a burgeoning field of research, but in many cases robots are operating in "safe" environments that are well described (e.g. robots in factories). Innovations in software engineering and artificial intelligence are driving competitions like RoboCup and RoboCup@Home, in which teams compete to develop the best AI that can be implemented in limited on board processing for standardised robots in novel scenarios. The next stages are to think about how to conceptualise new approaches to thinking about human-robot interaction in less certain environments, and how to develop systems thinking around these problems.

We believe it is important to think about how to structure the representation of knowledge and understand how to build a common representation that can be updated and be resilient to delays in communication. This problem has already been faced in other operational environments, but it needs to be adapted for feedback from the robot and the human. A recent position paper by Caldwell et al. (2022) proposes an agile new research framework for thinking about hybrid human-AI teams. As these authors note, this is an important area of research that is evolving.

And on a final note, we urge the reader to remember the "human" in human-machine teaming. The focus on teams and teaming often centres around abstraction – how can performance be captured and quantified and translated for computers. We must also remember that human teams at their best are entities that transcend the abilities of an individual – they work in unison, they dynamically support each other, and they often do this with humour and a lot of trust and respect. We must not forget that humans working with machines will be cast into a stressful environment if it is one where these social cues are completely absent.

Acknowledgements The authors wish to thank members of the Andy Thomas Space Resource Centre Deep Space Habitation Group, and Jean-Philippe Diguet and Cedric Buche for helpful discussions.

References

Abbass, A., Tang, J., Amin, R., Ellejmi, M., & Kirby, S. (2014). Augmented cognition using real-time EEG-based adaptive strategies for air traffic control. In *Proceedings of the Human Factors and Ergonomics Society Annual Meeting* (Vol. 58, No. 1, pp. 230–234). SAGE Publications.

Allison, R. S., Harris, L. R., Jenkin, M., Jasiobedzka, U., & Zacher, J. E. (2001). Tolerance of temporal delay in virtual environments. *Proceedings IEEE Virtual Reality, 2001*, 247–254. https://doi.org/10.1109/VR.2001.913793

Caldwell, S., Sweetser, P., O'Donnell, N., Knight, M. J., Aitchison, M., Gedeon, T., Johnson, D., Brereton, M., Gallagher, M., & Conroy, D. (2022). An agile new research framework for hybrid human-AI teaming: Trust, transparency, and transferability. *ACM Transactions on Interactive Intelligent Systems, 12*(3), 1–36. https://doi.org/10.1145/3514257

Comstock, J. R., & Amegard, R. J. (1992). The multi attribute task battery for human operator workload and strategic behaviour research. *NASA Technical Memorandum No. 104174.*

Cong, P., Zhou, J., Li, L., Cao, K., Wei, T., & Li, K. (2020). A survey of hierarchical energy optimization for Mobile edge computing: A perspective from end devices to the cloud. *ACM Computing Surveys, 53*(2), Article 38. https://doi.org/10.1145/3378935

Crawford, I. A. (2012). Dispelling the myth of robotic efficiency. *Astronomy & Geophysics, 53*(2), 2.22–2.26.

Crusan, J. C., Craig, D. A., & Herrmann, N. B. (2017). NASA's deep space habitation strategy. *IEEE Aerospace Conference, 2017*, 1–11. https://doi.org/10.1109/AERO.2017.7943624

de Winter, J. C. F., Happee, R., Martens, M. H., & Stanton, N. A. (2014). Effects of adaptive cruise control and highly automated driving on workload and situation awareness: A review of the empirical evidence. *Transportation Research Part F: Traffic Psychology and Behaviour, 27*, 196–217. https://doi.org/10.1016/j.trf.2014.06.016

Dehais, F., Peysakhovich, V., Scannella, S., Fongue, J., & Gateau, T. (2015). "Automation surprise" in aviation: Real-time solutions. *Proceedings of the 33rd Annual ACM Conference on Human Factors in Computing Systems – CHI '15*, 2525–2534. https://doi.org/10.1145/2702123.2702521

Di Nocera, F., Camilli, M., & Terenzi, M. (2007). A random glance at the flight deck: Pilots' scanning strategies and the real-time assessment of mental workload. *Journal of Cognitive Engineering and Decision Making, 1*(3), 271–285. https://doi.org/10.1518/155534307X255627

Diez, M., Boehm-davis, D. A., Holt, R. W., Pinney, M. E., & Hansberger, J. T. (2001). *Tracking pilot interactions with flight management systems through eye movements*. Ohio State University.

Endsley, M. R. (2017). From here to autonomy: Lessons learned from human–automation research. *Human Factors, 59*(1), 5–27. https://doi.org/10.1177/0018720816681350

Howard, R. L. (2018). Justification of crew function and function capability for long duration deep space habitation. *2018 AIAA SPACE and Astronautics Forum and Exposition*. 2018 AIAA SPACE and Astronautics Forum and Exposition, Orlando, FL. https://doi.org/10.2514/6.2018-5357

Matthews, G., Neubauer, C., Saxby, D. J., Wohleber, R. W., & Lin, J. (2019). Dangerous intersections? A review of studies of fatigue and distraction in the automated vehicle. *Accident; Analysis and Prevention, 126*, 85–94. https://doi.org/10.1016/j.aap.2018.04.004

Ma-Wyatt, A., Abbass, H., & Fidock, J. (2018a). Quantifying and predicting performance for human-autonomy teaming. *International Conference on Science and Innovation for Land Power.*

Ma-Wyatt, A., Johnstone, D., Fidock, J., & Hill, S. (2018b). Cognitive implications of HMIs for tele-operation and supervisory control of robotic ground vehicles. *Companion of the 2018 ACM/IEEE International Conference on Human-Robot Interaction* (pp. 189–190). https://doi.org/10.1145/3173386.3177043.

Ma-Wyatt, A., Fidock, J., & Hill, S. (2019). Cognitive implications of supervisory control and tele-operation of robotic ground vehicles. *Final report for ITC-PAC RDECOM grant*, funded by the US Department of Defence.

Neubauer, C., Matthews, G., Langheim, L., & Saxby, D. (2012). Fatigue and voluntary utilization of automation in simulated driving. *Human Factors, 54*(5), 734–746. https://doi.org/10.1177/0018720811423261

Poole, A., & Ball, L. J. (2006). Eye tracking in human-computer interaction and usability research: Current status and future prospects. 13. *Encyclopedia of Human Computer Interaction* (pp. 211–219). IGI Global.

Regis, N., Dehais, F., Tessier, C., & Gagnon, J.-F. (2012). Ocular metrics for detecting attentional tunnelling. 12. *Proceedings HFES Europe Chapter Conference Toulouse.*

Scannella, S., Peysakhovich, V., Ehrig, F., Lepron, E., & Dehais, F. (2018). Assessment of ocular and physiological metrics to discriminate flight phases in real light aircraft. *Human Factors, 60*(7), 922–935. https://doi.org/10.1177/0018720818787135

Schaefer, K. E., Chen, J. Y. C., Szalma, J. L., & Hancock, P. A. (2016). A meta-analysis of factors influencing the development of trust in automation: Implications for understanding autonomy in future systems. *Human Factors, 58*(3), 377–400. https://doi.org/10.1177/0018720816634228

Schmidt, J., Laarousi, R., Stolzmann, W., et al. (2018). Eye blink detection for different driver states in conditionally automated driving and manual driving using EOG and a driver camera. *Behavior Research Methods, 50*, 1088–1101. https://doi.org/10.3758/s13428-017-0928-0

Shen, S., & Neyens, D. M. (2017). Assessing drivers' response during automated driver support system failures with non-driving tasks. *Journal of Safety Research, 61*, 149–155. https://doi.org/10.1016/j.jsr.2017.02.009

Solís-Marcos, I., Galvao-Carmona, A., & Kircher, K. (2017). Reduced attention allocation during short periods of partially automated driving: An event-related potentials study. *Frontiers in Human Neuroscience, 11*. https://doi.org/10.3389/fnhum.2017.00537

Svensson, Å. (n.d.). Analysis of work patterns as a foundation for human- automation communication in multiple remote towers. 10.

Ulutas, B. H., Özkan, N. F., & Michalski, R. (2020). Application of hidden Markov models to eye tracking data analysis of visual quality inspection operations. *Central European Journal of Operations Research, 28*(2), 761–777. https://doi.org/10.1007/s10100-019-00628-x

Waltemate, T., Senna, I., Hülsmann, F., Rohde, M., Kopp, S., Ernst, M., & Botsch, M. (2016). The impact of latency on perceptual judgments and motor performance in closed-loop interaction in virtual reality. *Proceedings of the 22nd ACM Conference on Virtual Reality Software and Technology* (pp. 27–35). https://doi.org/10.1145/2993369.2993381

Wilson, G. F., Russell, C. A., Monnin, J. W., Estepp, J. R., & Christensen, J. C. (2010). How does day-to-day variability in psychophysiological data affect classifier accuracy? *Proceedings of the Human Factors and Ergonomics Society Annual Meeting, 54*(3), 264–268. https://doi.org/10.1177/154193121005400317

Chapter 5
Legal and Ethical Planetary Protection Frameworks for Crewed Missions

Melissa de Zwart, Stacey Henderson, and Rachel Neef

Abstract The Artemis Accords foreshadow a return of humans to the Moon, after a prolonged absence, and from the Moon on to Mars. Much has been learned from continuous human presence in Low Earth Orbit but the habitation of humans on the Moon and Mars will create new challenges. This includes not only the existential issues of sufficient nutrition, air, water, and a sustainable habitat, but also the potential for contamination of the Moon and Mars environment and of return of harmful contamination to Earth. The potential for both 'forward' and 'backward' contamination has been recognized since the dawn of space exploration. Guidelines are already in place which prescribe protection mechanisms and processes for accessing 'special regions' of Mars. This chapter will outline the application of existing laws regarding 'harmful contamination' in the context of the plan to send humans to Mars in the near future and consider the need for ethical and legal frameworks for crewed missions beyond Low Earth Orbit. It will also consider the growing interest in addressing the potential human impact on Mars as a unique environment addressing ethical, as well as environmental and scientific, concerns.

5.1 Introduction

5.1.1 Return to the Moon and on to Mars

In 2019 NASA announced the Artemis Accords, inviting other states to join with NASA and commercial providers in the return of humans to the Moon and then on to Mars. As of September 2022 there are 21 signatories of the Artemis Accords: Australia, Bahrain, Brazil, Canada, Colombia, France, Israel, Italy, Japan, the

M. de Zwart (✉) · S. Henderson
College of Business, Government and Law, Flinders University, Adelaide, SA, Australia
e-mail: melissa.dezwart@flinders.edu.au

R. Neef
Adelaide Law School, The University of Adelaide, Adelaide, SA, Australia

© The Author(s), under exclusive license to Springer Nature Singapore Pte Ltd. 2023
M. de Zwart et al. (eds.), *Human Uses of Outer Space*, Issues in Space, https://doi.org/10.1007/978-981-19-9462-3_5

Republic of Korea, Luxembourg, Mexico, New Zealand, Poland, Romania, Saudi Arabia, Singapore, Ukraine, the United Arab Emirates, the United Kingdom, and the United States. Current time frames for NASA's Artemis project involve the November 2022 launch of Artemis 1, the uncrewed mission test launch of the Space Launch System (SLS) rocket carrying the Orion spacecraft, and the orbit of Orion around the Moon and back to Earth, prior to use of the SLS for crewed missions. Artemis 2, planned for 2024, will be a minimum 8 day crewed mission to further test Orion in orbit around the Moon. After the success of this mission, Artemis 3 is planned as early as 2025 (although this timeline is likely to be extended) and will return humans to the surface of the Moon. Underpinning this program is the plan to use the expertise gained from long-term habitation on the Moon, to send a crewed mission to Mars.

In September 2022, NASA released a more detailed articulation of its Moon to Mars Objectives (NASA, 2020). These Objectives are expressed to 'develop and document an objectives-based approach to its human deep space exploration efforts'. These Objectives highlight the unique focus on the involvement of humans in these activities, including the conduct of lunar science and exploration, as well as the sustained presence of humans on the Moon and Mars. Included in the Recurring Tenets of these Objectives is the commitment to 'Responsible Use' identified as the Obligation to 'conduct all activities for the exploration and use of outer space for peaceful purposes consistent with international obligations, and principles for responsible behaviour in space'. The Objectives also affirm that 'high priority planetary science questions…are best accomplished by on-site human explorers on and around the Moon and Mars, aided by surface and orbiting robotic systems.' This need for human engagement in planetary activities brings both enormous benefits and risks.

Establishing a crewed base on Mars is a long-term goal of the Artemis partners, as well as featuring in the plans of space entrepreneurs like Elon Musk. Musk, CEO of Space X, a leader in commercial space flight, aims to send humans to Mars by 2026 (Vega, 2020). In 2020, Musk tweeted about his thoughts on the possibility of finding alien life: 'Doesn't seem to be any life in this solar system. Maybe under the ice of Europe or extremophile bacteria below the surface of Mars' (Musk, 2020). Despite this possibility, the billionaire has plans to send humans to Mars, with no current publicly available planetary protection policies. In fulfilment of his belief that humans should be an 'interplanetary species', SpaceX will establish a 'self-sustaining city on Mars' (Etherington, 2019). According to Musk, creating that city will require approximately 1000 Starships over a period of 20 years, to deliver crew, supplies, and infrastructure to make 'Moon Base Alpha' sustainable. Musk has also expressed his support for terraforming of Mars, involving the detonation of nuclear bombs over the Mars ice caps (Wall, 2019). Whilst it is unclear both whether Musk is serious about this concept (which even if successful would only result in potential changes in support of human life long after his lifetime) and indeed if these terraforming efforts would be ineffectual or even catastrophically destructive, the floating of such ideas challenges current thinking around who may determine if such ideas are ethically desirable or legally permissible.

Within this allure of sending humans to Mars to live for an extended period lies the potentially competing objects of learning more about the Red Planet and its potential as a host of new lifeforms and the challenge for humans to adapt to not only survive but thrive in such a hostile environment without destroying that environment. It is clear that: 'the possible presence of life of Mars is one of the main drivers as well as one of the main obstacles to Mars exploration' (Changela et al., 2021).

In addition to these plans for the human exploration and potential settlement of space, there are numerous robotic missions under development to various destinations in the solar system which have been identified as capable of hosting some form of life (Sherwood et al., 2019). These destinations may include the icy moons of Jupiter and Saturn. The potential for life on these worlds too necessitates the need to consider the potential for, and consequences of, forward contamination.

All of these possibilities give rise not only to the question of how such issues should be tackled, but also the ethics-based consideration of whether missions that have the possibility of contaminating unexplored environments should be undertaken at all. A question for explorers may also be what steps to take in the event that evidence of life is obtained only after establishment of a long-term habitat (Cazallo, 2021). What are the scientific and ethical considerations that should be engaged in planning for and conducting such missions?

This chapter will identify the principles of planetary protection and address non-binding and binding obligations imposed on states in conducting activities on Mars. It will propose the need to expand the discussion around responsible planetary protection behaviours to address broader ethical and environmental issues for all human missions beyond Low Earth Orbit.

5.1.2 Planetary Protection

Planetary protection concerns itself with both the protection of hazards to space from Earth ('forward contamination') and from space to Earth ('backward contamination'). The potential for contamination of the Moon, Mars, and Earth by 'forward' and 'backward' contamination has been recognized since the early days of space exploration. Robotic exploration of Mars has resulted in detailed guidelines being created to prescribe protection mechanisms and processes for 'special regions' of Mars, discussed below. Further, it is widely recommended that prior to human habitation, further robotic studies should be undertaken of proposed habitation sites.

The COSPAR Policy on Planetary Protection defines the scope for that policy as follows:

> The conduct of scientific investigations of possible extra-terrestrial life forms, precursors, and remnants must not be jeopardized. In addition, the Earth must be protected from the potential hazard posed be extra-terrestrial matter carried by a spacecraft returning from an inter-planetary mission/target planet combinations, controls on contamination shall be imposed in accordance with issuances implementing this policy. (COSPAR, 2021)

A 2017 Interim Report by the Space Studies Board suggested the following working definition of planetary protection was consistent with US obligations under the Outer Space Treaty, as well as COSPAR and NASA approaches:

> Planetary protection involves at least three fundamental activities—policy formulation, policy implementation, and compliance and validation. It encompasses those goals, rationales, policies, processes, and substantive requirements that are intended to ensure that any interplanetary space mission does not compromise the target body for a current or future scientific investigation and does not pose an unacceptable risk to Earth (in the case, for example, of sample return missions). (National Academies of Sciences, 2017)

The Interim Report proposed a further additional statement which may be considered for inclusion in the (never produced) final report:

> Further, in the course of ensuring the biological safety of the Earth and other bodies, planetary protection has a role in safeguarding the scientific objectives of future investigations, specifically investigations aimed at ascertaining the possible occurrence and nature of life on other solar system bodies. (National Academies of Sciences, 2017)

The Report stressed that, whilst the rationale and goals of planetary protection remained mostly unchanged since the beginning of space exploration, such a definition should remain a 'work in progress'. Further, the Interim Report made it clear that the purpose of such a policy was to promote space exploration rather than prohibit it. The Report acknowledged the broad range of disciplines who would be involved in planetary protection, including science, engineering, management, mission design, cost and risk assessment, and others. Whilst there has been no further progress on this Report, it is clear that the concept of Planetary Protection remains under scrutiny. What is less clear is whether such consideration extends beyond the scientific community.

5.1.3   Microbes in Space

NASA has extensive research programs examining microbiology within the context of its human spaceflight and exploration programs. Whilst the Office of Planetary Protection is not concerned with forward or backward contamination from Low Earth Orbit, activities on the International Space Station (ISS) provide important insights into the survival of microorganisms in space (Ott et al., 2014). NASA monitors the bacteria growth on the ISS and has reported that, as of March 2021, three new species of bacteria have been found inside the ISS. Those bacteria had originated from Earth but had undergone changes in the ISS environment. Bacteria placed on the outside of the ISS was found to have survived after 3 years of exposure (Bijlani et al., 2021).

It is clear that despite the harshness of the space environment, there is the possibility for the continued survival of microbes that could contaminate and even damage the Mars environment. Whilst there is a growing recognition that crewed missions to Mars will be able to undertake tasks that are not possible for autonomous rovers and robots, the presence of humans will bring with it unique environmental challenges. Unlike robots, humans cannot be perfectly sterilised. Nor is there any possibility of them operating in a perfectly enclosed environment once on the Mars surface. Humans bring with them a need for nutrition and respiration, which create inevitable waste (Jet Propulsion Laboratory, 2005). Therefore, it has been accepted that there will be some inevitable forward contamination of Mars from crewed missions (Rummel et al., 2014).

This chapter will consider what legal steps have and may be taken to minimise and address this risk. It will also highlight some ethical considerations which should be addressed to inform the approach to planetary protection.

5.2   Historical Context

Calls for planetary protection were first raised in 1956 at the International Astronautical Federation 7th Congress in Rome (National Academies of Sciences, 2017). In 1958, the International Council of Scientific Unions (ICSU) formed the Committee on Contamination by Extra-terrestrial Exploration (CETEX), which recommended that a code of conduct be established for space missions and research (National Academies of Sciences, 2017). Adopting these recommendations, the ICSU established the Committee on Space Research (COSPAR, 2021) to coordinate space research globally; one of the matters of concern being planetary protection. After the formation of the United Nations Committee on Peaceful Uses of Outer Space (COPUOS) in December 1958, discussions on how to legally regulate outer space gained momentum.

Despite there being no legal obligation to follow planetary protection protocols, the 1961 Lunar Ranger project lead by NASA was the first mission that followed a sterilization procedure (Barengoltz, 2005). This was in light of declarations of the ICSU that all countries launching space experiments which could have a potential adverse effect on future scientific research should provide the ICSU and COSPAR with the relevant information to evaluate the potential contamination (Barengoltz, 2005). COSPAR formed a Consultative Group on Potentially Harmful Effects of Space Experiments in 1962 to assist with conducting these evaluations (National Academies of Sciences, 2017).

The Apollo missions also followed planetary protection protocols, the 1969 Apollo 11 mission famously being the first time humans stepped foot on the lunar surface. Planetary protection concerns at this time, however, were largely related to *backward* contamination and fears that the astronauts would be bringing back potentially harmful extra-terrestrial matter to Earth. The astronauts were subject to a 21-day quarantine upon their return to Earth (Barengoltz, 2005). After the Apollo 14 mission, quarantine for lunar missions was discontinued as unnecessary. It is largely accepted that the Moon does not contain an environment that could host life (COSPAR, 2021); as such, the planetary protection protocols that are recommended are lower. A Moon landing is a Category II mission 'where there is only a remote chance that contamination carried by a spacecraft could compromise future investigations' (COSPAR, 2021).

The Apollo 12 mission highlights some of the practical difficulties of planetary protection. The Surveyor III probe was brought back from the Moon to Earth as part of the Apollo 12 mission. Upon examination of the camera of the probe, scientists claimed to have isolated a colony of *Streptococcus mitis* bacteria; however, other components did not contain any viable terrestrial bacteria (National Academy of Sciences, 2017). It was suggested that the bacterium was deposited in the camera prior to its launch and survived its time on the lunar surface (Mitchell & Ellis, 1971). It has been noted that the presence of bacteria could have been a result of poor contamination protocols within the laboratory upon return and *not* an issue of sterilization prior to launch (Rummel et al., 2011). Regardless, the situation highlights the confusion that can occur with terrestrial contamination and possible detection of life outside of our planet (Glavin et al., 2004).

Early Soviet Mars Missions also evidence compliance with at least the concept of planetary protection policies. Mars 1 (1962), 2 (1971) and 3 (1971) missions — the first a flyby mission and the next two orbital-lander missions — claimed to have followed planetary protection protocols equivalent to those set out by COSPAR, but no data was made available at the time of the missions (National Academies of Sciences, 2017). The Viking projects lead by NASA followed strict planetary protection protocols in their search for life on Mars. In 1975 two orbiters and landers undertook the first in-situ search and experiments for life detection on Mars. NASA followed the guidance of COSPAR implementing strict sterilization methods, estimated to be 10% of the budget for the USD 4.4 billion landers (National Academies of Sciences, 2017).

Since these missions, science and technical standards have continued to develop. The explicit adoption and use of these non-binding standards is relevant to the development of State practice but do not themselves represent binding law, with *opinio juris* noticeably absent.

The next part of the chapter identifies the legal obligations of States under international space law.

5.3   International Space Law

5.3.1   The UN Space Treaties

International space law consists primarily of five treaties: the *Treaty on Principles Governing the Activities of States in the Exploration and Use of Outer Space, Including the Moon and Other Celestial Bodies* (OST, 1967); the *Agreement on the Rescue of Astronauts and the Return of Objects Launched in Outer Space* (Rescue and Return Agreement, 1968); the *Convention on International Liability Caused by Space Objects* (Liability Convention, 1972); the *Convention on*

Registration of Objects Launched into Outer Space (Registration Convention, 1976); and the *Agreement Governing the Activities of States on the Moon and Other Celestial Bodies* (Moon Agreement, 1979). The Moon Agreement articulates a more advanced environmental approach to space, but due to its poor uptake by States — with only 18 State Parties— it is regarded as a 'failed treaty' and its effect in international law is very limited (Cheney et al., 2020).

The OST articulates the framework principles regulating State activities in outer space. Article IX creates a 'proscriptive positive legal obligation' for States to avoid harmful contamination stating that:

> States Parties to the Treaty shall pursue studies of outer space, including the moon and other celestial bodies, and conduct exploration of them so as to avoid their harmful contamination and also adverse changes in the environment of the Earth resulting from the introduction of extraterrestrial matter and, where necessary, shall adopt appropriate measures for this purpose. (OST, 1967)

The planetary protection obligations found in Article IX reflect further duties found in that article that States shall conduct their space activities 'with due regard to the corresponding interests of all other States Parties to the Treaty.' The extent of the concept of 'due regard' remains unclear, however, State practice, as evidenced by compliance with the COSPAR Policy on Planetary Protection, discussed in the next section, indicates that it is at least in part concerned with biological contamination where there is life or the potential of life (Cheney et al., 2020).

There are more recent efforts to link concepts of due regard with environmental responsibility in outer space (Cheney et al., 2020). Growing threats of space debris as well as the potential competing projects to create habitats and extract resources on the Moon, give rise to environmental concerns. The space environment is fragile and, in many cases, not susceptible to natural restoration. Therefore, it may be timely to expand the consideration of these issues under Article IX and the COSPAR Policy on Planetary Protection.

5.4 COSPAR

COSPAR was created to explore concerns that the scientific community had with the use and exploration of space. COSPAR was involved in the drafting process of the OST, attending meetings and creating reports for the COPUOS Legal Sub-Committee, but could not vote on the articles or sign the treaty document (Coustenis et al., 2019). Despite being a scientific body that cannot create or enforce legal obligations on States, several spacefaring States have readily taken up COSPAR's planetary protection policies within their own domestic regimes, including NASA and JAXA.

The ISCU, now the International Scientific Council (hereinafter ISC), created COSPAR in 1958. COSPAR is a scientific international non-governmental organization whose purpose is to promote research in space on an international level. One of their primary focus areas is planetary protection related to both forward and backward contamination. COSPAR's current planetary protection policy stresses both the need to avoid biological contamination of outbound space objects, which could impact the search for extra-terrestrial life, and hazards posed to Earth by returning missions. As discussed above, the rationales and objectives of planetary protection were reviewed by the Space Sciences Board in 2017. That review concluded that the original rationales, including protection of Earth and other places in space from biological contamination and avoiding compromising scientific investigations, including the search for life off-Earth, remained valid (National Academies of Sciences, 2017).

The recommendations set forth by COSPAR are in no way binding on States or indicative of their legal obligations under the OST. Nevertheless, they played a significant role in the development of Article IX OST and subsequent domestic policies of States. In 1969, COSPAR adopted guidelines, which replaced the previous 1964 interim framework. These guidelines prescribed limits on space activities to reduce the probability that a celestial body would be contaminated during a mission. These policies have been reviewed regularly over the years, with amendments being released in 1984, 1994, 2002, 2008, 2017, 2020, and 2021 (COSPAR, 2021). Many of these changes were made in line with NASA policies and recommendations, highlighting the strong relationship between States and COSPAR.

The current COSPAR Policy divides missions into five categories:

- Category I missions are those where the target body is not of direct interest to the study of the evolution or origin of life and no planetary protection is warranted and no requirements are imposed.
- Category II missions are those where there is a significant interest in the search for life; however, there is only a remote chance that contamination would compromise future investigations. Only documentation requirements are imposed on these missions, involving the preparation of short planetary protection plans detailing intended target, pre- and post-launch analyses addressing impact strategies and a post-encounter and end-of-mission report, providing location of impact if applicable.
- Category III missions (largely fly-by and orbiter) are those where there is an interest in the origin of life and there is a consensus that there is a significant chance of contamination that could comprise future investigations. These missions require more extensive documentation and also the implementation of some protection mechanisms such as cleanroom assembly and biological testing.
- Category IV missions comprise probe and lander missions to a target body with an evolution or origin of life interest with a significant chance of contamination which would compromise future investigations. These require sterilization, cleanrooms, and other protection mechanisms on a case-by-case basis, as well as more detailed documentation and implementing procedures.
- Category V missions comprise all return to Earth missions that require prevention against backward contamination. This includes protection of the Moon, to ensure unrestricted Earth to Moon travel. Except where the return is from a body

designated 'unrestricted Earth return', these missions prohibit destructive impact on return to Earth and strict containment procedures.

Where a mission/target is not covered by any of these categories, advice may be sought from Member National Scientific Institutions of COSPAR. Further, where such guidance is not available, COSPAR may provide advice through its Panel on Planetary Protection or through an ad hoc multidisciplinary committee 'formed in consultation with its Member National Scientific Institutions and International Scientific Unions' (COSPAR, 2021).

Missions to Mars in Categories III, IV and V have additional requirements, as this is recognized as an environment in which it is possible that life exists or once existed. In particular, COSPAR has demarcated 'special regions' on Mars which are 'region[s] within which terrestrial organisms are likely to replicate. Any region which is interpreted to have a high potential for the existence of extended martian life forms is also defined as a special region' (COSPAR, 2021). These missions have the highest requirements for sterilization. Despite being the sites where it would be most likely for missions to find life, due to the high cost of sterilization procedures, currently no missions have conducted a search for life in these areas. This is of concern because with human missions to Mars beginning to be planned, it will be increasingly difficult to keep Mars free from Earth microorganisms. As such, it is becoming urgent for robotic missions to search for life on Mars, particularly in designated 'special regions' before human missions commence.

The COSPAR Policy provides specific principles and guidelines for human missions to Mars, stating:

> The intent of this planetary protection policy is the same whether a mission to Mars is conducted robotically or with human explorers. Accordingly, planetary protection goals should not be relaxed to accommodate a human mission to Mars. Rather, they become even more directly relevant to such missions—even if specific implementation requirements must differ. (COSPAR, 2021)

Despite this, COSPAR recognizes that human missions will be carrying microbial populations and that in landed missions, it will be not possible for operations to be conducted in entirely closed systems. COSPAR appreciates that there is a 'greater capability of human explorers [that] can contribute to the astrobiological exploration of Mars,' with the caveat though only if 'human-associated contamination is controlled and understood'. COSPAR recommends that a conservative approach be taken for initial human missions and, further, that any uncharacterized Martian site be evaluated by robotic missions as a precursor to human access (COSPAR, 2021).

The COSPAR policies are recommendations of a scientific body and not legally binding on States. They are a soft law instrument that does much to address the concerns of astrobiologists but little to consider the rapid development of the space industry, particularly as private industry becomes more and more involved. The legal and scientific positions must be better connected to ensure that the fundamental principle of free exploration and connected idea of preventing harmful contamination is not breached. The soft law nature of the COSPAR principles provides flexibility to adapt to changes and new information about space exploration, as they have done over the decades. It should also be understood that these guidelines remain under constant review and they are not absolute or binding standards. They should be assessed and revised as circumstances warrant. For example, whilst assessments suggest that the potential of microbial contamination from samples to be returned to Earth from the moons of Mars from a JAXA mission planned for launch in 2024, are within acceptable limits, COSPAR has 'strongly recommended' a re-evaluation of this risk analysis before the return of the samples to Earth (Changela et al., 2021).

Despite being soft law, NASA, the European Space Agency (ESA) (ESA, 2017), and the Japanese Aerospace Exploration Agency (JAXA) (JAXA, 2019) have all adopted COSPAR recommendations as part of their planetary protection policies. For example, NASA's policy, elaborating on COSPAR's recommendations, finds that:

(a) 'Safeguarding the Earth from potential back[ward] contamination is the highest planetary protection priority in Mars exploration.'
(b) 'The greater capability that human explorers can contribute to the astrobiological exploration of Mars is only valid if human-associated contamination is controlled and understood.'
(c) 'For a landed [human] mission conducting surface operations, it will not be possible for all human-associated processes and mission operations to be conducted within entirely closed systems.'
(d) '[Humans] exploring Mars, and/or their support systems, will inevitably be exposed to martian materials.' (NASA, 2020)

The COSPAR Policy on Planetary Protection has played a significant role in shaping the landscape of planetary protection policies. There is however some scope to argue that the policies themselves do not reflect a significant diversity of interests. The policy and thinking behind the principles have been contributed by current space-faring nations through member national and international scientific institutions. However, it might be useful to open-up the policies to greater scrutiny and debate from nations yet to engage in space technology and particularly to those in the private sector who may be involved in implementing such policies. Musk's claims regarding SpaceX's planned activities on Mars demonstrate the growing interest in activities on Mars, and without binding legal force, there is nothing constraining actions to comply with COSPAR Policy, unless they have been implemented in national domestic space regulation.

With this in mind, the divergence over the past decades between regimes of the legal and scientific communities has been of concern. With only limited State practice on the issue, the stricter scientific policies have failed to be clearly integrated into international law and may soon be left aside. This makes it even more important for a strong clarification of the legal obligations under Article IX so that States can ensure they act in accordance. Given the irreversible effects that contamination could have, States need to be aware of what measures should be adopted to comply with their legal obligations and to ensure future use and access to all the benefits of space exploration, in particular, human missions to the Moon and Mars. NASA has announced that there will be a 'reframing of the application of the COSPAR Policy in the context of the Artemis Accords' (NASA, 2020). It is not clear whether this will reflect a tightening or loosening of current practices. Given the nature of Artemis as an agreement between NASA and a growing number of international partners, this may not even result in a consistency of approach across all projects.

Under Article VI of the OST States are responsible for the activities of their nationals in outer space. The Registration Convention and the Liability Convention provide further guidance for establishing jurisdiction and responsibility for activities in outer space. Commercial actors, however, are only required to follow the legal regime applicable to the domestic law they are operating in; they themselves are not bound by either treaty obligations or soft law recommendations. The 2019 crash landing on the Moon by Israeli company Beresheet, with a payload that held tardigrades (a phylum of microscopic organisms) illustrates the difficulty of regulating private actors (Weisberger, 2019; Cheney et al., 2020). As commercial entities increase their access to space, it is important that there is a clear understanding of State obligations under international space law to facilitate consistent approaches in domestic laws implementing those obligations.

There has been limited legal debate on the implementation of Article IX thus far as the key space-faring States have acted in compliance with strict planetary protection protocols. Despite being subject to supervision under Article VI, unless domestic legislation enforces planetary protection protocols, commercial actors could be subject to lower standards than national space agencies bound by their own policies.

There are also questions regarding whether sufficient views are being included in the development of such guidelines: as society changes and new missions become possible, should views beyond those of scientists be taken into account?

5.5 Ethical Considerations

Given the number and range of missions being planned to the Moon, Mars, and other destinations, it seems timely to consider whether limiting our considerations regarding mission risk and planning to scientific and legal principles is sufficient. Identifying the limited number of 'ocean worlds' which have the capacity of hosting non-Earth lifeforms within our solar system, and hence accessible with currently known technology, Sherwood et al. (2019) advocate for a multi-generational approach to mission planning. They suggest a multifaceted conversation, addressing the following:

1. Humankind's potential to contaminate the ocean worlds (technical probabilities)
2. The implications of doing so (science-based and ethics-based discussions and decisions)
3. Acceptable ways of managing this risk (program planning and execution) and would therefore require collaboration by a diverse community of technical and non-technical stakeholders. (Sherwood et al., 2019)

In particular, given the length of time required to plan, build, and execute such missions, in some case decades, the generations that would inherit and implement the missions and their consequences, should be involved in such discussions. Further, they suggest that much broader ethical issues should be included in such a consideration, including matters such as should humans seek to establish permanent settlements outside of Earth and what are the consequences of destroying or altering any lifeform that may be found beyond Earth? Our understanding of lifeforms has grown exponentially in the last 50 years, as too has our understanding of human impact on our own planet. This highlights the need for a more comprehensive discussion regarding our values, including a consideration of whether the promotion of scientific exploration remains the prime objective of space exploration. This may include reconsideration of the risk of interference with, or destruction of, habitats which are very different from Earth, even if such actions fall short of active terraforming.

Some work has been done on ethical dimensions of planetary protection, with a workshop being held at Princeton in 2010 to examine:

- The ethical implications and responsibility to explore Mars in a manner that minimizes the harmful impacts of those activities on potential indigenous biospheres (whether suspected or known to be extant),
- Whether revision to current planetary protection policies is necessary to address these concerns, and.
- How best to involve the public in such a dialogue about the ethical aspects of planetary exploration. (Rummel et al., 2012)

In particular, the Workshop sought to address 'whether planetary protection measures and other practices should be extended to protect other aspects of planetary environments within an ethical and practical framework that goes beyond "science protection"' and what the bases for such policy and ethical framework would be (Rummel et al., 2012) The Workshop concluded that there was a need for further study of the relevant ethical considerations and COSPAR should establish a group to undertake a study of such considerations. Further, the need for greater inclusiveness in communication and consultation was recognised, stating 'scientists need to undertake public dialogue to communicate widely about these future policy deliberations and to ensure public involvement in decision making' (Rummel et al., 2012). However, pending these further actions, no change was made to the COSPAR Policy on Planetary Protection.

Clearly there is a need for broader voices to be included in the consideration of human missions to Mars. These considerations should extend beyond planetary protection to the profound impact that such missions will have on humanity, Earth, and Mars. Human contact with Mars will inevitably change that planet and environmental and existential concerns should be addressed before the mission becomes possible. Mars will also change us, physically, emotionally, and mentally. Various ethical lenses may assist in preparing us for such changes beyond the biological. It is suggested that it is now timely for the work of the Princeton workshop discussed above be resumed with a broad range of stakeholders (Sherwood et al., 2019). In particular, it may be useful to draw upon principles of environmental ethics, considering responsibility for stewardship of the new and unique environments humans will encounter (Norma & Reiss, 2021).

5.6 Conclusion

To date, the responsible uses of space have been facilitated by adherence by States to the COSPAR Policy on Planetary Protection, as amended from time to time. That Policy gives form to the legal requirement under Article IX of the Outer Space Treaty to avoid harmful contamination of outer space and adverse changes in the environment of Earth from extraterrestrial matter. However, as more States, and wealthy individual and commercial actors become involved in space, and major international projects are planned it may be time to consider whether the COSPAR Policy is sufficient both to discharge obligations under Article IX and also to engage the broader community in consideration of the rules which should guide settlement of other planets.

Much of our consideration of what life on Mars may be like for humans has been derived from science fiction, which enables us to explore what might be possible in these new environments. Kim Stanley Robinson's *Mars* trilogy explores a vast range of ethical, political, biological, and scientific issues which may beset humanity in forging sustained life on a new planet. It also juxtaposes the beliefs of the Red Mars believers, like Ann Clayborne, who is resolutely against human modification of Mars and those, such as Saxifrage Russell, who exemplifies the 'scientific' view that terraforming is justifiable to support life and who favours drastic environmental modification (Robinson, 1992). These positions become incompatible and set the scene for major conflict and environmental disaster. Learning from this vast space opera, we should direct our energies now to undertake a more inclusive consideration of the rules that we will take with us to Mars and how they may be implemented across multiple settlements.

This chapter has outlined the context for the COSPAR Planetary Protection Policy and identified the underpinning legal obligations imposed on States by the OST. It has assessed that process and the resulting Policy within the context of a foreshadowed crewed mission to Mars. It has identified a range of ethical, equity, and environmental issues that it is suggested be included in the process going forward, in line with the draft recommendations of the 2010 Ethics workshop. The time has come to revisit the suggestions emerging from that work, as well as the 2017 Interim Report by the Space Studies Board, which viewed the definition of 'planetary protection' as a work in progress. All of the issues discussed are compatible with and relevant to current considerations of responsible behaviours in outer space and various projects to send humans to the Moon, including Artemis (Swiney & Hernandez, 2022).

The current framework may require a broader ethical framework to prepare us for the questions we may face once we arrive on Mars. These issues, as well as the scientific ones, need to be considered before we go.

References

Agreement Governing the Activities of States on the Moon and Other Celestial Bodies. (1979) Available at https://www.unoosa.org/oosa/en/ourwork/spacelaw/treaties/intromoon-agreement.html. Accessed 2022, February 24 ('Moon Agreement').

Agreement on the Rescue of Astronauts, the Return of Astronauts and the Return of Objects Launched into Outer Space. (1968). Available at https://www.unoosa.org/oosa/en/ourwork/spacelaw/treaties/introouterspacetreaty.html. Accessed 2022, February 22 ('Rescue and Return Agreement').

Barengoltz, J. (2005). Jet Propulsion Laboratory, National Aeronautics and Space Administration. A review of the approach of NASA projects to planetary protection compliance. https://trs.jpl.nasa.gov/bitstream/handle/2014/40515/04-3484FN.pdf?sequence=3. Accessed 2022, October 28.

Bijlani, S., et al. (2021). Methylobacterium ajmalii sp. nov. Isolated from the International Space Station. *Frontiers in Microbiology, 12*, 7.

Cazallo, R. (2021). Plants under the moonlight: The biology and installation of industrial plants for lunar settlements. In M. Rappaport & K. Szocik (Eds.), *The human factor in the settlement of the Moon* (pp. 75–96). Springer. https://doi.org/10.1007/978-3-030-81388-8_5

Changela, H., et al. (2021). Mars: New insights and unresolved questions. *International Journal of Astrobiology, 20*(6), 394–426. https://doi.org/10.1017/S1473550421000276

Cheney, T., et al. (2020). Planetary protection in the new space era: Sciences and governance. *Frontiers in Astronomy and Space Sciences, 13*. https://doi.org/10.3389/fspas.2020.589817

Convention on International Liability for Damage Caused by Space Objects. (1972). Available at https://www.unoosa.org/oosa/en/ourwork/spacelaw/treaties/introliability-convention.html. Accessed 2022, February 22 ('Liability Convention').

Convention on Registration of Objects Launched into Outer Space. (1976). Available at https://www.unoosa.org/oosa/en/ourwork/spacelaw/treaties/introregistration-convention.html. Accessed 2022, February 22 ('Registration Convention').

COSPAR. (2021). Cospar policy on planetary protection. 3 June 2021. https://cosparhq.cnes.fr/assets/uploads/2021/07/PPPolicy_2021_3-June.pdf. Accessed 2022, October 28.

Coustenis, A., et al. (2019). The COSPAR panel on planetary protection role, structure and activities. *Space Research Today, 205*(14), 18.

Musk, E (@elonmusk). (2020). TWITTER (Oct. 16, 2020, 6:14PM), https://twitter.com/elonmusk/status/1317008535075528704?ref_src=twsrc%5Etfw%7Ctwcamp%5Etweet embed%7Ctwterm%5E1317008535075528704%7Ctwgr%5E%7Ctwcon%5Es1_&ref_url=https%3A%2F%2Fwww.foxbusiness.com%2Ftechnology%2Fspacexs-elon-musk-alien-life-in-these-two-spots. Accessed 2022, October 3.

Etherington, D. (2019). Elon Musk says building the first sustainable city on Mars will take 1,000 Starships and 20 years. *Tech Crunch.* 8 November 2019. https://techcrunch.com/2019/11/07/elon-musk-says-building-the-first-sustainable-city-on-mars-will-take-1000-starships-and-20-years/. Accessed 2022, October 28.

European Space Agency. (2017). ESA planetary protection policy. https://www.esa.int/Science_Exploration/Human_and_Robotic_Exploration/Exploration/ExoMars/Planetary_protection. Accessed 2022, January 21.

Glavin, D., et al. (2004). Biological contamination studies of lunar landing sites: Implications for future planetary protection and life detection on the Moon and Mars. *International Journal of Astrobiology, 3*(3), 265–271.

Japan Aerospace Exploration Agency. (2019). Planetary Protection Program Standard.

Jet Propulsion Laboratory. (2005). Planetary protection and contamination control technologies for future space science missions. Available at https://solarsystem.nasa.gov/resources/294/planetary-protection-and-contamination-control-technologies-for-futurespace-science-missions/

Mitchell, F., & Ellis, W. (1971). Surveyor III: Bacterium isolated from lunar-retrieved TV camera. *Proceedings of the Second Lunar Science Conference, 2*, 2721.

NASA. (2020). NASA updates planetary protection policies for robotic and human missions to Earth's Moon and future human missions to Mars, NASA (2020, July 10). https://www.nasa.gov/feature/nasa-updates-planetary-protection-policies-for-robotic-and-human-missions-to-earth-s-moon

National Academies of Sciences. (2017). engineering and medicine: The goals, rationales, and definition of planetary protection: Interim Report 2.

National Aeronautics and Space Administration (NASA). (2020). Biological planetary protection for human missions to Mars 4. https://nodis3.gsfc.nasa.gov/OPD_docs/NID_8715_129.pdf

Norma, Z., & Reiss, M. (2021). The emergence of an environmental Ethos on Luna. In M. Rappaport & K. Szocik (Eds.), *The human factor in the settlement of the Moon* (pp. 221–232). Springer. https://doi.org/10.1007/978-3-030-81388-8_14

Ott, M., et al. (2014). Space habitation and microbiology: Status and roadmap of space agencies. *Microbes and Environments, 29*(3), 239–242. https://doi.org/10.1264/jsme2.ME2903rh

Robinson, K. S. (1992). *Red Mars*. Random House.

Rummel, J., et al. (2011). A microbe on the Moon? Surveyor III and lessons learned for future sample return missions. https://www.lpi.usra.edu/meetings/sssr2011/pdf/5023.pdf

Rummel, J., et al. (2012). Ethical considerations for planetary protection in space exploration: A workshop. *Astrobiology, 12*(11), 1017–1023. https://doi.org/10.1089/ast.2012.0891

Rummel, J. D., et al. (2014). A New Analysis of Mars "Special Regions": Findings of the Second MEPAG Special Regions Science Analysis Group (SR-SAG2). *Astrobiology, 14*(11). https://doi.org/10.1089/ast.2014.1227

Sherwood, B., et al. (2019). Forward contamination of ocean worlds: A stakeholder conversation. *Space Policy, 48*, 1–13.

Swiney, G., & Hernandez, A. (2022). Lunar landing and operations policy analysis. NASA. Office of Technology, Policy and Strategy. 2022, September 30.

Treaty on Principles Governing the Activities of States in the Exploration and Use of Outer Space, including the Moon and other Celestial Bodies. (1967). Available at https://www.unoosa.org/oosa/en/ourwork/spacelaw/treaties/introouterspacetreaty.html. Accessed 2022, February 22 ('Outer Space Treaty').

Vega, N. (2020). Elon Musk pledges to put humans on Mars by 2026. *New York Post* (2020, December 2). https://nypost.com/2020/12/02/elon-musk-pledges-to-put-humans-on-mars-by-2026/. Accessed 2022, October 28.

Wall, M. (2019). Elon Musk floats 'Nuke Mars' idea again (He Has T-Shirts). *Space.com*, 2019, August 17. https://www.space.com/elon-musk-nuke-mars-terraforming.html. Accessed 2022, October 28.

Weisberger, M. (2019). Thousands of tardigrades stranded on the Moon after Lunar lander crash. *Space.com*, 2019, August 7. https://www.space.com/tardigrades-moon-israeli-lander.html. Accessed 2022, October 28.

Chapter 6
Moon Resources and a Proposition for Supply Chains

Manuel Varon Hoyos, Nigel J. Cook, and Volker Hessel

Abstract Humans are exploring outer space with ever-greater scope and are continually pushing the limits of scientific and technological development. Technology readiness has reached a level at which a perspective on commerce and trade in space processing is reasonable. A central element of commerce is the provision of resources to make products and to distribute those to customers, which means the proposition of a supply chain.

Supply chains make possible the harmonious flow of both materials and information throughout the various stages necessary for the production of goods and the provision of services. Through properly structured processes and based on the principles of Supply Chain Management (SCM), suppliers, manufacturers, distributors and customers contribute to a reduction of costs and implicitly, improvement of profits in a given supply chain.

The environmental conditions in space pose enormous challenges to any production and supply chain, a situation amplified by the logistical obstacles involved in transporting manufactured goods to customers. The long distances involved in space travel demand major technological innovations. The technology leap needed likely requires a partnership between the governmental and private sectors.

The Moon, the natural satellite of the Earth, represents the first opportunity for the implementation of economic activities in outer space. Its proximity to Earth, the information that is already available about this celestial body and the ready availability of some of its natural resources puts it in a prime position to structure space supply chains for goods. This may include space between the Moon and Earth, defined as 'cislunar' space.

M. V. Hoyos · V. Hessel (✉)
School of Chemical Engineering and Advanced Materials, The University of Adelaide, Adelaide, SA, Australia
e-mail: volker.hessel@adelaide.edu.au

N. J. Cook
School of Civil, Environmental and Mining Engineering, The University of Adelaide, Adelaide, SA, Australia

© The Author(s), under exclusive license to Springer Nature Singapore Pte Ltd. 2023
M. de Zwart et al. (eds.), *Human Uses of Outer Space*, Issues in Space, https://doi.org/10.1007/978-981-19-9462-3_6

79

A perspective for the structuring of supply chains conceived on the Moon and cislunar space will imply the development of manufacturing capacities for the required space products, as well as the emergence of specialized space suppliers, and space marketers.

6.1 Introduction

This chapter initially addresses, in general terms, the concept of supply chains by understanding aspects such as their characteristics, components and classification. Next, the importance of supply chain management is explored as a fundamental element for the structuring of adequate logistics systems, emphasizing the scope of the supply chain operations reference model (SCOR), which is the most applied and recognized conceptualization on this topic at the international level.

Once the importance of supply chains is established as one of the thematic axes of this chapter, we proceed to a look at the space industry, seeking to understand its most relevant aspects, the impact of the space economy on our current lifestyle and the nature of the transformation that this industry has undergone in recent years. This transformation in particular is of the utmost importance since it allows us to understand why it is currently crucial to implement space supply chains that have a favorable impact, not only on the environment outside the Earth, but also on the planet itself.

Later, the reader will find a vision that integrates supply chains and the space industry through a review of the challenges posed by the expansion of the knowledge frontier of space reflected in initiatives such as the return to the Moon, and exploration of Mars, among others. Currently, the supply chains at the space industry level are completely dependent on the Earth, a situation that ought to be reconsidered if what is wanted is to have access to increasingly remote destinations.

After addressing the importance of supply chains in the space industry, this chapter focuses on the place considered most promising for the beginning of the expansion of the frontiers of civilization: the Moon. In this case, the reader is given a perspective about the potential in terms of resources that our natural satellite has, the possible uses of them, and the way in which they could be exploited, emphasizing In-Situ Resource Utilization (ISRU) as a strategy for implementation.

Finally, this chapter identifies the way in which space supply chains less dependent on the Earth might be implemented, taking cislunar space as a reference zone, through the definition of a number of components that would be essential for the proper functioning of such supply chain.

6.2 Supply Chains

A supply chain can be understood as a system that is predominantly made up of all those entities in charge of the commercialization, production, and distribution of all types of goods and services, whose existence implies the transformation of initial materials or ideas and the sending of products or the provision of services anywhere in the world (Ernst & Haar, 2019). Therefore, in a supply chain, the entities or organizations involved interrelate with each other through various logistics processes, including transportation, stock storage, supply of goods and demand planning (Deckert, 2020).

A supply chain is composed of a series of stages that can be clearly differentiated from one another and that, depending on their specific characteristics, may or may not be present in their entirety. Essentially, most supply chains are networks in which the following stages can be distinguished:

- Suppliers (who can supply raw materials or components)
- Manufacturers
- Distributors (or wholesalers)
- Retailers
- Customers (Chopra, 2013)

On the other hand, there are different ways to classify supply chains (Fig. 6.1). A first form of classification is based on the physical structure, that is, on the way materials flow through the chain, which influences the decisions that need to be made, especially in terms of inventories (Goetschalckx, 2011). Depending on its physical structure, a supply chain can be a serial system, that is, a system in which there is a series of levels along which the flow of materials occurs, from the highest to the lowest (Goetschalckx, 2011). There may also be assembly systems based on the supply of materials from various nodes of a higher level to a single node of a lower level. A supply chain can also be a distribution system that functions on the basis of materials flow from a single node at a higher level to multiple nodes at a lower level, this being the opposite of an assembly system (Goetschalckx, 2011).

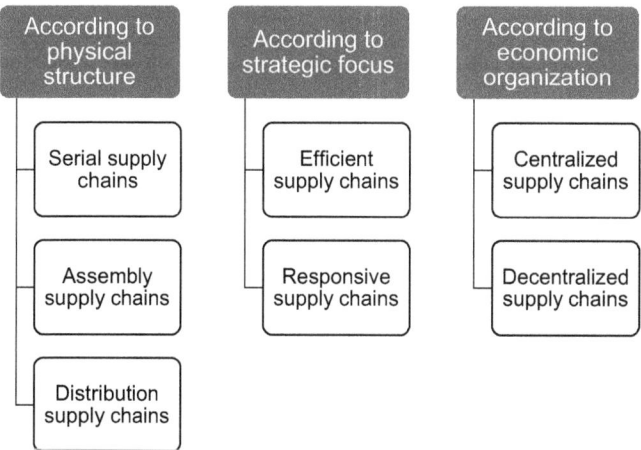

Fig. 6.1 Classifications of supply chains (Goetschalckx, 2011)

From the point of view of the strategic focus, a supply chain can be either efficient or responsive. An efficient supply chain is based on the production and processing of goods at low cost, which is ideal for obtaining products with long life cycles and little variety. A responsive supply chain, on the other hand, is built on speed, making it more suitable for products with shorter life cycles and greater variety, such as clothing and electronics (Goetschalckx, 2011).

Finally, supply chains can be classified based on their economic organization, that is, based on the level at which they are centralized or decentralized from the economic point of view (Goetschalckx, 2011). Therefore, a supply chain is considered centralized if it is completely controlled by a single party or owner, while one that is decentralized will have several actors involved in the decision-making process. In practice, there are currently no supply chains in the world that can be considered entirely centralized (Goetschalckx, 2011).

6.2.1 Composition of a Supply Chain

Generally speaking, a supply chain in its basic form is made up of three elements. These are the company or organization, the provider, and the consumer (Hugos, 2018). Now, the existence of these elements or actors can occur in different ways. It is possible that, for example, there are companies in a supply chain that are also producers, distributors and even wholesalers. It may also be the case that consumers are themselves retailers or companies that are simultaneously providers of various services (Hugos, 2018).

Considering that the members or participants of a supply chain can fulfill different functions, they can belong to one or more of the following categories (Fig. 6.2):

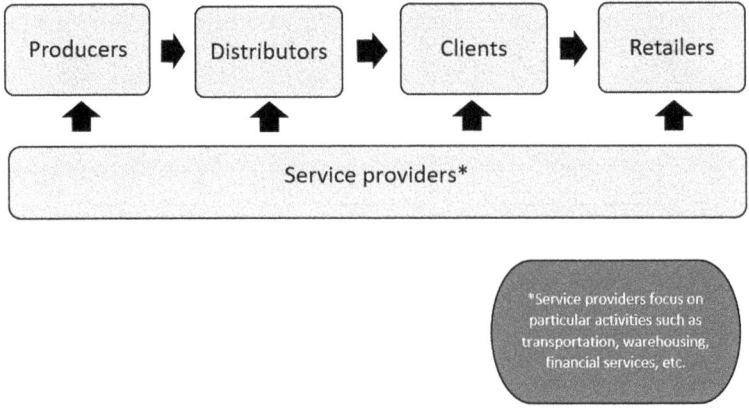

Fig. 6.2 Participants of a supply chain (Hugos, 2018)

1. *Producers*

   These are entities or organizations that produce or manufacture products, whether they are raw materials, goods resulting from industrial processes, intangible goods (music, entertainment, software, etc.), and even services (Hugos, 2018).

2. *Distributors*

   These are organizations that purchase large volumes of products and build inventories of them to subsequently sell them on to smaller retailers. Distributors can also perform functions of storage, transportation of products, and after-sales service, among others (Hugos, 2018).

3. *Retailers*

   Like distributors, retailers stock inventories and sell products, these sales being directly to the consumer (the general public), which is why it is common for them to use different strategies to maintain and attract new buyers (Hugos, 2018).

4. *Clients*

   Clients are all organizations or individuals that acquire products, either to use them as supplies or raw materials necessary for the production of other products or to consume them (Hugos, 2018).

5. *Service providers*

   There are organizations specialized in providing services, both to producers and distributors, retailers and customers. In terms of expertise, efficiency and prices, supply chains are favored by the existence of providers of transportation, storage, financial and marketing services, among others (Hugos, 2018).

A supply chain must have a previous design, which is essential for the fulfillment of tasks and objectives. At the time of design, it must be taken into account that, at a minimum, three types of main actors must be considered that will inevitably be involved. The first is the organization (for example, a production plant), the second is the organization's supplier, and the third is the consumer. These actors are related to one another through the activities or flows of the supply chain (Nel & Badenhorst-Weiss, 2010).

Moreover, the design and planning of any supply chain must be based on the structuring of a series of fundamental objects or components, which should be established correctly, since correct planning results in successful administration (Goetschalckx, 2011).

These components are:

- **Products**

  It is necessary to properly handle the product or products related to a supply chain. This is achieved from an understanding of the product life cycle, because this is a sequence of stages that goes from conception through design, manufacturing, maintenance and end of life or final disposal (Ganesan, 2015). Likewise, analysis of which products are a priority or suitable and are considered to generate better income allows us to improve the design through tools such as Pareto analysis (Ganesan, 2015).

- **Suppliers and vendors**
  All those agents that provide the necessary goods for the supply chain are called suppliers. Depending on the specific characteristics of the supply chain, suppliers may also require vendors, likewise, suppliers may require part of the supply chain, whether they belong to the organization or not (Ganesan, 2015).
- **Processing facilities**
  They are physical assets such as production or assembly plants and distribution centers. In relation to production plants, these facilities are responsible for the manufacture of products, while distribution centers have the task of responding to the demand for products based on available stocks or inventories (Ganesan, 2015). Planning of the location and characteristics of the facilities is a critical task due to the implications that these will have in terms of managing suppliers and costs related to their start-up (Ganesan, 2015).
- **Transport channels**
  These are the components that make it possible to move goods between different facilities. Factors such as capacity, costs or freight, the means used for transport and the required frequency of transportation are essential to define a certain transport channel in a supply chain (Ganesan, 2015).

Likewise, it is pertinent to point out that the design phase of a supply chain seeks to meet two specific objectives. These objectives are, in the first place, the maximization of profits and the minimization of costs (Goetschalckx, 2011). Profits are maximized to the extent that the accumulated net cash flows, after discounting taxes, are optimal according to the circumstances that are considered to take place in the planning horizon (Goetschalckx, 2011). On the other hand, the costs are minimized if their reduction in net present value is achieved throughout the planning horizon (Goetschalckx, 2011).

6.2.2 Supply Chain Management

Management of supply chains is a field of action whose organized study is relatively recent yet accelerated rapidly between the 1980s and the 1990s (Nel & Badenhorst-Weiss, 2010; Ganesan, 2015; Hilmola, 2018; Sindi & Roe, 2017). Supply Chain Management (SCM) can be defined as a set of tasks that allows appropriate coordination of the way in which materials, information and financial flows take place on behalf of the work of suppliers, transporters, manufacturers, distributors, and traders (Nel & Badenhorst-Weiss, 2010; Lourenço & Ravetti, 2018; Stadtler, 2005). SCM seeks to harmonize the way in which the various flows of a supply chain occur, in order to achieve, as primary objectives, the satisfaction of consumer expectations and the optimization of competitiveness (Stadtler, 2005).

Worldwide, the best-known reference framework for processes related to SCM is the model called SCOR (Supply Chain Operations Reference) developed by the

Table 6.1 Management processes according to SCOR model (Kurbel, 2013)

Process	Description
Planning	It allows definition of the capacities and difficulties in terms of resources by assessing the needs of consumers, the availability of resources and the ways in which the difficulties in obtaining resources can be addressed.
Sourcing	It establishes the way in which goods and services are handled, defining aspects such as reception mechanisms, activity programming, and billing management, among others. Management tasks such as evaluating the performance of suppliers and capital goods are also part of this set of activities.
Making	It addresses all the processes associated with the production of goods and services, more specifically all manufacturing activities or those that involve the transformation of materials.
Delivery	The activities related to the management of customer orders (from receipt to billing) are described in this case.
Returning	Everything related to the return of goods is established in this topic, from the justification of a certain return to the reception of the returned goods.

Supply Chain Council (SCC), a non-profit organization founded in 1996, which institutes globally required standards (Kurbel, 2013). According to the SCOR model, the entire supply chain must be managed based on planning, sourcing, making, delivering, and returning processes (Table 6.1).

Based on what is established in the SCOR model, every SCM system fulfills a series of tasks, which are listed below (Kurbel, 2013).

- **Strategic level tasks**
  From the strategies of the different companies that are presumed to be, or will be part of the supply chain, the definition of the network of suppliers and buyers is undertaken (Kurbel, 2013). This implies making decisions related to the supply capacity, strategic investments, and cost evaluation, among other aspects. Therefore, at the strategic level, it is necessary to use simulation tools that allow for evaluation of scenarios to identify the one that best suits the chain's specific needs (Kurbel, 2013).
- **Planning level tasks**
  In general terms, as far as planning is concerned, these tasks are carried out with consideration of the medium and long term (Kurbel, 2013). This implies the existence of planning activities, both for high hierarchical levels and for lower levels. Regarding high levels, planning is based on the fulfillment of tasks such as estimation of demand, safety inventories and an appropriate supply and distribution network (Kurbel, 2013). At lower levels, planning tasks are usually production planning, transportation planning, route planning, and detailed scheduling (Kurbel, 2013).
- **Execution-level tasks**
  At this level of any supply chain there are two fundamental tasks: event management; and performance management (Kurbel, 2013).

6.2.3   Supply Chain Event Management (SCEM)

This is the set of actions that allows, both within and between the different organizations that are part of a supply chain, the monitoring of its operation (Kurbel, 2013). This work requires obtaining and constantly updating data about everything that happens throughout the supply chain, leading to the adoption of two important strategies, such as tracking and tracing. These allow, in the first case, for monitoring the location of an object in a logistics process, and in the second case, for information about the status of an object at hand throughout the business processes (Kurbel, 2013). Monitoring of the supply chain also allows the verification of the information obtained and the creation of events or notifications that can lead to a better and quicker resolution of any problems as they occur (Kurbel, 2013).

6.2.4   Supply Chain Performance Management (SCPM)

Unlike SCEM, SCPM is applied at higher levels since it depends on the data previously processed by SCEM, which allows it not only to analyze aspects such as the causes and frequency of events, but also to identify trends (Kurbel, 2013). Likewise, to the extent that adequate information is available, SCPM can contribute to generation of indicators and thresholds that, in turn, contribute to improving the evaluation of the performance of a supply chain (Kurbel, 2013).

6.3   Space Industry: Features and Current Trends

The space industry is a particularly special one, due to unique aspects such as the set of actors that participate in space exploration and exploitation projects, as well as the requisite participation of various scientific disciplines given the technological complexity of the aforementioned projects (Yazıcı & Darıcı, 2019).

Space is increasingly creating social and economic impact worldwide, which is dependent on impetus given by governments (PWC, 2019). Indeed, national states and multinational consortia like European Space Agency (ESA) fulfill various tasks in the value chain, promote alliances with private companies and finance research and development initiatives, among others (Highfill & MacDonald, 2022). The exploitation of gas and oil, agriculture, telecommunications, the implementation of smart cities and defense and security, among other activities, increasingly benefit from the advances of space exploration (PWC, 2019) and from technologies that can be adopted on Earth.

Space economy refers to the set of actors made up of those who work in the research, development and construction of space devices and equipment (satellites, vehicles, ground equipment, among others), suppliers of specialized products, providers of services and customers, which are therefore part of a long value-added

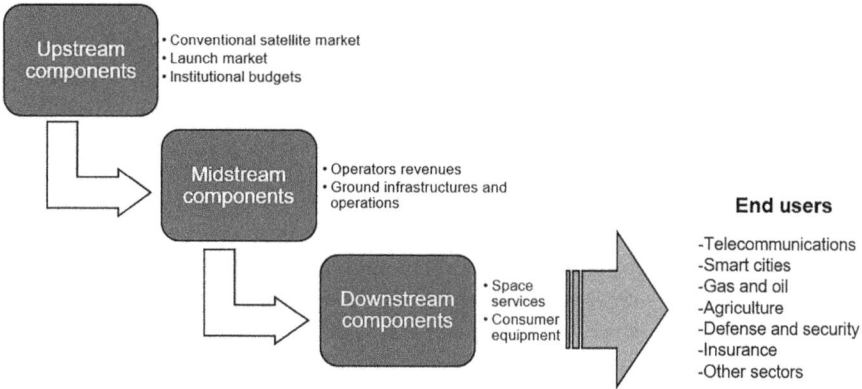

Fig. 6.3 Components of space economy (PWC, 2019)

chain (Fig. 6.3) (Paladini et al., 2021). Therefore, the goods and services related to the space industry are all those that are used in the space environment. These include those that support goods and services used in space, those that require inputs from space or support those activities, or all those that are associated with space research (Wooten & Tang, 2018). The most important economic sectors in the production of goods and services related to space exploration and exploitation are the following (Wooten & Tang, 2018):

- Information industry (telecommunications, broadcasting and software)
- Professional Services (research and Development, Computer Systems, Geophysics, Mapping and Engineering)
- Manufacturing industry (satellites, ground equipment, weapons systems, Global Positioning Systems (GPS) equipment, positioning, navigation and timing (PNT) equipment and spacecraft).
- Construction (space installations and observatories).
- Government sector (personnel specializing in exploration, satellite services and weapons systems).
- Other sectors (launch services, insurance, educational services).

The exploration and exploitation of space has experienced significant growth in its activities and relevance, which is reflected in a considerable increase of global investment in the field, increasing from 3667 million US dollars in 2012 to 10,238 million US dollars in 2017 (Yazıcı & Darıcı, 2019), a three-fold increase in just five years. Therefore, it is necessary to advance in the normative regulation of the space activity and market and in the structuring of better cooperation mechanisms between the public and private sectors (Yazıcı & Darıcı, 2019). Likewise, this industry has begun to experience changes in the way it approaches and enables the exploration of outer space. In this sense, the emergence of private companies with the capacity to launch rockets can promote the emergence of new ideas such as commercial space travel, exploration and use of resources from the Moon (for example, through mining) and, including colonization (Orlova et al., 2020).

The opening of the space sector to private initiative was favored by circumstances such as the modification of the special legislation of the United States in 2015 by which the possibilities of space-related commercial activity were promoted, encouraging activities such as launch systems, tourist travel and resource exploitation (Vedda & Hays, 2018). Likewise, the end of the space shuttle program in 2011 and the existence of the International Space Station (ISS) led to the appearance of new business possibilities, and therefore, of new companies that carried out tasks that had been previously the exclusive purview of entities such as the National Aeronautics and Space Administration (NASA) of the United States (Orlova et al., 2020). In this order of ideas, activities such as the construction of spacecraft, the manufacture of specialized resources and the facilitation of logistics for launches are currently taking place with the help of new private firms, such as Virgin Atlantic, Blue Origin, Space X, and Made In Space, among many others (Orlova et al., 2020). Likewise, the opening of the space sector has implied an increase in the number of spacecraft launches worldwide in recent years (Orlova et al., 2020).

It is clear then that, in the future, the scope of space activity will continue to expand. Apart from the contribution of the private sector and its investments, it is presumed that other factors will influence the diversification of the space industry, such as the fascination with the unknown, advances in technological capability, and the need to supply resources to satisfy growing demand (Orlova et al., 2020).

- **Fascination with the unknown**
  By nature, human societies have curiosity as the driver of many of their activities. Everything that is considered unknown inevitably challenges people and outer space is a prime example of this (Orlova et al., 2020).
- **Scientific and technological advances**
  The exploration of space has required the advancement of science in various fields. These advances, in general terms, have been thanks to research techniques and groups with capacity for innovation. In turn, these have allowed, over time, for science applied to space to promote the development of new products, mainly manufactured, as well as useful technologies for various aspects of daily life, such as medicine, the spread of the Internet, information technology and the management of natural resources and the environment, among others (Paladini et al., 2021; Orlova et al., 2020).
- **Supply and demand**
  The demand for natural resources necessary for the development of various activities of human societies has increased progressively over time. This situation has been favored by factors such as population growth, the increase in the general longevity of people and the increase in consumption due to greater economic power, all of which are expected to continue in the near future (Orlova et al., 2020).

Apart from the above, the increasingly limited access to resources such as arable land, fresh water, fossil fuels and minerals, as well as the impact of climate change make it necessary to adopt strategies that alleviate pressures on finite resources available on Earth. This can be done either by adopting measures that reduce consumption or by increasing the supply of available natural resources (Orlova et al., 2020).

Eventually, the increase in the supply of resources that satisfy demand could occur, for example, through the establishment of human settlements in space, in turn allowing the exploitation of minerals that are increasingly scarce on Earth, but available in large quantities on asteroids and planets (Paladini et al., 2021). Likewise, there is great potential in terms of energy sources and the space required for human activities such as housing and facilities for agriculture and waste management (Orlova et al., 2020).

6.4 Supply Chains in the Space Industry

More and more actors see space as a favorable environment for business. The growth in the number of organizations interested in space activities is a reflection of the so-called "democratization of space" (Galluzzi et al., 2006), which also implies the need to structure parameters and regulations that allow the favorable development of space exploration and exploitation.

Consequently, the consolidation of space as a field of economic action will require various obstacles to be overcome. First of all, space travel involves huge distances. For example, the Moon's orbit is just over 400,000 kilometers from Earth while Mars is at least 55,000,000 kilometers away. It is not only about how to reach such remote places, but also to think about the conditions of human existence when there (Orlova et al., 2020). Another important aspect that becomes a challenge is gravity, since the design and manufacture of ships that allow this condition to be overcome are very expensive, especially given the need for high speed capability (more than 40,000 kilometers per hour) (Orlova et al., 2020).

The crucial importance of hostile environmental conditions of space should also be noted. These environments are characterized by little or no natural availability of water, air, or food for humans, high levels of radiation, and a complete lack of gravity in many places (Orlova et al., 2020). Finally, the flow of information must be optimized by reducing dependence on the use of equipment located on the ground, improving communications and reducing the risks posed by space debris (Orlova et al., 2020).

While acknowledging and understanding that the aforementioned difficulties will eventually have to be overcome, increasingly complex activities will be carried out in space in the future. These will require proper management of both materials and processes, as well as information. Therefore, and taking into account recent technological advances, the establishment of complete and robotic supply chains in space is a practical and accessible possibility (Metzger, 2016). Without proper supply chains in place beyond the Earth, space exploration will not be sustainable (Galluzzi et al., 2006).

It is thus pertinent to promote the planning, control and administration of space activities in order to integrate and anticipate the different flows of the supply chains, taking into account the simultaneous execution of new space programs, such as those related to the Moon and Mars (Galluzzi et al., 2006). Therefore, to the extent that a supply chain management system is implemented at the space industry level, everything related to the selection of supply sources, the execution of manufacturing and acquisition appropriate to the conditions of the demand, forecasting supply and demand and measuring performance indicators will become increasingly important (Galluzzi et al., 2006).

6.4.1 Areas of Action for the Implementation of Supply Chains in Space

The supply chains necessary for the development of space activities, bearing in mind the challenges imposed by the environmental conditions of space, will require clear progress in various aspects of an operational nature. These are highlighted below (Fig. 6.4).

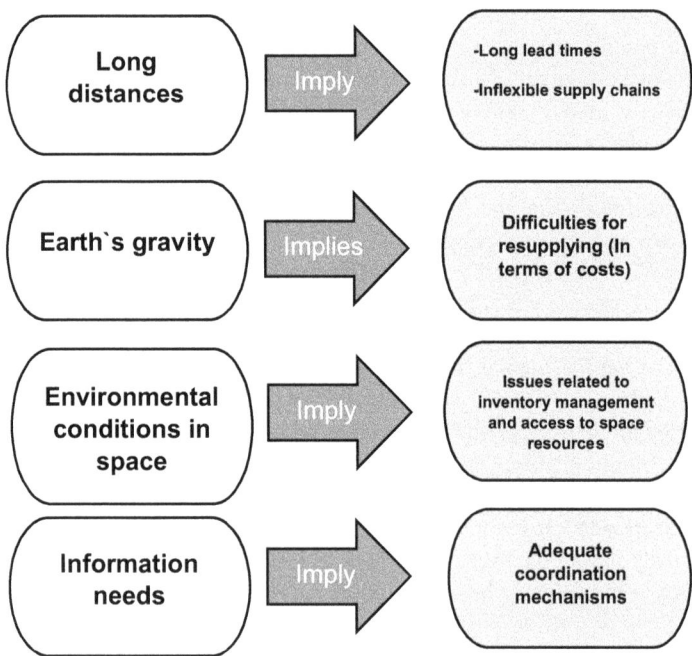

Fig. 6.4 Relationship between spatial context conditions and future supply chain development (Wooten & Tang, 2018)

- **Delivery times**

  While it currently takes a few minutes for a rocket to reach low Earth orbit after being launched, docking with the ISS can take hours or even days (Wooten & Tang, 2018). Likewise, the previous set-up of a spacecraft requires a reasonable time that must be strictly respected for the good of the mission. Traveling to the farthest reaches of space such as the Moon and Mars make this aspect even more vital (Wooten & Tang, 2018). The complexity of space travel negatively affects the delivery times of supplies, which must be taken into account when designing supply chains.

  Long lead times will, in turn, negatively impact on the flexibility of a supply chain to the extent that they can affect its ability to respond to risks (Wooten & Tang, 2018). To counteract these difficulties, it is probably useful to design supply chains based on a made-to-order basis in order to offer customized solutions (Wooten & Tang, 2018).

- **Costs**

  The flow of parts and specialized equipment transported in low volumes can result in high costs since supply chains, in general, base their operation on handling large quantities (Wooten & Tang, 2018). Given that the most sophisticated elements required for the space economy will likely not be present in large volumes, supply chain design must address this, along with risks and uncertainties, while seeking to reduce costs (Wooten & Tang, 2018).

- **Inventories**

  Inventory management in space can become problematic due to factors such as the lack of gravity, which can lead to items being lost due to improper storage, inadequate tracking, inefficient management of required spare parts, and related issues (Wooten & Tang, 2018).

- **Access to space resources**

  Development of adequate supply chains for the needs of future space exploration and exploitation requires, by necessity, a reduction of dependence on the goods and services offered by planet Earth (Wooten & Tang, 2018; Carpenter et al., 2016). At present, the presence of abundant amounts of minerals and water is known on the Moon, as well as on some asteroids. Utilization of these resources, in addition to promoting the consolidation of space as an economic environment endowed with its own supply chains, can contribute to improving the economy on Earth itself (Wooten & Tang, 2018).

- **Coordination between stakeholders**

  Opening of the space sector to private initiative has fostered the emergence of numerous companies, which translates into a growing interaction between public and private entities in a business environment with more and more opportunities, albeit with greater competition. Interaction entails the need to advance coordination, which requires configuring, optimizing and integrating information flows. Given the complexity and the particular characteristics of space activities, the use of modeling is a fundamental tool since it can help establish joint work schemes appropriate to specific situations (Wooten & Tang, 2018). Along with coordination, improvement of communication systems over long distances must be advanced if the way in which information flows is to be improved (Wooten & Tang, 2018).

6.5   Moon Resources

Outer space provides an immense amount of resources in the form of matter and energy. The Moon, the closest celestial body to Earth, has this characteristic. In view of its proximity to our planet, the Moon can be an ideal testing ground to understand how the potential of non-terrestrial natural resources can be harnessed (Carpenter et al., 2016; Spudis, 2011a).

Based on information from numerous missions supported by remote sensing teams over many years, we can conclude that the natural resources of the Moon may eventually have three types of use (Crawford, 2015). First, the resources could be used as support materials to facilitate exploration of the Moon itself. A second possibility would be the performance of economic and scientific activities, both in the so-called "cislunar space" (which includes the area between the Earth and the Moon), and in other areas of the solar system. A third and final use would be the export of resources to the Earth in order to contribute to economic development on our planet (Crawford, 2015).

6.5.1   Use of Resources for Lunar Exploration

Construction of lunar bases will require the use of regolith, a layer of unconsolidated rocky material that covers the entire lunar surface, and which has been formed over millions of years. The importance of this material lies in the fact that it can facilitate the construction of structures that provide protection against cosmic rays (Crawford, 2015). Regolith can also be used for manufacture of ceramics and facilities for plant growth. Likewise, the production of rocket fuel and the production of nuclear energy can be favored by the existence of other components within the regolith, such as oxygen, hydrogen, helium and metals such as iron, aluminum, and titanium, as well as silicon (Taylor, 1992).

6.5.2   Use of Resources for Activities in Cislunar Space

The existence of abundant amounts of water and the almost permanent availability of sunlight in regions near the lunar poles may allow the creation of a transport system that allows travel through cislunar space (Spudis & Lavoi, 2011). It will be necessary to begin with demonstrative processes for the production of water and oxygen in small quantities that allow the required techniques to be perfected. Later on, usable products (mainly drinking water, air and construction materials) can be obtained in larger quantities. It will then be possible to refine rocket fuel, which, when produced in large quantities, will enable surplus fuel that can be taken to deposits located between the Earth and the Moon, thus opening the way for the creation of a cislunar economy (Spudis, 2011b).

6.5.3 Use of Exportable Resources for the Economy of the Earth

The economy of planet Earth can be advantaged by the exploitation of resources found in outer space. It should, however, be noted that this will require some conditions to be met. The importation of extraterrestrial resources to Earth can be viable if a specific commodity (for example metals such as platinum or gold) has a high market value, if transportation costs from space are low enough to do this profitably and if said resource becomes unavailable on our planet (Henckens, 2021; Duke et al., 2006).

From a geological point of view, the Moon has two main zones: the highlands and the mares. The highlands are light-colored, ancient rock formations, while the mares are darker and predominantly circular (Crawford, 2015). The highlands are characterized by being rich in chemical elements such as calcium, aluminum, silicon and oxygen. The mares, in contrast, contain an abundance of magnesium, iron and titanium (Crawford, 2015).

However, both the highlands and the mares are, in turn, covered by regolith, which formed over millions of years by countless impacts of meteorites and micrometeorites (Crawford, 2015) and by the action of the solar wind (Rapp, 2018). Regolith is abundant and therefore the fundamental raw material around which the processes of exploration and economic exploitation of the Moon could be implemented (Crawford, 2015). Regolith can serve as a raw material for the production of oxygen, the construction of houses and roads, the production of glass and various alloys, among other activities (Kuhn et al., 2022).

We can thus talk about the following natural resources of the Moon as having economic potential:

- **Silicates**
  They are mainly found in the highlands in the form of pyroxene, plagioclase and olivine. These are, the most common minerals in the lunar crust and mantle (Kuhn et al., 2022; Chen, 2018). The importance of silicates lies in the fact that they typically have an oxygen content greater than 40% (Spudis & Lavoi, 2011). However, at least at present, extraction of oxygen implies the need to identify a method that allows the strong silicate bonds to be broken, requiring very high

temperatures to achieve extraction (Duke et al., 2006). For this reason, an autonomous processing unit equipped with suitable reactors would have to be developed to perform all tasks, from excavation to final disposal of the waste regolith (Rapp, 2018).

- **Iron oxide**
  Fe-oxides are abundant in the regolith found in the mares (on average the regolith can contain 14% Fe-oxides) (Rapp, 2018). Obtaining the iron oxide present in the Moon requires a reduction process based on hydrogen, which can be carried out under more favorable conditions than the process required for the reduction of silicates (Rapp, 2018).

- **Atoms from the solar wind**
  They are found mainly in the form of hydrogen and helium ions on the surface of the regolith grains, and are most abundant in the very fine material. The lack of atmosphere on the Moon and the high speed at which these atoms move facilitates their entry to the surface (Rapp, 2018). Hydrogen ions occur in low quantities on the Moon, so their use would require utilization of large volumes of regolith. However, it is considered that hydrogen can be used as rocket fuel, as a reducing agent, and perhaps most importantly, as a raw material for the production of water (Heiken et al., 1991). For its part, helium ions are also found in limited quantities on the Moon (Helium-3 (^{3}He), approximately between 10 to 20 µg/g He), but still in greater abundance than on Earth. This, together with the fact that Helium-3 can be used for the generation of nuclear energy through fusion, have positioned ^{3}He as a significant potential resource (Heiken et al., 1991).

- **Water in the form of ice in the craters near the poles**
  Based on the data available so far, water ice is present in the dry regolith of the north and south poles, covering an area of approximately 1850 km^2 at each pole (Rapp, 2018). This is because temperatures are high on the rest of the Moon's surface due to the lack of an atmosphere, which means that the non-polar regions are exposed to direct sunlight. On the other hand, the poles, being dark areas, meet the conditions conducive to the existence of ice at the bottom of the craters (Rapp, 2018) since these do not point in the direction of the sun. Sunlight has not reached these areas in the last 2 billion years (Zhao & Chen, 2020).

- **Aluminum**
  Aluminum occurs in plagioclase feldspar, a mineral present in highland areas either in the form of fragments or in rocks. Aluminum present on the Moon has the potential to be used as a material for lightweight structures, it can also serve as a reflective or coating material, and as possible rocket fuel. However, the complex processing of this mineral means that its extraction must be considered in the medium or long term (Heiken et al., 1991).

- **Oxygen**
  Its presence on the Moon as free gas is almost zero, so it will eventually have to be extracted from rocks, more specifically from silicate or oxide minerals. The most promising mineral for oxygen extraction is considered to be ilmenite

(FeTiO$_3$), since its use would require the use of relatively low amounts of energy. The importance of oxygen lies in the fact that it would be a fundamental support for human life outside of the Earth; Likewise, it is considered that it can be a component of rocket fuels (Heiken et al., 1991).

6.6 In-Situ Resource Utilization (ISRU)

Exploitation of natural resources in outer space can reduce dependence on the limited resources of Earth and help make space exploration profitable. In this sense, the emergence of the concept of In-Situ Resource Utilization (ISRU) represents a step in the right direction. ISRU refers to the use of materials available in situ, that is, in places of celestial bodies other than the Earth in order to produce goods and services necessary for various activities, whether they are carried out by humans or machines (Crawford et al., 2014; McConnell & Tolley, 2016; Grier & Rivkin, 2019; Anand et al., 2012; Sacksteder & Sanders, 2007; Linee et al. 2017). Likewise, ISRU seeks to reduce costs, mass and level of risk that exploration may entail, as well as improve the performance of space missions (Sanders & Larson, 2012). ISRU is based on the development of five areas that are considered of great interest (Sanders & Larson, 2012):

1. Characterization and mapping of resources
2. Production of consumables for the development of missions (goods and raw materials)
3. Civil engineering and surface constructions
4. Generation, storage and transmission of energy
5. Manufacture and repair using local resources

A system for taking advantage of the natural resources available on the Moon, Mars, or other celestial bodies such as asteroids, implies the fulfillment of the following tasks or stages (Linne et al., 2017; Kleinhenz & Sanders, 2021):

- **Resource assessment (Prospecting)**
  Evaluation and mapping of the various available resources (physical, chemical, geological, water, etc.). This can be carried out either on the ground or from the orbit of the celestial body concerned. It is considered pertinent that surveying from space helps to make initial and general measurements, while the ground survey yields more specific data (Linne et al., 2017; Kleinhenz & Sanders, 2021).
- **Resource Acquisition**
  This task is based on obtaining, via excavation, drilling or other methods, materials present in the soil and in the atmosphere and their preparation before processing (Linne et al., 2017; Kleinhenz & Sanders, 2021).
- **Resource processing/Consumable production**
  Conversion of resources into useful products or into raw materials required for construction or the manufacture of new products, such as consumables for mis-

sions (thrusters, products designed for the life support of humans and supplies for fuel cells) (Linne et al., 2017; Kleinhenz & Sanders, 2021).

- **On-Site Manufacturing**
  Production of various goods using locally available materials. These can include spare parts, machinery and other complex products (Linne et al., 2017; Kleinhenz & Sanders, 2021).
- **In-Situ Construction**
  This includes all those activities that involve the construction of infrastructure using only local materials. In-Situ construction will allow the placement of facilities such as anti-radiation shelters, roads, houses and structures for the landing and take-off of spacecraft, among others (Linne et al., 2017; Kleinhenz & Sanders, 2021).
- **In-Situ Energy**
  The manufacture of energy generation and storage equipment and the generation of energy itself using resources available in the immediate environment (Linne et al., 2017; Kleinhenz & Sanders, 2021).

Likewise, integration in the ISRU systems of mobility schemes that allow the movement of resources and goods produced between the different facilities, and between these and the points of consumption of final products, as well as the development of autonomous technologies that allow the operation of infrastructures and equipment for long periods of time will be essential elements for the start-up of facilities for the ISRU (Linne et al., 2017; Kleinhenz & Sanders, 2021).

6.7   Structuring of Supply Chains for the Use of the Resources of the Moon

The implementation of supply chains based on the use of lunar resources will require extensive prior research on Earth and involve the most faithful simulation possible of the unique conditions of the Moon. In general terms, these are the abundance of regolith, absence of gravity, presence of vacuum and extreme temperature changes (International Space Exploration Coordination Group, 2021). In addition, it will be important to establish to what extent the exploitation of lunar resources can be sustainable. Currently, it would seem that production of oxygen from various minerals is the single economic process that has a high probability fulfilling one of the main objectives of the ISRU approach, the production of goods and services in space based on extraterrestrial raw materials (Ellery, 2020).

With regard to the actual functioning of the possible supply chains in space, it is worth highlighting the importance that aspects such as the dynamic nature of supply and demand of the network, changes in load configurations, transportation costs and unforeseen events pose. The way in which the mobilized goods will be stored, distributed and used should also be taken into account (Galluzzi et al., 2006).

Despite the existence of certain information gaps at present, this chapter addresses ways in which supply chains in outer space are likely to be structured. The cislunar region will be taken as spatial reference since because of its proximity to Earth. It is expected that this will be the first region of space that must have an adequate supply of goods and services, with capacities for transportation of them to and from the Moon and with the necessary infrastructure to carry out lunar and deep space missions. The strategic importance of this area is thus considered to be growing (Kaplan, 2020).

6.7.1   Cislunar Space

Cislunar space refers to the area that receives the influence of gravity, both from the Earth and from the Moon, also covering various orbits such as low Earth orbit (LEO), medium Earth orbit (MEO), geosynchronous orbit (GSO), geostationary orbit (GEO), and highly elliptical orbit (HEO) (Fig. 6.5). Cislunar space is made up of the Earth-Moon libration points (or Lagrange points) and the lunar low orbit (LLO) (Bobskill & Lupisella, 2012; Johnson, 2022). At present, cislunar space is of great importance for human beings, since all satellites and structures that support space activity are located there, distributed in almost all its zones as follows:

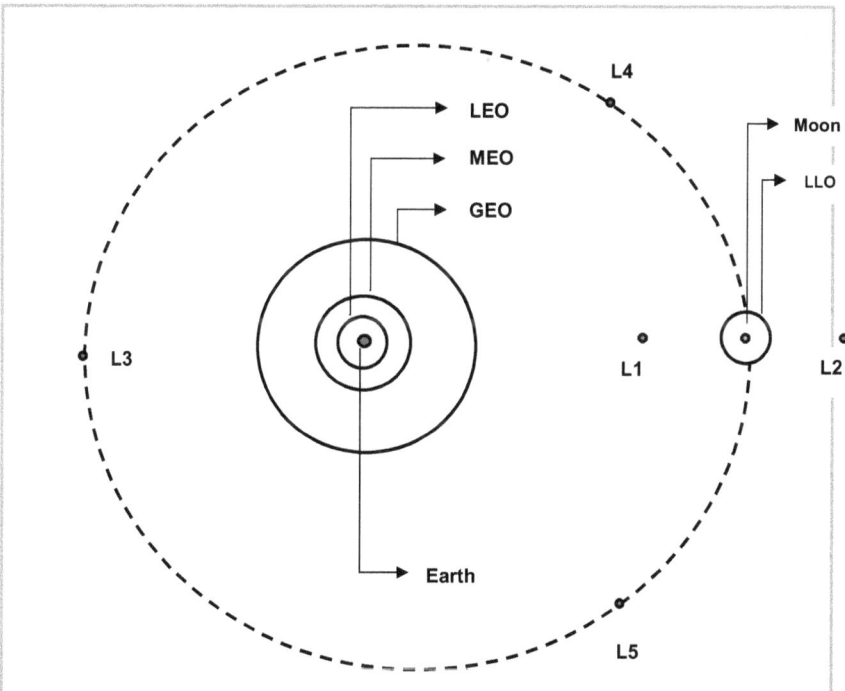

Fig. 6.5 Cislunar space

- **LEO** is the area closest to the Earth (between 180 and 2000 km altitude) (Duffy & Lake, 2021). Most of the satellites and facilities (temporary and permanent) launched from Earth operate in it (typically at heights of 200 to 300 km), mainly carrying out remote orbital sensing missions of the Earth and its atmosphere (Spudis, 2011b).
- **MEO** is located between 2000 and 35,780 km altitude (Duffy & Lake, 2021). Satellite constellations used for global positioning systems (GPS) mainly operate in this region due to the suitable conditions for activities that require visibility for long periods of time (Spudis, 2011b).
- **GEO and GSO** make up an area of approximately 35,780 km high used for activities related to communications, climate monitoring and observation (Spudis, 2011b).
- **HEO** is a highly elongated orbit and thus has very long orbital periods. This class of orbit is mainly used for communications, satellite radio and remote sensing (Spudis, 2011b).
- **Earth-Moon libration points** are also known as Lagrange points. These are areas even further away than GEO in which the combined gravitational forces of two large celestial bodies, in this specific case the Earth and Moon, equal the centrifugal force of a much smaller body (Howell, 2017), making them suitable for the location of facilities for transport and logistics (Spudis, 2011b). It has been determined that there are five libration points, of which three are considered unstable (L1, L2 and L3) while points L4 and L5 are stable (Duffy & Lake, 2021). These zones have already been used for space activities, such as observation and monitoring of climatic variables (Howell, 2017).
- The **LLO** zone is easily accessible from GEO or from the libration points (Spudis, 2011b).

6.7.2 Supply Chains in Cislunar Space

Cislunar space can have a supply chain that is structured based on the definition of four critical aspects, which, as established in the initial section of this chapter, would be its components: the products; the suppliers and marketers; the facilities; and the transport channels.

6.7.2.1 Products

The missions to be carried out in cislunar space will not only facilitate transportation to and from the Moon, but also the development of technological capabilities that make it possible, in the future, to carry out increasingly complex lunar missions and the commencement of deep space missions (Kaplan, 2020). Therefore, the exploration of cislunar space will require the availability of various goods, products or supplies, to give life support to the crews and to facilitate scientific and economic activities.

First, provisions will be required for crews in the early phases of exploration and for larger assemblages of people as off-Earth human settlements become established. Air, water, food, items for hygiene and personal use, and medicines will all be needed, together with essential tools for daily life and to maintain health and the proper functioning of support items such as clothing and electronic equipment (Lee et al., 2018; National Space Society, 2018a; Gralla et al., 2006). Apart from the development of the ISRU, this will require, implementation of agricultural, manufacturing, and air and material recycling techniques that are adapted to vacuum conditions and low gravity (National Space Society, 2018a). Therefore, it will be important to have facilities and implementation protocols to enable proper waste management.

The supply of facilities for housing and infrastructure, such as mobility systems, equipment for electricity generation, robotic systems and habitats will also be of great importance and will require the implementation of agile manufacturing techniques (such as 3D printing) that allow the use of materials such as regolith or recycled parts from dismantled space vehicles (Lee et al., 2018; Hendrixson, 2022).

Likewise, it will be necessary to have transport equipment, propellants and fuels to enable the required rockets and ships to move. This is a vital aspect of space exploration since, unlike the supply chains that we know from Earth, the propellant can represent most of the ship's mass (Gralla et al., 2006). The use of cislunar space will also require, not only the availability of specific equipment for exploration and scientific research, but also for communications and the stowage and securing of supplies (Gralla et al., 2006).

6.7.2.2 Suppliers and Marketers

Operation of supply chains at the cislunar level should include organizations that undertake activities in the following areas:

Transportation

The promotion of cislunar space exploration will bring with it the need to transport people and materials necessary for the various missions. Space vehicles traversing the different Earth and lunar orbits and Lagrange points are expected to drop off and pick up goods, robotic equipment and humans where they are needed (Vedda, 2018). However, spacecraft launch costs need to come down enough that it will eventually be cheaper to produce, for example, water and propellants for spacecraft on the Moon than to provide such goods from the Earth (Colvin et al., 2020).

Building

The construction of habitats for the crews of the missions as well as other infrastructures is another essential task that should be taken into account. Structures such as inflatable habitats and capsules, surface habitats (3D printed structures for example) (Colvin et al., 2020), as well as more complex facilities such as hotels, factories and laboratories must be put into operation, each adapted to the particular conditions of space and taking advantage of locally available resources (National Space Society, 2018a).

In-Situ Resource Utilization

In this sense, companies will engage in two types of ISRU: prospecting, extraction and processing of lunar resources; and the use of resources to manufacture or produce various goods (Colvin et al., 2020).

Communications

Communications and navigation services will become essential as activities in cislunar space become more frequent. The companies that provide these services must strive to guarantee their security, reliability and scalability (Vedda, 2018).

Private Goods and Services

It is estimated that a market will be created based on the offer of services such as the disposal of mortal remains on the lunar surface, the creation of objects (for example jewelry) based on lunar materials and space tourism, which is considered feasible on the satellite itself or in the form of paths along an orbit (Colvin et al., 2020).

Production of Goods for the Supply Chain

The production of goods such as batteries, fuel cells, motors, support systems and electronic equipment for activities such as the ISRU must take place through specialized companies (Colvin et al., 2020).

Scientific Investigation

The companies involved in this field will focus on the collection of scientific information and the supply of specialized remote sensing equipment (Colvin et al., 2020).

6.7.2.3   Facilities

The facilities that must be built for the structuring of supply chains in cislunar space must be adapted, among others, to conditions of temperature, solar radiation and gravity, all of which represent an unprecedented challenge from a logistical point of view. In this order of ideas, the existence of possible facilities is required,such as:

ISRU Plants

These structures will have elements such as tank trucks, special vehicles for the terrain, an electricity generation plant and a processing plant for the raw materials to be exploited (Ishimatsu et al., 2016). It is estimated that these systems will work automatically or through the work of robots and that their maintenance and productivity will be scalable over time (Ishimatsu et al., 2016).

In-Space Manufacturing Facilities

They will serve as sites for the production of goods for space exploration as well as structures that would be considered too large to be manufactured on Earth and carried into space (National Space Society, 2018a).

Space Stations

Their main purpose would be to facilitate the flow of space vehicles allowing their arrival and departure, mainly those that transport crews and supplies between the Earth, the Moon and the Lagrange points (Vedda, 2018; Lizy-Destrez et al., 2021).

Facilities for the Permanence of People and the Performance of Scientific Activities

To guarantee the sustainable presence of personnel necessary for the operation of the supply chain, there will be facilities that allow said personnel to carry out their activities protected from various space phenomena such as cosmic radiation and events related to solar activity (Bobskill & Lupisella, 2012).

In-Space Logistics Bases

They will be located especially in places such as the lunar orbit and the Lagrange points (L1 and/or L2) and will be used for the transfer and storage of propellants and cargo (National Space Society, 2018b).

6.7.2.4 Transport Channels

Transport in a supply chain of goods and services in cislunar space will be influenced by various disturbances of celestial bodies, mainly those related to their gravitational forces, which are estimated to affect the determination of routes (Lizy-Destrez et al., 2021). Likewise, the availability of adequate places for the arrival of vehicles, the development of navigation and the improvement of transfer times will affect the performance of mobility systems (Lizy-Destrez et al., 2021).

Suitable transport channels for supply chains in cislunar space will need to be conceptualized around four fundamental aspects addressed below.

Capacity

In the initial phases of deeper space exploration (fundamentally based on the use of LEO), small and medium-sized vehicles will be used, which, as far as possible, will be reusable and will serve to transport passengers and supplies (Snead, 2006). Later, in the medium term, it will be possible to have vehicles with greater capacity, which will not only move people and merchandise, but also assembly and/or repair facilities for elements such as satellites, becoming hangars or temporary bases located in a certain orbit (Snead, 2006).

In terms of specific capacities, it is possible that there will be small vehicles with payloads of around 10 tons, while medium vehicles will be able to load up to 20 tons. Likewise, there would be large vehicles capable of transporting up to 50 tons and even still larger vehicles with capacities of 70 and even 110 tons (Merrill et al., 2012).

Costs or Freights

It is hoped that vehicle launch costs will be significantly reduced by the development of reusable propellants. Likewise, launches will be sought to be more efficient and reliable so that their success rates are higher (National Space Society, 2018a). Likewise, efforts should be made to reduce costs by more efficient use of vehicles, for example, in relation to cargo transport, vehicles with more capacity are used to transport larger loads and use vehicles with less capacity for logistics and resupply tasks (Merrill et al., 2012).

Means of Transport

Vehicles such as lunar landers will be useful for trips between orbital stations and the surface of the Moon as they are designed to land smoothly and safely (Lizy-Destrez et al., 2021). On the other hand, for cargo transportation purposes, it is expected that the vehicles destined for these tasks will work, in the shorter term, with propulsion systems based on fuels of a chemical nature, given that the use of these can be done in small, large and medium-sized vehicles. Although production systems based on electric motors can already be developed, these could only be implemented in small and medium-sized vehicles (Merrill et al., 2012).

Frequencies

Transport and delivery times in cislunar space can be quite long considering the long distances between possible locations (Fayez et al., 2006). The high costs that transportation off Earth can have must also be taken into account. Therefore, if costs can be reduced through, for example, ISRU propellant production, this may create greater demand for cislunar transport and the need for increased frequencies (Kutter & Sowers, 2016).

6.8 Conclusions

The production of goods and the provision of services will require the conjunction of numerous events and the collaboration of many participating entities. One circumstance that will ensure the proper functioning of the economy is the existence of supply chains, which, based on the participation of suppliers, manufacturers, distributors and customers, makes it possible for a product or service to be provided to those who need it in the time and conditions required.

Every supply chain must therefore be sufficiently well planned that, to the maximum extent possible, it covers both the initial stages in which the idea that will govern said chain is developed, and the period in which the various economic activities take place. The structured management of a supply chain must then be governed by the parameters established by the Supply Chain Management (SCM).

The economic activities carried out by humans that relate to the exploration of outer space are also likely to be planned conscientiously and indeed even more so if the particular conditions of environments outside of the Earth are taken into account. Earth. Situations such as low or zero gravity, solar radiation and the enormous distances to be traveled, among others, require greater care when defining the way in which material resources are going to be used and the number of humans, if any, that will be required.

Despite the enormous challenges that the exploration and exploitation of space entail, there is enormous potential in celestial bodies such as the Moon and Mars in terms of natural resources whose availability is less and less on Earth or in some cases, is almost zero. The Moon thus becomes a place that will enable the parameters and conditions to be established that are required to expand the frontiers of humanity.

In view of the proximity of the Moon to Earth, the region between the two celestial bodies known as cislunar space has begun to be used consistently (mainly in the area closest to the Earth) through the positioning of satellites and more complex space installations. It is, however, necessary to take advantage of the space closest to the Moon in which there are also areas with potential for carrying out activities and, therefore, for the creation of supply chains.

Achieving establishment of a cislunar economic structure and supply chains that allow improved profits and reduced costs will take time since substantial work will need to be carried out. This will include the creation of both products and organizations with qualified personnel, as well as infrastructure, and not least through design of special transport vehicles that can cope with the harsh conditions of space.

References

Anand, M., Crawford, I. A., Balat-Pichelin, M., Abanades, S., van Westrenen, W., Péraudeau, G., Jaumann, R., & Seboldt, W. (2012). A brief review of chemical and mineralogical resources on the moon and likely initial in situ resource utilization (ISRU) applications. *Planetary and Space Science, 74*(1), 42–48. https://doi.org/10.1016/j.pss.2012.08.012

Bobskill, M., & Lupisella, M. (2012, May 22). *The role of cis-lunar space in future global space exploration.* Global space exploration conference (Washington, DC). https://ntrs.nasa.gov/citations/20120009459

Carpenter, J., Fisackerly, R., & Houdou, B. (2016). Establishing lunar resource viability. *Space Policy, 37* (Part 2), 52–57. https://doi.org/10.1016/j.spacepol.2016.07.002

Chen, S. (2018). Surface of the moon, distribution of materials and structures. In B. Cudnik (Ed.), *Encyclopedia of lunar science* (pp. 1–6). Springer. https://doi-org.ezproxy.utp.edu.co/10.1007/978-3-319-05546-6_44-1

Chopra, S. (2013). *Supply chain management: Strategy, planning, and operation.* Pearson.

Colvin, T., Crane, K., Lindbergh, R., & Lal, B. (2020). *Demand drivers of the lunar and cislunar economy.* IDA Science & technology policy institute. https://www.ida.org/-/media/feature/publications/d/de/demand-drivers-of-the-lunar-and-cislunar-economy/d-13219.pdf

Crawford, I. A. (2015). Lunar resources: A review. *Progress in Physical Geography: Earth and Environment, 39*(2), 137–167. https://doi.org/10.1177/0309133314567585

Crawford, I., Joy, K., & Anand, M. (2014). Chapter 25 – Lunar exploration. In T. Spohn, D. Breuer, & T. V. Johnson (Eds.), *Encyclopedia of the solar system* (pp. 555–579). Elsevier. https://doi.org/10.1016/B978-0-12-415845-0.00025-6

Deckert, C. (2020). Supply chain. In S. Idowu, R. Schmidpeter, N. Capaldi, L. Zu, M. Del Baldo, & R. Abreu (Eds.), *Encyclopedia of sustainable management* (pp. 1–4). Springer. https://doi-org.ezproxy.utp.edu.co/10.1007/978-3-030-02006-4_132-1

Duffy, L., & Lake, J. (2021). Cislunar Spacepower. *The New Frontier Space Force Journal,* Issue II by sfj december 31, 2021. https://spaceforcejournal.org/3859-2/

Duke, M., Gaddis, L., Taylor, G. J., & Schmitt, H. (2006). Development of the Moon. *Reviews in Mineralogy and Geochemistry, 60*(1), 597–655. https://doi.org/10.2138/rmg.2006.60.6

Ellery, A. (2020). Sustainable in-situ resource utilization on the moon. *Planetary and Space Science, 184,* 104870. https://doi.org/10.1016/j.pss.2020.104870

Ernst, R., & Haar, J. (2019). Supply chains. In *Globalization, competitiveness, and governability* (pp. 125–144). Palgrave Macmillan. https://doi-org.ezproxy.utp.edu.co/10.1007/978-3-030-17516-0_6

Fayez, M., Cope, D., Kaylani, A., Callinan, M., Zapata, E., & Mollaghasemi, M. (2006). Earth to orbit logistics and supply chain modeling and simulation for NASA exploration systems. *Proceedings of the 2006 winter simulation conference* (pp. 1462–1469). https://doi.org/10.1109/WSC.2006.322914

Galluzzi, M., Zapata, E., de Weck, O., & Steele, M. (2006) *Foundations of supply chain management for space application*, AIAA 2006-7234. Spaceflight 2006. https://doi.org/10.2514/6.2006-7234

Ganesan, R. (2015). Introduction. In *The profitable supply chain*. Apress. https://doi-org.ezproxy.utp.edu.co/10.1007/978-1-4842-0526-6_1

Goetschalckx, M. (2011). Supply chain systems. In *Supply chain engineering* (International series in Operations Research & Management Science) (Vol. 161). Springer. https://doi-org.ezproxy.utp.edu.co/10.1007/978-1-4419-6512-7_11

Gralla, E., Shull, S., & de Weck, O. (2006). *A modeling framework for interplanetary supply chains*. AIAA 2006-7229. AIAA Space 2006 Conference and Exposition, San Jose, California.

Grier, J., & Rivkin, A. (2019). Chapter 12 – Future exploration. In J. A. Grier & A. S. Rivkin (Eds.), *Airless bodies of the inner solar system* (pp. 255–273). Elsevier. https://doi.org/10.1016/B978-0-12-809279-8.00012-3

Heiken, G., Vaniman, D., & French, B. (1991). *Lunar sourcebook a user's guide to the moon*. Cambridge University Press. https://www.lpi.usra.edu/publications/books/lunar_sourcebook/pdf/LunarSourceBook.pdf

Henckens, T. (2021). Chapter 2 – The availability of mineral resources. In T. Henckens (Ed.), *Governance of the world's mineral resources* (pp. 9–35). Elsevier. https://doi.org/10.1016/B978-0-12-823886-8.00010-5

Hendrixson, S. (2022, May 3). *6 reasons space exploration will need additive manufacturing*. Additive Manufacturing. https://www.additivemanufacturing.media/articles/6-reasons-space-exploration-will-need-additive-manufacturing

Highfill, T., & MacDonald, A. (2022). Estimating the United States space Economy using input-output frameworks. *Space Policy, 60*, 101474. https://doi.org/10.1016/j.spacepol.2021.101474.CD

Hilmola, O. P. (2018). Introduction. In *Supply chain cases* (pp. 1–6). Palgrave Pivot. https://doi-org.ezproxy.utp.edu.co/10.1007/978-3-319-71658-9_1

Howell, E. (2017, August 22). *Lagrange Points: Parking places in space*. Space. https://www.space.com/30302-lagrange-points.html

Hugos, M. (2018). Key concepts of supply chain management. In M. Hugos (Ed.), *Essentials of supply chain management*. https://doi-org.ezproxy.utp.edu.co/10.1002/9781119464495.ch1

International Space Exploration Coordination Group. (2021). *In-situ resource utilization gap assessment report*. https://www.globalspaceexploration.org/wordpress/wp-content/uploads/2021/04/ISECG-ISRU-Technology-Gap-Assessment-Report-Apr-2021.pdf

Ishimatsu, T., de Weck, O. L., Hoffman, J. A., Ohkami, Y., & Shishko, R. (2016). Generalized multicommodity network flow model for the earth–moon–Mars logistics system. *Journal of Spacecraft and Rockets, 53*(1), 25–38. https://doi.org/10.2514/1.a33235

Johnson, K. (2022). *Fly me to the moon worldwide Cislunar and lunar missions*. A Center for strategic and international studies. https://csis-website-prod.s3.amazonaws.com/s3fs-public/publication/220215_Johnson_FlyMe_Moon.pdf?eBOSyAKB1ite5cort60IluuBQWvYyADa

Kaplan, S. (2020, July 13). *Eyes on the prize. The Strategic Implications of Cislunar Space and the Moon*. Aerospace Security. A Project of the Center for Strategic and International Studies. https://aerospace.csis.org/strategic-interest-in-cislunar-space-and-the-moon/

Kleinhenz, J., & Sanders, G. (2021, April 19). *Lunar in-situ resource utilization concept to reality*. Pre-conference short course: Engineering and construction on the moon. ASCE Earth and Space Conference *(Virtual)*.

Kuhn, L., Schingler, J. K., & Hubbard, K. M. (2022). Res Lunae: Characterizing diverse lunar resource systems using the social-ecological system framework. *New Space, 10*(2), 155–165. https://www.liebertpub.com/doi/full/10.1089/space.2021.0054

Kurbel, K. E. (2013). SCM: Supply chain management. In *Enterprise resource planning and supply chain management. Progress in IS* (pp. 221–247). Springer. https://doi-org.ezproxy.utp.edu.co/10.1007/978-3-642-31573-2_8

Kutter, B. F., & Sowers, G. F. (2016, September 13-16). *Cislunar-1000: Transportation supporting a self-sustaining space economy*. AIAA SPACE 2016 Long Beach, California. https://doi.org/10.2514/6.2016-5491

Lee, G., de Weck, O., Armar, N., Jordan, E., Shishko, R., Siddiqi, A., & Whiting, J. (2018, September 9–11). *SpaceNet: Modeling and simulating space logistics.* AIAA SPACE 2008 Conference & Exposition San Diego, California. https://arc.aiaa.org/doi/10.2514/6.2008-7747

Linne, D. L., Sanders, G. B., Starr, S. O., Eisenman, D. J., Suzuki, N. H., Anderson, M. S., & Araghi, K. R. (2017, September 25–29). *Overview of NASA technology development for in-situ resource utilization (ISRU).* 68th International Astronautical Congress (IAC), Adelaide, Australia. https://ntrs.nasa.gov/citations/20180000407

Lizy-Destrez, S., Guardabasso, P., Beauregard, L., & Blazquez, E. (2021, June 14). *Towards the moon and beyond: preparing for the future of cislunar and solar system exploration.* GLEX – 2021, 14 June 2021–18 June 2021. Saint Petersburg, Russian Federation.

Lourenço, H. R., & Ravetti, M. G. (2018). Supply chain management. In R. Martí, P. Pardalos, & M. Resende (Eds.), *Handbook of heuristics* (pp. 1241–1258). Springer. https://doi-org.ezproxy.utp.edu.co/10.1007/978-3-319-07124-4_54

McConnell, B., & Tolley, A. (2016). Ceres and in situ resource utilization. In *A Design for a Reusable Water-Based Spacecraft Known as the Spacecoach* (SpringerBriefs in Space Development) (pp. 77–82). Springer. https://doi-org.ezproxy.utp.edu.co/10.1007/978-3-319-22677-4_12

Merrill, R., Goodliff, K., Mazanek, D., & Reeves, J. (2012, May 22). *Cis-lunar base camp.* Global space exploration conference (Washington, DC). https://ntrs.nasa.gov/citations/20120009357

Metzger, P. (2016). Space development and space science together, an historic opportunity. *Space Policy, 37*(Part 2), 77–91. https://doi.org/10.1016/j.spacepol.2016.08.004

National Space Society. (2018a). *NSS Roadmap to Space Settlement (3rd Edition 2018) Part One: General Milestones.* NSS. https://space.nss.org/nss-roadmap-to-space-settlement-3rd-edition-2018-part-1/

National Space Society. (2018b). *NSS roadmap to Space Settlement (3rd Edition 2018) Part two: Utilization and Development of Cislunar Space.* NSS. https://space.nss.org/nss-roadmap-to-space-settlement-3rd-edition-2018-part-2/

Nel, D., & Badenhorst-Weiss, J. (2010). Supply chain design: Some critical questions. *Journal of Transport and Supply Chain Management, 4.* https://doi.org/10.4102/jtscm.v4i1.68

Orlova, A., Nogueira, R., & Chimenti, P. (2020). The present and future of the space sector: A business ecosystem approach. *Space Policy, 52,* 101374. https://doi.org/10.1016/j.spacepol.2020.101374

Paladini, S., Saha, K., & Pierron, X. (2021). Sustainable space for a sustainable earth? Circular economy insights from the space sector. *Journal of Environmental Management, 289,* 112511. https://doi.org/10.1016/j.jenvman.2021.112511

PWC. (2019). *Main trends and challenges in the space sector.* [PowerPoint slides]. https://www.pwc.fr/fr/assets/files/pdf/2019/06/fr-pwc-main-trends-and-challenges-in-the-space-sector.pdf

Rapp, D. (2018). Lunar ISRU. In *Use of extraterrestrial resources for human space missions to moon or Mars* (pp. 187–196). Springer Praxis Books/Springer. https://doi-org.ezproxy.utp.edu.co/10.1007/978-3-319-72694-6_2

Sacksteder, K., & Sanders, G. (2007, January 8–11). *In-situ resource utilization for lunar and mars exploration.* 45th AIAA Aerospace Sciences Meeting and Exhibit, 08–11 January 2007 Reno, Nevada.

Sanders, G. B., & Larson, W. E. (2012). Progress made in lunar in-situ resource utilization under NASA's exploration technology and development program. *Earth and Space* (JSC-CN-26038).

Sindi, S., & Roe, M. (2017). The evolution of supply chains and logistics. In *Strategic supply chain management* (pp. 7–25). Palgrave Macmillan. https://doi-org.ezproxy.utp.edu.co/10.1007/978-3-319-54843-2_2

Snead, M. (2006). A space logistics infrastructure for the near term. *Aerospace America, 44,* 39–42. https://www.researchgate.net/publication/298538842_A_space_logistics_infrastructure_for_the_near_term

Spudis, P. (2011a). Lunar resources: Unlocking the Space Frontier. *Ad Astra, 23*(2, Summer), 30–34. https://space.nss.org/lunar-resources-unlocking-the-space-frontier/

Spudis, P. (2011b). The moon: Port of entry to Cislunar Space Paul. In C. D. Lutes & P. L. Hays (Eds.), *Toward a theory of Spacepower* (pp. 241–251). Institute For National Strategic Studies, National Defense University Press. https://www.spudislunarresources.com/Papers/12SpudisNDU.pdf

Spudis, P., & Lavoi, T. (2011). *Using the resources of the moon to create a permanent Cislunar Space Faring System*. In Annual Meeting of the Lunar Exploration Analysis Group, p. 80. LPI Contribution No. 1646, Lunar and Planetary Institute, Houston. https://www.lpi.usra.edu/lpi/contribution_docs/LPI-1646.pdf

Stadtler, H. (2005). Supply chain management and advanced planning—Basics, overview and challenges. *European Journal of Operational Research, 163*(3), 575–588. https://doi.org/10.1016/j.ejor.2004.03.001

Taylor, L. A. (1992, September 1) *Resources for a lunar base: Rocks, minerals, and soil of the moon*. NASA. Johnson Space Center, The Second Conference on Lunar Bases and Space Activities of the 21st Century, Volume 2.

Vedda, J. (2018). Cislunar development: What to build—And why. *The Aerospace Corporation. Center for Space Policy and Strategy, 1–10.* https://csps.aerospace.org/papers/cislunar-development-what-build-and-why

Vedda, J., & Hays, P. (2018). *Major policy issues in evolving global space operations*. The Mitchell Institute for Aerospace Studies. Air Force Association.

Wooten, J., & Tang, C. (2018) Operations in space: Exploring a new industry. *Decision Sciences, 49*, 999– 1023. https://doi.org/10.2139/ssrn.3107707

Yazıcı, A., & Darıcı, S. (2019). The new opportunities in space Economy. *İnsan ve Toplum Bilimleri Araştırmaları Dergisi, 8*(4), 3252–3271. Retrieved from http://www.itobiad.com/tr/issue/49747/615134

Zhao, L., & Chen, S. (2020). Lunar permanently shaded areas. In B. Cudnik (Ed.), *Encyclopedia of lunar science* (pp. 1–4). Springer. https://doi-org.ezproxy.utp.edu.co/10.1007/978-3-319-05546-6_53-1

Chapter 7
CSR/ESG in Commercial Space Operations and the Artemis Accords

Francesco de Zwart, Stacey Henderson, and John Culton

Abstract With space activities increasingly dominated by commercial space actors, this chapter explores whether there is a need for Corporate Social Responsibility in space and what that might mean for large commercial space actors. With a focus on the Artemis Accords, this chapter concludes that corporate social responsibility and environment social governance areas, activities, principles, and disclosures risk being displaced with unintended consequences for the corporate shareholder purpose of corporate actors.

7.1 Introduction

7.1.1 Existing and Space-Based CSR/ESG Principles and the Corporate Shareholder Purpose

The sphere of space is becoming increasingly commercialised. The Artemis Accords were announced by NASA in October 2020, with eight founding member states signing the Accords on 14 October 2020.[1] The Accords are a series of bilateral

---

[1] The founding members are Australia, Canada, Italy, Japan, Luxembourg, United Arab Emirates, United Kingdom, and the United States of America. As at 13 May 2022, the Accords have also been signed by Ukraine, South Korea, New Zealand, Brazil, Poland, Mexico, Israel, Romania, and the Kingdom of Bahrain.

F. de Zwart (✉)
Adelaide Law School, The University of Adelaide, Adelaide, SA, Australia
e-mail: francesco.dezwart@adelaide.edu.au

S. Henderson
College of Business, Government and Law, Flinders University, Adelaide, SA, Australia

J. Culton
Andy Thomas Centre for Space Resources, The University of Adelaide,
Adelaide, SA, Australia

M. de Zwart et al. (eds.), *Human Uses of Outer Space*, Issues in Space,
https://doi.org/10.1007/978-981-19-9462-3_7

109

agreements between NASA and signatory states which, as in the preamble, seek to 'implement the provisions of the Outer Space Treaty and other relevant international instruments and thereby establish a political understanding regarding mutually beneficial practices for the future exploration and use of outer space'. The Accords signpost the way for 'agency-to-agency' and 'agency-to-private operator' commercial operation, heralding even greater involvement of commercial actors in space activities in the future. They have been discussed in the context of international space law (de Zwart, 2021). As stated in section 1 of the Accords, the purpose is:

> to establish a common vision via a practical set of principles, guidelines, and best practices to enhance the governance of the civil exploration and use of outer space with the intention of advancing the Artemis Program. Adherence to a practical set of principles, guidelines, and best practices in carrying out activities in outer space is intended to increase the safety of operations, reduce uncertainty, and promote the sustainable and beneficial use of space for all humankind.

Our purpose in this chapter is to examine the Accords to consider which sections may be open – in the corporate purpose sense – to the operation of Corporate Social Responsibility/Environment Social Governance (CSR/ESG) areas, activities, principles and disclosures either Earth-based or space-based. In other words, which sections, mechanisms or principles of the Accords leave room for or invite the operation of CSR/ESG areas, activities, practices and disclosures? Contrastingly, which do not allow – or at least appear to be restrictive of or contrary to – an implication of those CSR/ESG outcomes? And how will the corporate shareholder purpose of corporate actors – either acting for those governments and agencies under the Accords or on their own behalf – be affected by implementation or operation of the Accords?

This chapter demonstrates four themes or factors in relation to the Artemis Accords. First, that additional – *specific space-based* – CSR/ESG definitions, areas, activities, principles and disclosures will be introduced by the Accords. Second, that the purpose of many of the provisions of the Accords resonates with the purposes and objectives of CSR/ESG. Third, that an interpretation or construction of the Accords is required in order to determine the status, nature and scope of the space-based CSR/ESG definitions, areas, activities, principles and disclosures. In other words, the drafting of which Accord sections on their face admit CSR/ESG definitions, areas, activities, principles and disclosures and which such sections (or parts of sections) exclude or curtail CSR/ESG to all or some degree? Fourth, what are the implications of these space-based CSR/ESG definitions, areas, activities, principles and disclosures for corporate actors contractually bound to Signatory-governments or Signatory-agencies to perform obligations under the Accords? Or those not acting for such governments and agencies but on their own behalf in the civil commercial outer space environments? In other words, what are the ramifications for corporate purpose – in Australian law generally the best interests of the shareholders – of superimposing the CSR/ESG definitions, areas, activities, principles and disclosures suggested or enhanced (or restricted) by the Accords' provisions?

7.1.2   'Shareholder Primacy' and the 'Stakeholder Model' Distinguished

7.1.2.1   'Nexus of Contracts', Agency Theory, the Shareholder Wealth-Maximisation Principal

Shareholder primacy – that the management of a company should act in the best interests of shareholders – is actually comprised of a number of principles or components.

The 'nexus of contracts' theory of corporate law – still well in vogue – provides that a corporation is a collection, intersection or 'nexus' of contracts between various parties involved in the existence and operation of the corporation such as employees, creditors, shareholders, the directors and management (Bainbridge, 1993).

'Agency theory' is a separate building block. It provides that – when exercising a discretion or exercising a power – the directors and management are the 'agents' of the shareholders which appear in nexus theory. For Jensen and Meckling, the agents should act in the interests of the principals (in this case, the shareholders) but, instead, their self-interests lead to behaviours of shirking, empire building, claims for increased compensation and claims for more (non-transparent) perks (Jensen & Meckling, 2000; Charreaux, 2004; Licht, 2003, 2004).

Jensen and Meckling, and, separately, Charreaux and Licht explain that the 'shareholder primacy' model of corporate governance denotes that the shareholders are the only 'residual claimants' on the assets and cash flows of the company after payment of all the company's liabilities and, at that point, the interests of shareholders and the managers of the company are aligned by the 'shareholder wealth-maximisation principle (Jensen & Meckling, 2000; de Zwart, 2015). This principle is said to be derived (there is disagreement) from the United States corporate law decision in *Dodge v Ford Motor Co* (Stout, 2007). For Rhee, this principle links the nexus of contracts and agency theory as a 'default standard' of behaviour (Rhee, 2008).

This is reinforced in Australian corporate law by the provisions of the *Corporations Act 2001* (Cth) (and the equivalent duties at common law and in equity) which provides, in subsection 181(1), the duty to act in the best interests of the corporation and the duty to act for a proper purpose. For subsection 181(1), Australian corporate law generally considers, under the High Court case of *Walker v Wimborne*, that the best interests of the corporation (apart from situations of insolvency or near insolvency) are the interests of its shareholders.

7.1.2.2 'Stakeholder' Model of Corporate Governance, 'Corporate Social Responsibility' ('CSR'), 'Environmental, Social and Governance' ('ESG') and 'Triple-Bottom-Line' Reporting

The Corporations and Markets Advisory Committee (CAMAC) explains the 'current interest' in the social responsibility of corporations – way back in 2006 – which now resonates with the explosion of private space operators such as SpaceX and Blue Origin:

> There is a wave of interest in issues relating to the social responsibility of corporations, including calls by community groups and others for companies to give greater attention to the environmental, social and economic impacts of their activities and to report more fully on their performance in this regards.

> The current interest reflects in part the success of the corporation as a vehicle for productive enterprise and the visibility of corp[orate business activities. The degree of responsibility displayed by particular companies in the course of theior business affairs is understandably a matter of public interest (Corporations and Markets Advisory Committee, 2006).

CAMAC tells us there is no precise meaning of CSR:

> The term 'corporate social responsibility' does not have a precise or fixed meaning. Some descriptions focus on corporate compliance with the spirit as well as the letter of applicable laws regulating corporate conduct. Other definitions refer to a business approach by which an enterprise takes into account the impacts of its activities on interest groups (often referred to as stakeholders) including, but extending beyond, shareholders, and balances longer-term societal impacts against shorter-term financial gains. These societal effects, going beyond the goods and services provided by companies and their returns to shareholders, are typically subdivided into environmental, social and economic impacts (Corporations and Markets Advisory Committee, 2006).

CSR is largely derived from the stakeholder model of corporate governance. The stakeholder model is the opposite of (or, more precisely, as it includes shareholders and others, goes beyond) the shareholder primacy model. Indeed, Licht disagrees that the shareholders are the residual claimants of the corporation (Licht, 2003). For Jensen, 'managers should make decisions that take account of the interests of *all* the stakeholders in a firm' (Jensen, 2002). Maher and Andersson give an indication of the wide range of interests denoted by the shareholder model:

> [o]ther stakeholders may include contractual partners such as employees, suppliers, customers, creditors, and social constituents such as members of the community in which the firm is located, environmental interests, local and national governments, and society at large (Maher & Andersson, 2000; Corporations and Markets Advisory Committee, 2006).

7.1.2.3 'Environmental, Social and Governance' ('ESG') Is Derived from CSR and 'Triple-Bottom-Line' Reporting

ESG – short for 'environment, social, and governance'(Diligent, n.d.) – evolved from CSR and 'Triple-Bottom-Line' reporting (Elkington, 2018; Kleeman & de Zwart, 2022). A wide variety of ESG areas, activities, principles and disclosures is adopted by Diligent:

Environmental
Preservation of our natural world

- Climate change
- Carbon emission reduction
- Water pollution and water scarcity
- Air pollution
- Deforestation

Social
Consideration of humans and our interdependencies

- Customer success
- Data hygiene and security
- Gender and diversity inclusion
- Community relations
- Mental health

Governance
Logistics and defined process for running a business or organization

- Board of directors and its makeup
- Executive compensation guidelines
- Political contributions and lobbying
- Venture partner compensation
- Hiring and onboarding best practices (Diligent, n.d.)

Diligent explains the huge attraction of 'ESG-orientated' investing. ESG activities enhance financial performance (operating profit) and stock/share prices (with less volatility) and attract investor attention leading to increased value in intangible reputational assets and therefore total asset values:

> For investors, environmental, social and governance considerations are a growing priority—and with good reason. ESG performance has been shown to correlate strongly with financial performance; companies in the S&P 500 that ranked in the top quintile for ESG factors outperformed those in the bottom quintile by more than 25 percentage points between the start of 2014 and the end of June 2018.
>
> Stock prices of companies with high ESG rankings also tend to be less volatile, whereas "high ESG controversy" events can cause a company's stocks to underperform the market for as long as two years.
>
> With ESG scores and rankings increasingly being published in the public domain, the importance of investing in ESG-focused organizations is growing. And it's not just published ESG metrics that are attracting investor attention; the reputational value of a proactive approach to environmental, social and governance issues is also being recognized. Today, intangible assets like reputation account for more than 80% of an organization's S&P asset value. Not surprising, then, that ESG-oriented investing has experienced a meteoric rise in recent years (Diligent, n.d.).

Many of the ESG activities identified also arise in the context of space activities. One risk in ESG-orientated investing – both on Earth and in commercial space operations – is 'greenwashing':

> But increased reporting does not inherently translate to meaningful stewardship. Greenwashing – a practice in which sustainability pledges are used as marketing to give the appearance of acting in environmentally responsible ways, rather than representing meaningful operational change or practice – exists (Christensen, 2022).

7.1.2.4 The Artemis Accords Provide for CSR/ESG Areas, Activities, Principles and Disclosures That Are Space-Specific

That there are other definitions, areas, activities, principles and disclosures for CSR/ESG is of course clear, but the areas, activities, principles and disclosures adopted from Diligent highlights the wide expanse. Although these areas are clearly *not* space-specific, many of them also arise in the context of space activities.

Christensen gives a number of space-specific examples of 'voluntary commitments' to ESG in space activities including initiatives published by the Space Safety Coalition (SSC), Satellite Industry Association (SIA), the Consortium for Execution of Rendezvous and Servicing Operations (CONFERS), SpaceX, and OneWeb among others (Christensen, 2022). His overview is one of inconsistency and lack of measurability to operational or financial performance:

> The voluntary commitments that industry actors are making to space sustainability – while laudable – are inconsistent across individual operators and groups, and are in many cases not clearly or measurably tied to operational and/or financial performance (Christensen, 2022).

What is also space-specific – and is of much current focus – is *The Artemis Accords* signed by the eight foundational member states on 13 October 2020 and with a total of twenty-one member states at the time of writing. More states have now signed the Accords than are parties to the *Moon Agreement*.

The Artemis Accords, considered in overview, introduce or contribute to the following space-based CSR/ESG definitions, areas, activities, principles and disclosures for the purposes of this chapter:

- The revolving and evolving themes around the space treaties:

  Benefit of humankind;
  International and commercial sustainable human exploration;
  Coordination and cooperation;
  Benefits of space exploration and commerce;
  Collective interest in preserving outer space heritage;

- The relationship between 'civil space agencies' and domestic corporate space actors;
- The rescue and return of astronauts;
- 'Peaceful purposes';
- Transparency and release of scientific data;
- Informing the public and scientific community of space resources extraction;
- Interoperability;
- Registration of space objects;
- Preserving outer space heritage;
- Space resource use is not national appropriation under Article II Outer Space Treaty;

- Deconfliction of space activities – provisions of 'due regard', 'harmful interference' and 'safety zones'

  'Due regard', 'harmful contamination' and 'potentially harmful interference';
  Protection of public and private personnel, equipment, and operations;
  Principle of free access to all areas of celestial bodies under Outer Space Treaty;

- Mitigation of orbital debris:

  Planning for mitigation of orbital debris and limiting the generation of "new, long-lived harmful debris";
  Sources of orbital debris; and
  Relationship between safety zones and orbital debris.

Each of these space-based CSR/ESG definitions, areas, activities, principles and disclosures will be examined in turn.

7.2   The Purpose of the Artemis Accords

7.2.1   The Revolving and Evolving Themes Around the Space Treaties

- *benefit of humankind*
- *international and commercial sustainable human exploration*
- *coordination and cooperation*
- *benefits of space exploration and commerce*
- *collective interest in preserving outer space heritage*

The Preamble of the Accords immediately presents a number of principles demonstrating a juxtaposition – and sometimes a tension – between a number of revolving and evolving themes. First, what – like the Apollo program identified by the Accords – may be identified as purposes for the benefit of all humankind. Second, those purposes for "together with international and commercial partners, the sustainable human exploration of the solar system." Third, those purposes for "the necessity of greater coordination and cooperation between and among established and emerging actors in space". Fourthly, those purposes "recognizing the global benefits of space exploration and commerce" and, fifthly, "a collective interest in preserving outer space heritage".

As noted in the introductory Sect. 7.1 of this chapter, if compared to our examination of Earth-based CSR/ESG definitions, areas, activities, principles and disclosures, many of these themes represent commercial and/or social objectives in themselves.

These commercial and/or social themes operate in the Preamble in the context of – and affirming – the following existing space treaties:

- *Outer Space Treaty*;
- *Rescue and Return Agreement*;
- *Liability Convention*; and
- *Registration Convention*.

The *Moon Agreement*,[2] with few signatories but including Australia, is not in the list of treaties affirmed by the Accords. Indeed, it has been made clear that the United States does not consider the *Moon Agreement* to be reflective of customary international law.

7.2.2 The Relationship Between 'Civil Space Agencies' and Domestic Corporate Space Actors Enables the Operation of CSR/ESG Areas, Activities, Principles and Disclosures

A number of mechanisms are contemplated by the Accords in order to enable the activities – on behalf of Signatory-agencies – of already well-known corporate actors such as SpaceX and Blue Origin.

In this respect, the Accords apply "to civil space activities conducted by the civil space agencies of each Signatory" as established in section 1. Immediately, even in this purpose and scope section, the Accords establish that Signatories must "implement the principles set out in these Accords through their own activities by taking, as appropriate, measures such as mission planning and contractual mechanisms with entities acting on their behalf". We turn then to the implementation provisions.

7.2.2.1 The 'Implementation' Provision of the Accords and CSR/ESG

The 'implementation' provision – section 2 paragraph 1 – contemplates the operation of a number of instruments which are Government-to-Government and Agency-to-Agency. Australia is a signatory to the Artemis Accords, signed on its behalf by the Head of the Australian Space Agency. Importantly for our CSR/ESG purposes, the implementation section contemplates the operation of activities and existence of entities which are non-governmental and non-agency:

> (d) Each Signatory commits to taking appropriate steps to ensure that entities acting on its behalf comply with the principles of these Accords.

---

[2] The UN Office for Outer Space Affairs (UNOOSA) states: The Moon Agreement was considered and elaborated by the Legal Subcommittee from 1972 to 1979. The Agreement was adopted by the General Assembly in 1979 in resolution 34/68. It was not until June 1984, however, that the fifth country, Austria, ratified the Agreement, allowing it to enter into force in July 1984.

On one view – excluding the operation of CSR/ESG altogether – a corporate actor is not required to comply with the principles in the Accords if not acting for a signatory agency.

On an 'enabling view' of CSR/ESG – in a general sense here – the recognition of these entities will permit the operation of CSR/ESG definitions, areas, activities, principles and disclosures in the case of for-profit corporations where not otherwise excluded or restricted by the terms of the Accords. Indeed, this is the case even though the same CSR/ESG definitions, areas, activities, principles and disclosures would not apply to the relevant Signatory governments or subordinate agencies in general. In other words, while the operation of CSR/ESG-like definitions, areas, activities, principles and disclosures *in appearance* are imposed on signatory agencies, their source is not corporate law (and its attendant CSR/ESG principles) but instead the Accords and the treaties, agreements, conventions and guidelines referred to in Sect. 7.2.1 above.

There may well be an internally created limitation on the 'enabling view' in section 2 paragraph 1(d)– the drafting of this provision appears to limit the 'appropriate steps' to those which effect compliance "with the principles of these Accords". This would leave a much smaller sphere of operation for CSR/ESG definitions, areas, activities, principles and disclosures on the relevant corporate actors. But even on this more limited view, certain tasks or activities in the past usually conducted by signatory agencies – but now conceivably conducted by a corporate actor at that agency's behest or arising within the relationship between agency and corporate actor (whether contractually or otherwise, such as under tort law[3]) – may now fall within CSR/ESG definitions, areas, activities, principles and disclosures when conducted by the corporate actor.

7.2.2.2 Example of Rescue and Return of an Astronaut – the 'Implementation' Provision, the Abolition of the 'Ultra Vires' Doctrine in Corporate Law, and the 'Frustration' Doctrine in Contract Law

Let's take an example to illustrate this interplay of the 'implementation' provision in section 2 and a contractual agreement between the signatory agency and its corporate actor. The rescue and return of an astronaut – of an entity which is not the contracting party – during a corporate actor's activities may well fall within the scope of this concept, albeit that the agency has contractually bound the corporate actor to abide by the *Outer Space Treaty* and the *Rescue and Return Agreement*. Indeed, section 6 of the Accords on 'emergency assistance' clearly contemplates this rescue and return scenario:

---

[3] Here, putting aside what may be the operation of the Liability Convention.

The Signatories commit to taking all reasonable efforts to render necessary assistance to personnel in outer space who are in distress, and acknowledge their obligations under the Rescue and Return Agreement.

Conceptually, a corporate actor may contractually oblige itself to conduct CSR/ESG definitions, areas, activities, principles and disclosures which may not – either in concept or ultimately in practice – be of corporate (shareholder) benefit although of wider stakeholder benefit (in particular, for the personnel in distress and their launching agency).

Such an activity would be of legal effect in the corporate law sense as the *ultra vires* doctrine (the common law concept that an act or contract exceeding the terms of, or a limitation in, the company's constitution was void) – at least in Australia – has been abolished by the *Corporations Act 2001* (Cth) in ss 124 and 125 (Lipton et al., 2018).

Thus, the corporate actor cannot plead a case of *force majeure* or 'frustration' of contract suspending or voiding the contractual obligations between the signatory agency and the corporate actor by virtue of the 'illegality' of the act or contract or that it is 'beyond power'. In this respect, it is conceptually problematic to argue that the rescue and return of the astronaut – as a contractual obligation owed to the agency – can be a frustrating act in relation to the performance of the primary mission obligations because the contract itself contemplates the performance of the rescue and return obligation.

But would the directors of the company – despite the CSR/ESG justifications or contractual obligations of any action – breach the duties that the directors owe to the company? This is unclear.

7.2.2.3 Rescue and Return of an Astronaut – Directors' Duties Under the Corporations Act 2001 (Cth), the Approaches to CSR/ESG and the 'Business Judgement Rule'

Two directors' duties provisions of the *Corporations Act 2001* (Cth) (and their equivalent duties at common law and in equity) are of immediate relevance to the rescue and return of an astronaut by a corporate actor example – first, the subsection 181(1) duties to act in the best interests of the corporation and for a proper purpose, and second, the subsection 180(1) duty to exercise their powers and discharge their duties with the degree of care and diligence of a reasonable person.

The Provisions of Sections 181, 180(1) and 180(2) of the Corporations Act 2001 (Cth)

For subsection 181(1), Australian corporate law generally considers, under the High Court case of *Walker v Wimborne*, that the best interests of the corporation (apart from situations of insolvency or near insolvency) are the interests of its shareholders. Thus, a CSR/ESG definition, area, activity, principle or disclosure – or a contractual obligation compelling any such outcome – if not in the best interests of the shareholders – could render the directors open to a claim for breach. That the CSR/ESG-like obligation is imposed contractually on the company will not protect the directors if the contract itself (i.e., the entailing contractual obligations) is not in the best interests of the company under s 181(1).

What about the duty of care and diligence under section 180(1) *Corporations Act 2001* (Cth)? Would there be a breach in such a scenario? And can the 'business judgment rule' defence apply?

Unamended, the 'business judgement rule' defence is in subsection 180(2) of the *Corporations Act 2001*(Cth). It provides a defence for directors from an action for a breach of the duty of care and diligence under subsection 180(1), the common law and equity.[4]

CAMAC Views on Corporate Benefit and the 'Amended' Business Judgement Rule Defence

Can directors put CSR/ESG principles ahead – on one view – of the best interests of the shareholders?

In this respect, the CAMAC Social Responsibility Report (Corporations and Markets Advisory Committee, 2006) identified a number of approaches to CSR "each being directly or indirectly linked to corporate benefit (which includes avoidance of detriment)" (being the 'compliance', 'philanthropic' and 'business' approaches) and those approaches "not necessarily linked to corporate benefit' (being the 'social primacy' and 'social obligation' approaches) (Corporations and Markets Advisory Committee, 2006).

CAMAC justified the 'business approach' on the basis of long-term value to the corporation (Corporations and Markets Advisory Committee, 2006) as Diligent observed in the introductory chapter.[5]

---

[4] The 'business judgement rule' in s 180(2) *Corporations Act 2001* (Cth) provides that:

(2) A director or other officer of a corporation who makes a business judgment is taken to meet the requirements of subsection (1), and their equivalent duties at common law and in equity, in respect of the judgment if they:

(a) make the judgment in good faith for a proper purpose; and
(b) do not have a material personal interest in the subject matter of the judgment; and
(c) inform themselves about the subject matter of the judgment to the extent they reasonably believe to be appropriate; and
(d) rationally believe that the judgment is in the best interests of the corporation.

The director's or officer's belief that the judgment is in the best interests of the corporation is a rational one unless the belief is one that no reasonable person in their position would hold.

[5] See discussion in Sect. 7.1.2.3 above.

So the first point here is that three of the approaches to CSR/ESG that CAMAC examined were linked to corporate benefit (the best interests of the shareholders as a whole) while two methods do not.

CAMAC then turned to consider whether the *Corporations Act 2001* (Cth) should be amended to accommodate CSR/ESG principles and considerations and considered that no amendments were required to section 181(1) (best interests) or section 180(2) (business judgement rule defence) as these 'are sufficiently broad to enable corporate decision-makers to take into account the environmental and other social impacts of their decisions ...' (Corporations and Markets Advisory Committee, 2006).

But it is difficult to reconcile this view with the observation of CAMAC that two approaches to CSR/ESG – 'social primacy' and 'social obligation' – are not necessarily linked to corporate benefit. Those two approaches would appear on their face to be raising a risk of breaching those sections if corporate shareholder benefit is not achieved.

Yet, Bainbridge would agree with CAMAC that no or little amendment was required to corporations legislation stating that the business judgment rule defence would apply if shareholder 'wealth' is diminished (Bainbridge, 1993).

Opposing Arguments for S 181(1) Best Interests of the Corporation and S 180(2) 'Business Judgement Rule' Defence

The opposing argument to Bainbridge is that one of the paragraphs of the business judgement rule – paragraph 180(2)(d) – itself provides that the directors "(d) rationally believe that the judgment is in the best interests of the corporation". The subsection continues that "[t]he director's or officer's belief that the judgment is in the best interests of the corporation is a rational one unless the belief is one that no reasonable person in their position would hold".

Again, Australia's High Court decision in *Walker v Wimborne* considers the best interests of the corporation in s 181(1) are the interests of its shareholders. Thus, a CSR/ESG-like definition, area, activity, principle or disclosure – or contractual obligation compelling such an outcome – if not in the best interests of the shareholders would be likely to breach s 181(1) and would render the business judgement rule in s 180(2) inoperable.

Of course, on the basis of arguments in the introduction section of this chapter, it may be open to argue that a CSR/ESG definition, area, activity, principle or disclosure or relevant contractual obligation *which is in the interests of stakeholders is also in the interests of shareholders* and thus in the best interests of the corporation. This would require no alteration of the High Court's view in *Walker v Wimborne*. As noted above, CAMAC believed that any such amendment to the *Corporations Act 2001* (Cth) was not required.

Of further complication is the note to the sub-section 180(2) of the business judgement rule which provides:

This subsection only operates in relation to duties under this section and their equivalent duties at common law or in equity (including the duty of care that arises under the common law principles governing liability for negligence)—it does not operate in relation to duties under any other provision of this Act or under any other laws.

The exact effect of this on the interpretation of the above sections is unclear. The "other provision of this Act" point would seem to be that the business judgement rule cannot be used as a defence to a breach of another section of the Act, in this case subsection 181(1) – the duties to act in the best interests of the corporation and for a proper purpose. The other point is the reference to "under any other laws". This likely means that the directors cannot use the business judgement rule as a defence to a duty or obligation under the Accords (and their associated treaties, agreements, conventions and guidelines) or international law.

But is the reverse permitted? Can a duty or obligation under the Accords or international law be used as a pedestal to mount a business judgement rule defence argument? The probable answer is 'yes' against a breach of s 180(2) but not a breach of s 181(1).

No 'Frustration' of the Contract if the Obligation Merely Becomes More Difficult or Expensive

The directors' duties concerns under a scenario of rescue and return of an astronaut are complex. So, too, are the contract 'frustration' concerns. In both cases, what if the rescue and return of the astronaut causes the relevant space mission's primary object or purpose to be abandoned or fail due to what could be hugely expensive rescue and return costs? Not to mention the technological difficulties involved. Does this mean – at the outset – that the corporation's space vehicle or object must carry enough fuel, other resources and technical know-how and mechanical abilities to ensure that both the primary mission obligations and any rescue and return obligations (if they arise) can both be performed? In other words, what if it is impossible to perform the primary mission obligations?

But even that precaution – while one a reasonable person would arguably take – may not be sufficient to cover the eventuality. What if the recue and return is of such complexity that it causes the space vehicle to re-enter the atmosphere and scrub the primary mission obligations? We should recall that a contract is not frustrated merely because the performance of the obligation becomes more difficult (though short of impossible) or more expensive (as confirmed in *Codelfa Construction Pty Ltd v State Rail Authority of NSW* and *Davis Contractors Ltd. V. Fareham Urban District Council*), but that may result if the corporation has obliged itself to be bound to perform the obligations of the *Rescue and Return Agreement*.

7.2.3 Interpretation Assisted by 'Peaceful Purposes'

The 'peaceful purpose' provision in section 3 of the Accords reflects one of the foundational principles of the *Outer Space Treaty*. It provides an enabling or encompassing provision for the operation of CSR/ESG definitions, areas, activities, principles and disclosures if otherwise permitted by the Accords:

> The Signatories affirm that cooperative activities under these Accords should be exclusively for peaceful purposes and in accordance with relevant international law.

That any CSR/ESG definitions, areas, activities, principles and disclosures operating in relation to the use of the Moon, Mars, comets and asteroids should be peaceful and in accordance with international law is unproblematic. Indeed, it would be difficult to posit a properly constituted 'environmental', 'social' or 'governance' activity which is not peaceful or legal (putting aside for this purpose the characterisation of activities which are for sole 'military' or dual 'peaceful-military' purposes irrespective of their peace-keeping purposes or legality at international law) (Additional Protocol I, 1977).

7.3 Transparency and Release of Scientific Data

7.3.1 Section 4 Transparency and CSR/ESG Disclosures

The 'transparency' provision is contained in section 4. The requirements on Signatories – which those Signatories may impose on non-government and non-agency entities – involve a statement that:

- Signatories *are committed to transparency* in the broad dissemination of information regarding their national space policies and space exploration plans in accordance with their national rules and regulations [and]
- The Signatories *plan to share* scientific information resulting from their activities pursuant to these Accords with the public and the international scientific community on a good-faith basis, and consistent with Article XI of the Outer Space Treaty.

It is not clear that this provision – on its proper construction – contains any *proper* obligations at all. The Signatories are "committed to transparency" in broadly disseminating information and "plan to share scientific information". The first statement is subject to 'their national rules and regulations" and the second is on a "good faith basis". Whatever can be said about the nature of any proper obligations, there is no exclusion of CSR/ESG definitions, areas, activities, principles or disclosures *per se*. But the provisions of "national rules and regulations" may well contain restrictions.

In this respect – and by way of example – the implementation provision contains a related "expectation" widely drafted which would apply to that information:

(b) The Signatories' bilateral instruments referred to above are expected to contain other provisions necessary to conduct such cooperation, including those related to liability, intellectual property, and the transfer of goods and technical data;

Thus, dissemination or sharing of the types of information contemplated in section 4 would clearly be within CSR/ESG disclosures. But does section 2 paragraph (b)'s reference to provisions for intellectual property and the transfer of technical data limit section 4? Or must intellectual property including confidential information/know-how, copyrights and patents – none of which are expressly mentioned – be subject to provisions for copying, licensing, transfer, etc.? At what costs? And what is the corporate (shareholder) benefits of this?

This is much more straight-forward than the rescue and return of an astronaut. One (even corporate) benefit of dissemination and sharing in the sense contemplated by section 4 by all corporate actors is presumably that the corporate actor will receive this dissemination and sharing in return enhancing interoperability (see Sect. 7.4 below) and therefore commercialisation opportunities. Thus section 4 conceivably involves – at least some – dissemination and sharing scenarios of corporate benefit that will not require resort to CSR/ESG principles.

7.3.2   Section 8 Excludes Proprietary and/or Export-Controlled Information and Private Operations _Not_ on Behalf of a Signatory from CSR/ESG Disclosures

Section 8 – Release of scientific data – repeats some of the principles of section 4 but with potentially two very extensive exclusions.

7.3.2.1   Exclusion for Proprietary and/or Export-Controlled Information

Section 8 paragraph 1 contains a number of principles on the 'release of scientific data'. Here, the Signatories "intend to coordinate with each other" in the public release of information relating to the other Signatories' activities under the Accords. Again a very open expression of information sharing which would enhance CSR/ESG outcomes – but subject to "appropriate protection for any proprietary and/or export-controlled information" thus availing operators a way of curtaining the fullest release CSR/ESG would accommodate.

7.3.2.2 Exclusion for Private Sector Operations Not Being Conducted on Behalf of a Signatory

Following this, section 8 paragraph 2 repeats the "commit[ment] to the open sharing of scientific data". Yet again there is a reservation which may curtail the fullest release of information CSR/ESG disclosures would encourage – the commitment "is not intended to apply to private sector operations unless such operations are being conducted on behalf of a Signatory to the Accords". Thus there is a strong argument here that information sharing will exclude proprietary information of "scientific data" which is the proprietary interest of a (presumably) private operator and used exclusively privately. The difficulty will arise in identifying the demarcation point – when are private operations conducted on behalf of a Signatory and when are those private operations (again, presumably by private operators) being conducted privately? Thus the private side of the line would create a large exclusion of what would otherwise be CSR/ESG-enhanced disclosures. For example, if a private company is undertaking, as its core business model, a private activity (not on behalf of a Signatory) to prospect/explore/compile a detailed map of resources in a specific area of the Moon for the express purpose of selling this data to prospective private resource companies (again, not Signatories), there is a strong argument under the Accords that this activity will be considered "private" and thus the information will be considered – as between the private company and the Signatory – "proprietary" information and thus excluded from otherwise CSR/ESG-enhanced disclosures.

Of course, as noted in Sect. 7.2.2.1 of this chapter, the 'implementation' provision – section 2 paragraph 1(d) – has the effect of excluding the operation of CSR/ESG disclosures which might arise under the Accords. There, a corporate actor is not required to comply with the principles in the Accords if not acting for a signatory agency.

7.3.3 Informing the Public and Scientific Community of Space Resources Extraction

Section 10 on 'space resources', too, includes a requirement that Signatories inform "the public and the international scientific community of their space resource extraction activities in accordance with the Outer Space Treaty". On its face, this provision would permit CSR/ESG disclosures. Discussed below in Sect. 7.7 of this chapter, however, is an affirmation of the Signatories that this does *not* "inherently constitute national appropriation under Article II of the Outer Space Treaty".

7.4 Interoperability

The development of "interoperable and common exploration infrastructure and standards" is expressed to "enhance space-based exploration, scientific discovery, and commercial utilization" and expressed in section 5.

Those outcomes – as expressed and if realised – do not require resort to CSR/ESG definitions, areas, activities, principles or disclosures to undertake interoperable/common infrastructures as they are very likely to be justified on corporate (shareholder) benefit grounds for advancing the commercial advantages/gains of the corporation. Indeed, the provision itself refers to 'commercial utilisation'. So contractual provisions between Signatory-agencies and their contracted corporate entity for interoperability purposes would likely satisfy the duties of the directors to the corporation discussed in Sect. 7.2.2.3 above.

But if 'space-based exploration' and 'scientific discovery' is conducted in the absence of corporate (shareholder) commercial benefit – at the time of entry into the contract or in performance of the contract – the interoperability provision may offend sections 181(1) and 180(1) of the *Corporations Act 2001* (Cth).

7.5 Registration of Space Objects

Section 7 contemplates that Signatories will adhere to the *Registration Convention*. Here, non-party entities are expressly identified – the Signatories "intend to consult with that non-Party to determine the appropriate means of registration". While the intention to consult is vague, there appears (if the intention is fulfilled) a similar outcome to that which CSR/ESG definitions, areas, activities, principles and disclosures would point to – registration under the *Registration Convention* with the accompanying obligations.

7.6 Preserving Outer Space Heritage

Preserving space heritage including "historically significant human or robotic landing sites, artefacts, spacecraft and other evidence of activity" is set out in section 9. This expressed intention would support CSR/ESG definitions, areas, activities, principles and disclosures as presently exist for the environment and historical/cultural sites on Earth (*Convention for the Protection of the World Cultural and Natural Heritage*, 1975). This section is *not* expressed to be limited by any other section, including, for example, the space resources section 10 to which we now turn.

7.7 Space Resources Is <u>Not</u> National Appropriation Under Article II Outer Space Treaty

The extraction and utilisation of space resources from the Moon, Mars and other celestial bodies such as comets and asteroids of course already places the Accords in contentious territory in the context of an interpretation of the principle of non-appropriation in Article II of the *Outer Space Treaty* that distinguishes appropriation of component resources from the prohibited appropriation of a celestial body as a whole.

Section 10 of the Accords begins with an appeal which resonates with CSR/ESG definitions, areas, activities, principles and disclosures – that the extraction and utilisation of space resources "can benefit humankind by providing critical support for safe and sustainable operations". Interestingly, the location of those operations – on Earth, the Moon, Mars, or in outer space generally – is not specified.

Paragraph 2 is complex in both terms and effects. It states that extraction and utilisation must comply with the *Outer Space Treaty* – but the CSR/ESG possibilities are curtailed by an affirmation of the Signatories that this does *not* "inherently constitute national appropriation under Article II of the Outer Space Treaty". Paragraph 2 states that "contracts and other legal instruments relating to space resources" are required to also comply with the *Outer Space Treaty*. Thus the rise or fall of CSR/ESG definitions, areas, activities, principles and disclosures – as opposed to private appropriation – relating to the mining, extraction and utilisation of space resources lies within the rubric of the enforceability of these contracts and instruments vis-à-vis the *Outer Space Treaty*. Section 10 concludes in paragraph 4 with an intention to develop international practices and rules for the extraction and utilisation of space resources, an intention with CSR/ESG considerations similar to interoperability.

7.8 Deconfliction of Space Activities – Provisions of 'Due Regard', 'Harmful Interference' and 'Safety Zones' Allow for CSR/ESG Areas and Principles

This section of the chapter will examine the definition and determination of "due regard", "harmful interference" and "safety zones". On one view, these concepts – if used for their (to use a corporate law term from section 181(1) *Corporations Act 2001* (Cth)) 'proper' purpose – can extend into CSR/ESG definitions, areas, activities, principles and disclosures. What is evident, however, is that the width or expansion of these concepts can be used to quarantine or exclude a Signatory's space-based activities, or the area in which they are undertaken, from the "free access" provisions of the *Outer Space Treaty*.[6]

7.8.1 'Due Regard', 'Harmful Contamination' and 'Potentially Harmful Interference'

7.8.1.1 Article IX of the Outer Space Treaty and Section 11 of the Accords

Article IX of the *Outer Space Treaty* requires States Parties to conduct all activities in outer space including the Moon and other celestial bodies "with due regard to the corresponding interests of all other States Parties" and avoiding "harmful contamination and also adverse changes in the environment of the Earth resulting from the introduction of extraterrestrial matter" including adopting "appropriate measures". States Parties are further required to undertake prior "appropriate international consultations" in the event that an activity or experiment by it or its nationals "in outer space, including the Moon and other celestial bodies, would cause potentially harmful interference with activities of other States Parties in the peaceful exploration and use of outer space, including the Moon and other celestial bodies".

Now turning to section 11 of the Accords and putting aside the lack of precision in the terms 'due regard' and 'harmful interference' (von der Dunk, 2018; Lyall and Larsen, 2018), the Signatories to the Accords acknowledge and reaffirm the *Outer Space Treaty* and the provisions relating to due regard and harmful interference in paragraphs one and three, with again, a request for consultations in the case of the latter. Signatories are to refrain from "intentional actions" which may cause "harmful interference with each other's use of outer space in their activities under these Accords as specified in paragraph 4. Thus there is potential to enhance CSR/ESG outcomes in these two concepts.

There is specific mention in paragraph 2 of the "due consideration" of COPUOS Guidelines but with "appropriate changes" for operations *beyond* low-Earth orbit:

> The exploration and use of outer space should be conducted with due consideration to the United Nations Guidelines for the Long-term Sustainability of Outer Space Activities adopted by the COPUOS in 2019, with appropriate changes to reflect the nature of operations beyond low-Earth orbit.

Of note, the Article IX *Outer Space Treaty* reference to 'harmful contamination' is not further dealt with in section 11 of the Accords. This is somewhat strange given that "space resources" referred to in section 11 and section 10 of the Accords could conceivably include utilisation on Earth (as discussed in Sect. 7.7 above of this chapter).

---

[6]"Free access to all areas of celestial bodies" is referred to in *Section 11* [11] of the Artemis Accords.

7.8.1.2 Section 11 of the Accords Adds 'Safety Hazard' and 'Safety Zone' to Activities

Paragraph 5 of Section 11 of the Accords requires that Signatories provide each other "necessary information regarding the location and nature of space-based activities under these Accords" in the event of (again) harmful interference with and, this time, introducing the concept of a "safety hazard" to space-based activities. A safety hazard is not further elaborated in section 11.

Paragraph 6 refers to efforts to develop practices, criteria and rules for defining and determining "safety zones" and harmful interference. The issue of zones in space has become an increasingly important topic in recent years with plans for space resource utilisation (or space mining) and with the release of the Accords, and must be balanced with one of the fundamental principles of space law – that space is free for exploration and use by all (Stubbs, 2021).

Paragraph 7 describes an intention to "provide notification of their activities and commit to coordinating with any relevant actor to avoid harmful interference". The reference to "any relevant actor" is not limited in any way. Presumably, a Signatory must engage in notification and coordination with private operators from its own – not just other – nation. *This (conceivably) opens the concept to artificial manipulation by Signatories and their respective space agencies.* Interestingly, the obligation on the non-Signatory or non-agency actor is not mentioned. This, presumably, falls under section 2's implementation provision in section 2, paragraph 1(d) – that "[e]ach Signatory commits to taking appropriate steps to ensure that entities acting on its behalf comply with the principles of these Accords".

Returning to section 11 paragraph 7 a "safety zone" is defined as:

[t]he area wherein this notification and coordination will be implemented to avoid harmful interference…

And further to this, it is elaborated that:

A safety zone should be the area in which nominal operations of a relevant activity or an anomalous event could reasonably cause harmful interference.

Presumably, then, a safety zone is comprised of an area in which "nominal operations" ("nominal" is not defined but presumably would include operations such as above-ground and underground mining) take place and, in addition – using the "reasonably" term – a zone in which there may be a spill, blast, fallout or contamination (in Earth-terms) from the operations or area including a pathogen or a mechanical, technological or (non-orbital[7]) debris-causing 'anomalous event'.

---

[7] Orbital debris is governed by *Section 12 – Orbital Debris* of the Artemis Accords.

7.8.1.3 Principles Relating to Safety Zones

Section 11 Paragraphs 7 (a)–(e) set out a number of principles pertaining to the size, scope, nature and existence of safety zones including:

- the size and scope of the safety zone reflecting the nature of the operations and the environment;
- determination in a "reasonable manner leveraging commonly accepted scientific and engineering principles";
- the status of the operation and any change in nature;
- that safety zones are "ultimately temporary" ending when the relevant operation ceases; and
- notification of "the establishment, alteration, or end of any safety zone, consistent with Article XI of the Outer Space Treaty".

Paragraph 8 calls for providing a Signatory with the somewhat amorphous concept of the "basis for the area in accordance with the national rules and regulations applicable to each Signatory".

7.8.1.4 Protection of Public and Private Personnel, Equipment, and Operations Reflects CSR/ESG Outcomes But Subject to Proprietary and Export-Controlled Information

Paragraph 9 is reflective of CSR/ESG definitions, areas, activities, principles and disclosures requiring the protection of "public and private personnel, equipment, and operations from harmful interference" and the making available of information. But similar to section 8, information on the extent and general nature of the operations has a carve-out for "taking into account appropriate protections for proprietary and export-controlled information".

Paragraph 10 contains a commitment to respect "reasonable safety zones" to avoid harmful interference but this commitment contemplates that the safety zone is not absolute – the Signatories commitment to include "prior notification to and coordinating with each other before conducting operations in a safety zone established pursuant to these Accords". On its face, this would accommodate the activities of a Signatory in another Signatory's safety zone which would be consistent with the principle of free use of outer space enshrined in the space law treaties. Whether a corporate actor would be satisfied with this is another matter.

7.8.1.5 Principle of Free Access to all Areas of Celestial Bodies Under Outer Space Treaty

Under section 11 paragraph 11, safety zones are expected to "change, evolve, or end" based on the status of the activity and in a manner which encourages:

- "scientific discovery and technology demonstration"; and
- "safe and efficient extraction and utilization of space resources in support of sustainable space exploration and other operations".

Thus space exploration and other operations are to be "sustainable' without further explanation of this concept.

In addition, Signatories commit to the principle of "free access to all areas of celestial bodies and all other provisions of the Outer Space Treaty in their use of safety zones". Yet there is no indication of which principle has precedence in the event of conflict.

In other words, it remains to be seen whether the "safety zone" concept is (conceivably) manipulated by signatory agencies or their private operators to the detriment of CSR/ESG definitions, areas, activities, principles or disclosures. There is a commitment by Signatories "to adjust their usage of safety zones over time" which appears on its face to contemplate *both a reduction and increase* in the size and scope of a safety zone. Presumably, this must follow the principles in section 11 paragraph 7(a) – (d) noted above.

This raises a number of questions which may (again, conceivably) have the effect of excluding or reducing CSR/ESG definitions, areas, activities, principles and disclosures:

- can a number of safety zones be aggregated to create a much more extensive safety zone?
- in the case of the operations of a satellite, can the placement of a multitude of satellites in a particular position or area of orbit (whether geosynchronous orbit or otherwise) prevent the placement of any other signatory agency or private operator's satellite in that aggregated safety zone?
- can access to a particular physical area in space, the Moon or Mars be artificially denied because a signatory agency or their private operator must pass through another signatory agency or private operator's safety zone to reach it?

7.9 Mitigation of Orbital Debris

7.9.1 *Planning for Mitigation of Orbital Debris and Limiting the Generation of "New, Long-Lived Harmful Debris"*

Section 12 paragraph 1 sees the Signatories commit to plan for mitigation of orbital debris:

> The Signatories commit to plan for the mitigation of orbital debris, including the safe, timely, and efficient passivation and disposal of spacecraft at the end of their missions, when appropriate, as part of their mission planning process.

There is a further commitment to limit the generation of "new, long-lived harmful debris" from a number of sources including "normal operations" in paragraph 2:

> The Signatories commit to limit, to the extent practicable, the generation of new, long-lived harmful debris released through normal operations, break-up in operational or post-mission phases, and accidents and conjunctions, by taking appropriate measures such as the selection of safe flight profiles and operational configurations as well as post-mission disposal of space structures.

There appears, then, some inconsistency in the drafting between paragraph 1 and paragraph 2 – paragraph 1 refers to "orbital debris" while paragraph 2 omits the "orbital" reference and applies to "new, long-lived harmful debris". So does the latter debris need to be 'orbital' for the provision to apply to it?

7.9.2 Sources of Orbital Debris

What appears more straightforward from section 12 paragraph 2 above is that orbital debris may be released through:

- "normal operations";
- "break-up in operational or post-mission phases"; and
- "accidents and conjunctions".

A "conjunction" is not further defined but appears in the same phrase as "accidents and…" in paragraph 2. The Macquarie Dictionary includes in its definition of conjunction:

> *noun* **1.** the act of conjoining; combination.
> **2.** the state of being conjoined; union; association.
> **3.** a combination of events or circumstances.
> ...
> **5.** *Astronomy*
> **a.** the meeting of heavenly bodies in the same longitude or right ascension.
> **b.** the situation of two or more heavenly bodies when their longitudes are the same.

7.9.3 Relationship Between Safety Zones (Section 11) and Orbital Debris (Section 12) Is Unclear

What is not elucidated further is the relationship, if any, between this section 12 (orbital debris) and section 11 (Deconfliction of space activities) of the Accords discussed above in relation to 'due regard', 'harmful interference' and 'safety zones'. The point is, does a safety zone in section 11 extend to the 'reasonable' size and scope (a determination in a "reasonable manner leveraging commonly accepted scientific and engineering principles" from ss 7(b)) of 'orbital' or 'new, long-lived harmful' debris from 'normal operations' in section 12? Or is 'orbital debris' and/or 'new, long-lived harmful debris' separate to, excluded from, or included in, a section 11 safety zone?

7.9.3.1 'Orbital Debris' (Section 12) Reference to 'Normal' Operations Does Not Appear in Section 11 on 'Safety Zones'

This poses some difficulty in interpretation. Section 11 above specifically refers to (emphasis added):

- "the location and nature of *space-based activities* under these Accords" (para 5);
- "a safety hazard to its *space-based activities*" (para 5);
- "notification of *their activities*" (para 7);
- "[a] safety zone should be the area in which *nominal operations* of a *relevant activity* or an anomalous event could reasonably cause harmful interference" (para 7);
- "the nature of the *operations*" (para 7(a));
- "the extent and general nature of *operations*" (para 9);
- "avoid harmful interference with *operations* under these Accords" and "before conducting *operations* in a safety zone" (para 10); and
- "safety zones, which will be expected to change, evolve, or end based on the status of the *specific activity*" and the "efficient extraction and utilization of space resources in support of sustainable space exploration and *other operations*" (para 11).

Thus the term 'normal operations' in section 12 does not appear in section 11 on safety zones. Or does a 'normal operation' in section 12 include any activity or operation mentioned in section 11 or any activity or operation mentioned anywhere in the Accords?

What is at stake here is the determination of the nature, size and scope of a safety zone. And, again, this may have serious consequences for the scope of any CSR/ESG definitions, areas, activities, principles or disclosures. Can this safety zone be (artificially) enlarged to exclude other Signatories – and their space agencies and private operators – by reference to *either* 'orbital' or 'new, long-lived harmful' debris of *any* space operation or activity?

Even before a satellite's useful/operable life is spent and it is decommissioned and/or moved, does the safety zone around that satellite include any zone in which break-up debris of the satellite – or, indeed, the satellite itself – may *eventually* (i.e., long-term) be situated, whether orbiting debris or not? Can a number of spent, decommissioned or otherwise failing satellites be moved to an area which then, in aggregate, would constitute an artificially large safety zone even though the satellites have not yet broken-up in any way?

What we are left with is that the determination of the nature, size and scope of a safety zone cuts both ways for CSR/ESG definitions, areas, activities, principles or disclosures.

For example, combining the discussion in Sect. 7.8.1.2 and this Sect. 7.9.3.1, a safety zone may be comprised of an area in which "nominal operations" (section 11) or "normal operations" take place. These operations may therefore include operations such as:

- above-ground and underground mining or resource extraction; and
- zones in which there may be a spill, blast, fallout or contamination (in Earth-terms) from the operations;
- an area in which there is a pathogen or a mechanical, technological or (non-orbital[8]) debris-causing 'anomalous event'; and
- an area in which there is 'orbital' or 'new, long-lived harmful' debris of *any* space operation or activity.

Such an interpretation, on safety grounds for the person or equipment or operations of the agency-signatories or private operator, its personnel and other operators in the 'vicinity' (to use a neutral term) of the safety zone would enhance CSR/ESG definitions, areas, activities, principles or disclosures. Indeed, such safety grounds are – by avoiding an 'accident' (again, a neutral term) which may harm the person or equipment and operations of the agency-signatory or private operator, its personnel and other operators – also likely to produce enhanced commercial benefit which is therefore justified on shareholder corporate benefit grounds.

But interpretations of safety zones which artificially widen or aggregate the safety zone, may reduce CSR/ESG definitions, areas, activities, principles or disclosures as they (again) artificially exclude other agency-signatories or private operators from – as noted in Sect. 7.8.1.5 above – the principle of free access to all areas of celestial bodies under *Outer Space Treaty*.

7.10   Concluding Remarks

The use of bilateral agreements, such as the Artemis Accords, in relation to commercial space operations may lead to unintended consequences. Such consequences include, on the one hand, the encapsulation of CSR/ESG areas, activities, practices and disclosures and, on the other hand, the displacement of those same areas, activities, practices and disclosures. The outcome – depending on the interpretation of the Artemis Accords – will determine whether these consequences have a positive or negative impact on the corporate shareholder purpose of corporate actors involved in activities in outer space.

References

Agreement Governing the Activities of States on the Moon and Other Celestial Bodies, available at   https://www.unoosa.org/oosa/en/ourwork/spacelaw/treaties/intromoon-agreement.html. Accessed 24 Feb 2022 ('Moon Agreement').
Agreement on the Rescue of Astronauts, the Return of Astronauts and the Return of Objects Launched into Outer Space, consensus agreement reached in the General Assembly in 1967

---

[8] Orbital debris is governed by Section 12 of the Artemis Accords.

(resolution 2345 (XXII)) and entered into force in December 1968, available at https://www. unoosa.org/oosa/en/ourwork/spacelaw/treaties/introouterspacetreaty.html. Accessed 22 Feb 2022 ('Rescue and Return Agreement').

Bainbridge, S. M. (1993). In Defence of the Shareholder wealth maximization norm: A reply to Professor Green. *50 Washington & Lee Law Review, 1423,* 1426–1427, at SSRN: http://ssrn. com/abstract=303780. Accessed 3 Mar 2015 (footnote omitted).

Charreaux, G. J. (2004, January). *Corporate governance theories: From micro theories to national systems theories* (Universite de Bourgogne Fargo Working Paper No 1040101, p. 8), at SSRN: http://ssrn.com/abstract=486522. Accessed 3 Mar 2015.

Christensen, I. (2022, April). Commentary, 'Guarding against greenwashing in space' in SpaceNews Inc, *SpaceNews,* 33(4):25, available at https://SpaceNews.com

Codelfa Construction Pty Ltd v State Rail Authority of NSW [1982] HCA 24; (1982) 149 CLR 337 (11 May 1982) available at http://classic.austlii.edu.au/au/cases/cth/HCA/1982/24.html. Accessed 24 Apr 2022, per Brennan J, pp. 407–409, [29]–[34], citing British Movietonews Ltd. v. London and District Cinemas Ltd. (1952) AC 166, at p 185 per Viscount Simon.

Convention for the Protection of the World Cultural and Natural Heritage, adopted on 16 November 1972, by the General Conference of the United Nations Educational, Scientific and Cultural Organization, meeting in Paris from 17 October to 21 November 1972, at its seventeenth session, (entered into force 17 December 1975).

Convention on International Liability for Damage Caused by Space Objects, agreement reached in the General Assembly in 1971 (resolution 2777 (XXVI)) and entered into force in September 1972, available at https://www.unoosa.org/oosa/en/ourwork/spacelaw/treaties/introliability-convention.html. Accessed 22 Feb 2022 ('Liability Convention').

Convention on Registration of Objects Launched into Outer Space, adopted by the General Assembly in 1974 (General Assembly resolution 3235 (XXIX)) and entered into force on 15 September 1976, available at https://www.unoosa.org/oosa/en/ourwork/spacelaw/treaties/ introregistration-convention.html. Accessed 22 Feb 2022 ('Registration Convention').

Corporations and Markets Advisory Committee. (2006, December). *The social responsibility of corporations.* Report, Australian Government, Sydney, at http://www.camac.gov.au. Accessed 3 Mar 2015 ('CAMAC Social Responsibility Report').

Davis Contractors Ltd. v. Fareham Urban District Council [1956] UKHL 3; (1956) AC 696, at 729, per Lord Radcliffe.

de Zwart, F. (2015). *Enhancing firm sustainability through governance, the relational corporate governance approach* (pp. 91–92). Edward Elgar Publishing, available at https://www.e-elgar. com/shop/gbp/enhancing-firm-sustainability-through-governance-9781784715519.html

de Zwart, M. (2021). To the moon and beyond: The Artemis accords and the evolution of space law. In M. de Zwart & S. Henderson (Eds.), *Commercial and military uses of outer space* (pp. 65–80). Springer.

Diligent. (n.d.). What is environmental, social and corporate governance (ESG)? *ESG (Web Page),* available at https://insights.diligent.com/esg/. Accessed 13 Jan 2022.

Dodge v Ford Motor Co. (1919). 204 Mich 459, 507; 170 NW 668; 684 (per Ostrander J, Steere, Fellows, Stone and Brooke JJ concurring), available at http://au.westlaw.com. Accessed 16 May 2008.

Elkington, J. (2018, June 25). *25 years ago I coined the phrase "Triple Bottom Line." here's why it's time to rethink it.*" Capitalism, Harvard Business Review, available at https://hbr. org/2018/06/25-years-ago-i-coined-the-phrase-triple-bottom-line-heres-why-im-giving-up-on-it. Accessed 13 Jan 2022.

Jensen, M. C. (2002). Value maximization, stakeholder theory, and the corporate objective function. In J. Andriof et al. (Eds.), *Unfolding stakeholder thinking.* Greenleaf Publishing. Also published in (2001) 14(3) *Journal of Applied Corporate Finance* 8–21; (2001) 7 *European Financial Management* 297–317 and in M. Beer and N. Norhia (eds), *Breaking the Code of Change,* Cambridge, MA: Harvard Business Press, 2000 (October 2001), 8, at SSRN: http:// ssrn.com/abstract=220671. Accessed 3 Mar 2015 (emphasis in original).

Jensen, M. C., & Meckling, W. H, (2000, December). Theory of the firm: Managerial behavior, agency costs and ownership structure. In M. C. Jensen (Ed.), *A theory of the firm: Governance, residual claims and organizational forms*. Harvard University Press; (1976) *Journal of Financial Economics, 3*(4):5–6, at SSRN: http://ssrn.com/abstract=94043. Accessed 3 Mar 2015.

Kleeman, L. C., & de Zwart, F. (2022). The adoption of ESG into Australia's major banks: Evolving expectations or business as usual? *Australian Journal of Corporate Law*. (forthcoming).

Licht, A. N. (2003, November). *The Maximands of Corporate Governance: A theory of values and cognitive style* (ECGI – Law Working Paper No 16/2003), available at SSRN: http://ssrn.com/abstract=469801 and (2004) 29(3) *Delaware Journal of Corporate Law* 649–746, 4, at SSRN: http://ssrn.com/abstract=764025. Accessed 3 Mar 2015.

Lipton, P., Herzberg, A., & Welsh, M. (2018., para 4.75). *Understanding Company Law* (19th ed., pp. 113–114). LexisNexis NZ Limited.

Lyall, F., & Larsen, P. B. (2018). *The outer space treaty, 1967* (pp. 49–73). Routledge.

Stout, L. A. (2007, September). *Stout, 'why we should stop teaching dodge v. ford'* (UCLA School of Law, Law-Econ Research Paper No 07-11), at SSRN: http://ssrn.com/abstract=1013744. Accessed 3 Feb 2015.

Maher, M., & Andersson, T. (2000, February). Corporate governance: Effects on firm performance and economic growth (p. 5), at SSRN: http://ssrn.com/abstract=218490. Accessed 3 Mar 2015.

Protocol Additional to the Geneva Conventions of 12 August 1949, and relating to the Protection of Victims of International Armed Conflicts, opened for signature 8 June 1977, 1125 UNTS 3 (entered into force 7 December 1978) ('Protocol I').

Rhee, R. J. (2008). Corporate ethics, agency, and the theory of the firm. *Journal of Business & Technology Law, 3*(2), 1101. 1109–10, at SSRN: http://ssrn.com/abstract=1083478. Accessed 3 Mar 2015.

Stubbs, M. (2021). The legality of keep-out, operational, and safety zones in outer space. In C. Steer & M. Hersch (Eds.), *War and peace in outer space: Law, policy, and ethics* (p. 201). Oxford University Press.

Treaty on Principles Governing the Activities of States in the Exploration and Use of Outer Space, including the Moon and other Celestial Bodies, agreement reached in the General Assembly in 1966 (resolution 2222 (XXI)) available at https://www.unoosa.org/oosa/en/ourwork/spacelaw/treaties/introouterspacetreaty.html. Accessed 22 Feb 2022 ('Outer Space Treaty').

von der Dunk, F. G. (2018). *International space law*. Edward Elgar.

Walker v Wimborne [1976] HCA 7; (1976) 137 CLR 1.

Chapter 8
Back to the Moon: Cooperation and Conflict

Marco Aliberti, Vinicius Guedes Gonçalves de Oliveira, and Rodrigo Praino

Abstract After a decades-long hiatus, the Moon has re-emerged as the main target of the major space powers' human exploration activities. Unlike the cooperative approaches that characterized human spaceflight activities in the aftermath of the cold war, upcoming lunar exploration endeavours seem to feature a more competitive approach and lean towards a progressive polarisation of the international space community around two separate and potentially conflicting blocs. Against this background, this chapter looks at the growing competition dynamics between the three leading space powers (i.e., the United States, Russia and China) when it comes to the return of human flights to the Moon. It disentangles their national stances and programmatic initiatives for getting back to the Moon, and also looks at the difficult scenarios that will emerge once the three superpowers get to the Moon. This chapter also includes an analysis of several outstanding issues, ranging from the creation of safety zones on the lunar surface and the protection of cultural sites to the use and exploitation of its resources, that will confront the actors when a more stable and long-term human presence on the Moon is achieved.

8.1 Introduction

Fifty years after the concluding mission of NASA's Apollo programme, the Moon has re-emerged as a main target of the human exploration activities of the major spacefaring nations. The United States, China and Russia, as the three leading space powers, all have plans for landing their respective astronauts, taikonauts and cosmonauts on the lunar surface within the next decade. Although there is no substantive evidence that their planned missions are openly intended to counter one another, the

M. Aliberti (✉)
European Space Policy Institute, Vienna, Austria
e-mail: marco.aliberti@espi.or.at

V. G. G. de Oliveira · R. Praino
College of Business, Government and Law, Flinders University, Adelaide, SA, Australia

M. de Zwart et al. (eds.), *Human Uses of Outer Space*, Issues in Space,
https://doi.org/10.1007/978-981-19-9462-3_8

137

crafting of partnerships among the three behemoths remains inherently problematic, fraught by years of mistrust and broader geopolitical rivalry. In fact, it is evident that two mutually contending pathways for creating a (semi)permanent human presence on the Moon are emerging. Recent developments indeed signal a progressive bifurcation of the international space community around two contending – and potentially conflicting – exploration blocs: on the one hand, the Artemis programme led by the United States and, on the other, the International Lunar Research Station (ILRS) endeavour led by China and Russia. As these two large competing blocs emerge, the only option available in the foreseeable future to virtually all other spacefaring and emerging actors is to aggregate around one of these two competing plans. Competition is heightened further by the symbolic power of the upcoming lunar missions as well as by the considerable material benefits the major space power aim to extract from their long-term presence on the Moon. One of the two blocs will become the first to put a woman on the surface of the Moon, and it is very likely that there will be several other important symbolic and material achievements to claim.

In this chapter, we explore and assess the mixture of cooperation and competition dynamics associated with this next wave of human lunar exploration activities. We do so by looking at the current phase of preparation towards the human return to the Moon, and by exploring issues that will emerge once the two blocs meet on the Moon. In the following section we reflect on the complex political interplay among the planned missions of the two blocs and unravel the fallouts this interplay will generate on the way to the Moon. We then shed some light on the potential repercussions of this polarisation of the international space community once the major powers get to the Moon. The analysis will in particular reflect on the different issue-areas where future strategic interaction on the Moon can be expected to confront the actors with novel issues, including the extraction and exploitation of lunar resources, the creation of safety zones, and the possible militarization of the lunar environment.

8.2   The Way to the Moon: A Polarised Endeavour?

With over 100 cislunar and lunar activities from over 20 nations and multinational consortia planned over the next years (Johnson, 2022), a new era of lunar space exploration is rapidly unfolding. Unlike the first human exploration wave in the 1960s, such a new era will pave the way to a stable human presence on the Moon and, with that, to the emergence of what has been dubbed as *Luna politics*, or the continuation of terrestrial politics in this new environment. Just like politics here on Earth, this unfolding new era is already characterised by a mix of cooperation and competition.

8.2.1 An Enhanced Role for International Cooperation…

The extant role played by international cooperation is certainly one of the most striking features embodying the upcoming lunar exploration wave. International cooperation has indeed become a critical element to the successful implementation of the robotic and crewed exploration programmes of most worldwide space agencies. As also recognised by the Action Team on Exploration and Innovation established by the United Nations (UN) in the context of UNISPACE+50 under Thematic Priority 1: Global partnership in space exploration and innovation:

> No single space agency can invest heavily in all the areas of technology that are needed. That poses a key challenge for space exploration missions. By developing partnerships with common goals, entities with an interest in space exploration will be able to coordinate their investments and work together in ways that maximize returns on investments and enable earlier realization of common goals and objectives (UNCOPUOS, 2017).

Given these widely recognised benefits, it should come as no surprise that most of the current and future exploration programmes by space powers and emerging spacefaring nations entail the participation of foreign partners. This is particularly visible in the European, Japanese and Canadian contexts, by nature inclined – or compelled – towards an internationally integrated approach in the demanding area of human spaceflight. But even for the United States, the master of all things space, cooperation remains quintessential.

For the implementation of the Artemis programme, NASA is building a variety of partnerships that are intended to enable it to get to the Moon as quickly and sustainably as possible. These partnerships include not only the US domestic industry and academia (NASA, 2021), but also foreign space agencies and industrial contractors from third countries. From a programmatic perspective, the main partners remain the ones already cooperating on the ISS. These include ESA, the Japan Aerospace Exploration Agency (JAXA), the Canadian Space Agency (CSA), but not the Russian or the Chinese space agencies, which are increasingly ostracised by the US containment posture. An important corollary of this cooperative undertaking is represented by the Artemis Accords, a seven-page document detailing a set of principles that countries willing to participate in the US Artemis programme accept to adhere by. Whereas the accords are bilateral agreements, not binding instruments of international law, adherence with the accords is a requirement to join the Artemis programme. As of December 2022, more than 20 countries (Australia, Bahrain, Brazil, Canada, Colombia, France, Israel, Italy, Japan, South Korea, Luxembourg, Mexico, New Zealand, Nigeria, Poland, Romania, Rwanda, Singapore, Ukraine, the United Arab Emirates, the United Kingdom, and the United States) have already ratified the Accords with the underlying hope to have their national astronauts flying to the Moon.

Similarly, also China and Russia have been keen to instrumentalise cooperation for both diplomatic and programmatic purposes, albeit with mixed results. Their national exploration programmes have both seen some notable partnerships with European countries and their joint ILRS endeavour has been in 2021 opened to international contributions at all levels. This opening was formalised on the side-lines of the Scientific and Technical Subcommittee of the UN Committee on the Peaceful Uses of Outer Space (UNCOPUOS) in April 2021, when China National Space Administration (CNSA) and Roscosmos issued a Joint statement regarding cooperation for the construction of the ILRS (Jones, 2021). The statement was followed in June 2021 by the release of the guide for partnership of ILRS at the Global Space Exploration Conference in Saint Petersburg and the creation of an inter-agency joint-working group (China National Space Administration, 2021). Despite the declared interest of several emerging and spacefaring nations, the ILRS has not yet secured the official participation of third countries. The more recent opening of the ILRS to international partners may in part explain the limited partnership configuration of the ILRS. But equally evident is the fact that Russia and China's international outreach is not on par with that of NASA and the European states. In addition, none of their political allies is a major spacefaring nation.

8.2.2 …Amidst Stronger Competition Dynamics

Together with the growth in the role of cooperation, the next wave of exploration to the Moon also sees – and will increasingly see – latent competition dynamics accompanied by an exceedingly pervasive narrative about the advent of a new space race in the return to the Moon.

Admittedly, unlike the first space race between the US and the USSR, none of the space powers has openly portrayed its lunar ambitions as a one-upmanship contest that stands in opposition to an alleged contender (Johnson, 2022). And no official statement has been made by the space programme officials of different countries with respect to the intention to get to the Moon before other nations, despite the timeline of US Artemis missions does not seem accidental either.

However, it does not go unnoticed that there is basically no exchange among the two major programmatic initiatives under way and that the very crafting of partnerships among the three leading space powers remains inherently problematic, to say the least.

This is first and foremost the case of US-China space cooperation. China has, from the outset, been excluded from a possible participation in the US-led Artemis programme, as it was for the ISS in the late 1990s. What is more, the path of a US-China cooperation in space has been blocked by the US policy of Chinese exclusion, enacted pursuant the so-called Wolf Amendment of 2011 (US Congress, 2011). Named after the US senator Frank Wolf, this Amendment banned NASA and other US organisations from engaging in bilateral cooperation with China's space entities. Its enactment was supported by many constituencies in the US who saw rising Chinese ambitions as a direct challenge to the American leadership in space (US Subcommittee on Space, 2017). Given its legacy and top-tier position in the space club, the US has proved extremely sensitive to any potential alteration in the status quo (Hunter, 2019; Aliberti, 2015). As also pointed out by Zhang (2013), "the arrival of China as a great power has been under intense scrutiny by the US strategic gaze, especially since China's 2007 ASAT test. This strategic gaze extends US geopolitical envisioning of great power rivalries into space, the so-called fourth battlefield. This social inscription of space as a new battleground has produced an imaginary of China as a threatening other, bent upon pursuing relentlessly a military space strategy aimed at a contest of supremacy in space with the USA". Also in the field of human spaceflight, the US political debate has been dominated by competition advocates who have accused cooperation proponents of "naively helping China to win a new cold war" (Kulacki, 2011), citing Chinese ambitions as a justification for initiating a new Apollo-like programme that would revitalise American space leadership. It is in this context that the Space Policy Directive 1, issued in 2017 by the Trump administration and directing NASA to lead the return of humans to the Moon for their long-term presence, was conceived (Harrison & Johnson, 2017).

On its side, Russia too has declined a possible partnership with the US on Artemis. Unlike China, it was invited to join the programme and a first Memorandum in this sense was signed by Roscosmos and NASA at the 68th International Astronautical Congress in 2017. However, the fact that the US conceived cooperation with Russia in terms of Roscosmos' acceptance of what in the final analysis is a NASA programme, made it unacceptable for Moscow to join, drawing criticism from the then Head of Roscosmos, which dubbed NASA's Moon plans as being "too US-centric" (Foust, 2020). From here, Russia took the decision to partner with China instead.

Recent developments, including Russia's invasion of Ukraine, accelerated the breakdown of Roscosmos' cooperation with Western space agencies. Already in 2021 Moscow had announced the intention to withdraw from the ISS, a position that was further reiterated in 2022 (Russian News Agency, 2022). Following the invasion of Ukraine and the enactment of sanctions by G7 countries, Russia decided to suspend its cooperation on launchers and ExoMars with ESA and several European nations. On its side, ESA decided to cancel its participation in Russia's Luna programme (Foust, 2022). In parallel, Russia pursued a tightening of relations with Chinese space organisations, which have been traditionally keen in circumventing the isolation efforts of the US and extracting practical benefits from Russia's technological prowess (Aliberti, 2015).

These are important occurrences that are indeed signalling the inexorable polarisation of the international space community around two contending – and potentially conflicting – pathways for future lunar exploration: on the one hand, the US-led Artemis programme and the associated construction of a Lunar Gateway and Base Camp, and on the other, the ILRS endeavour led by Beijing and Moscow.

For all the other actors with no programmes of their own of comparable breadth the only option will be to aggregate around one of the two plans led by the space powers. Admittedly, both the Artemis programme and the Sino-Russian Moon base are in principle open to international partners at all levels. Hence participation in one of the two programmes would not *per se* preclude a possible participation in the other. However, the reality is that the two endeavours are to large extent mutually exclusive in terms of partnership configurations. For a signatory of the Artemis

Accords, it may prove politically difficult to extensively engage in the ILRS with substantial contributions, and vice-versa. Most countries will hence tend to band-wagon to either the Artemis or the ILRS endeavour. This is true even for an organisation like ESA, which has thus far maintained cooperative relations with both the United States on the one hand and China and Russia on the other, traditionally trying to position itself as an architect of a broader multilateral endeavour and even bridge builder between isolated powers (ESPI, 2019).

One such polarisation is obviously not happening in a vacuum and cannot be taken in isolation from the broader space ambitions and posture of the main powers involved. It needs to be embedded in the broader context of strategic rivalry *about* space and *in* space, that is stirred by political rivalry on Earth. Space politics, after all, is a continuation of terrestrial politics in a different medium (Bowen, 2020). Like in the bipolar world order, current earthly dynamics seem to be once more precipitating international space relations towards a new race scenario, becoming both cause and symptom of a deeper geopolitical split between the Euro-Atlantic community and Chinese-Russian partnership. Not surprisingly, catchwords like "the New Space Race" or "Space Race 2.0", have become more and more common within media outlets as well as among scholars and practitioners (Goswami, 2022; de Zwart & Stephens, 2019; Rajagopalan, 2018; US Subcommittee on Space, 2017; Seedhouse, 2010).

While there are striking differences that make a parallelism with the US-Soviet space race inappropriate and possibly misleading (Aliberti, 2015), many of the ingredients that defined competition in the original space race (competition for international prestige or soft power, competition for hard power and competition for the provision of public goods) (Suzuki, 2013), seem already present in the current dynamics. In addition, irrespective of whether current dynamics fit the parameters of a space race, the progressive bifurcation of the international space community around two different undertakings is in any case bound to amplify the current rhetoric, steering public perceptions towards one such scenario and further fuelling the already looming competition patterns.

As in the case of the first space race, such competition trends will not only materialise with regards to the achievements of space firsts (the first woman on the Moon, the first permanent outpost, the first commercial facilities, etc.), but also with regards to the role of "dispenser" of space cooperation. The opening of the ILRS to international cooperation clearly echoes the partnerships the United States is building through its Artemis Accords and already pinpoints this looming (zero-sum) competition for winning partners for their endeavours. Both the US and China/Russia have indeed already started to compete and instrumentalize programmatic cooperation by linking it to third countries' acceptance of their respective normative visions for managing exploration activities.

Through the Artemis Accords, the US has already signed bilateral agreements with several countries willing not only to engage with NASA on a programmatic level, but also disposed to accept US-defined principles, guidelines, and best practices to manage future lunar activities. With these Accords, the US has been more specifically providing a legal interpretation of international space treaties that is not universally shared and thus invoking for itself the role of norm legislator, an activity that would normally be carried through a more inclusive debate within the UN framework.

On their side, China and Russia have not yet secured the official participation of third countries, but within the inter-agency joint working group of the ILRS they have established a legal unit to look into the applicable international law and consider appropriate governance instruments for the future lunar activities.

Independently from the eventual outlook of the partnership configurations, the freezing of lunar activities around two concurrent undertakings can be more importantly expected to generate harmful spillover effects, amplifying the present state of mutual mistrust and misperceptions over respective space activities and in turn making current diplomatic efforts towards international norm- and rule-setting more cumbersome. The positioning and voting results of recent UN resolutions confirm this trend, with China and Russia voting against Western-sponsored resolutions, and US and friends opposing China and Russia initiatives (e.g., the UK-led process on "Reducing space threats through norms, rules and principles of responsible behaviours" versus the Russia-sponsored resolution "No first placement of weapons in outer space").[1]

The concurrent implementation Artemis and ILRS programmes may even lead to the implementation of potentially incompatible principles, norms and rules for managing future lunar activities. There are few governance structures for managing future lunar activities. With the Artemis Accords, the US has been trying to establish some set of norms and rules that can fill the void left by international law. Their content, however, remains contentious (even for some of the US closest allies) and has been widely criticised by Russia and China (ESPI, 2020). While it remains to be seen whether the ILRS project will be connected to the acceptance by future partners of specific governance principles in the same way the Artemis Accords did (and whether these principles will be fundamentally different from those promoted by the US) contention over outstanding issues such as space resources utilization/exploitation, creation of safety zone and the deconfliction of activities may be further exacerbated and create difficult scenarios once the three superpowers will eventually get to the Moon.

8.3   On the Moon: A More Challenging Interaction

The most important implications stemming from the freezing of future lunar exploration activities around two opposing blocs can indeed be expected once the three superpowers get to the Moon and strategic interaction among them will sensibly increase. The exploration and human settlement of uncharted territories has always

---

[1] A report of the positioning and voting within the UN First Committee can be found in West J (2021).

proved challenging, particularly when interaction among the actors involved is loosely regulated, as in the case of lunar exploration activities.

There are so far limited agreed-upon rules governing strategic interaction in space and on celestial bodies, including the Moon. The basic set of principles, norms and rules, or more simply regime (Krasner, 1982), for governing such interaction have been codified in the five international treaties found in UNOOSA (2017), which concluded between 1967 and 1979, namely: the 1967 *Outer Space Treaty*; the 1968 *Rescue and Return Agreement*; the 1972 *Liability Convention*; the 1975 *Registration Convention*; and the 1979 *Moon Agreement*. This latter agreement, which would provide more specific regulations for the management of celestial bodies and create a Seabed Authority-like organisation, has essentially been rejected by the international community, having been ratified by 18 states, all of which remarkably are not spacefaring nations. Other agreements and soft law instruments have in the following decades been adopted, but the core of the international space regime has remained more or less unaltered.

What is equally striking is that despite having been formulated more than 50 years ago, this regime has worked well to the present. From a neo-realist perspective, this resilience does not stem from the fact that all fundamental principles and norms have been embraced by everyone, nor by the fact that all issues have been solved. Rather it is because the limited number of actors operating in space and their low levels of interaction has not required the creation of a very intrusive regime (Aliberti & Krasner, 2016). For many space activities, including those related the Moon exploration, individual states have been basically able to do what they want without damaging the interests of others. Lunar activities, be them human or robotic, have thus far entailed situations characterised by a substantial harmony of interests, i.e., situations in which actors do not need to take into account the interests of others to maximise their own utility and that of the system as a whole.

One such configuration of interest, very rare in shared environments like the high seas, can be more specifically explained with the fact that strategic interaction in space has been historically limited and power asymmetries greater than in any other field of human interaction. This "situation has generally enabled the more powerful states to secure their first best outcome through unilateral action. Consequently, the incentives to establish and maintain international regimes have been lower and, not surprisingly, the institutional arrangements that have been agreed to in the basic space treaties have sanctioned the freedom of use and access to the space environment for civil, commercial and even military activities" (Aliberti & Krasner, 2016).

In those limited areas where individual decision-making could cause collective problems, relatively simple and self-enforcing coordination regimes have been established to ensure stability.[2] But even where more stringent restrictions have been accepted, these have not, at least to date, imposed real constraint upon the actors. For instance, according to Article IX of the OST, states need to observe due

---

[2]A clear case is offered by ITU regime for managing the allocation of the radio-spectrum and preventing signal interference that would leave all parties worse off.

regard for the activities of other actors. This principle, however, has never been clearly defined in terms of specific obligations and has not prevented states from engaging in activities they wanted (including debris-generating anti-satellite tests weapons that pose a threat to everyone's space safety). The OST also bars states party to the treaty from asserting sovereignty over bodies in outer space. While potentially impactful for the richest and most technologically advanced states, this concession has been so far costless, considering the state of technology. Similarly, according to article IV states cannot place weapons of mass destruction or create military instalments on celestial bodies. This provision, like denying sovereign claims in space, can greatly affect the powerful states but also, like the denial or sovereignty, the acceptance of this provision has at least to date been costless. Weapons of mass destruction in space or the establishment of military outposts on celestial bodies would be costly and would not alter the relative position of the competitors.

This relatively benign interaction, however, can neither be taken to mean that the present regime for space has eliminated potential for conflict nor that it can continue indefinitely. As space technology advances and missions to the Moon multiply, strategic interaction will increase, and with that the possibility that the interests of the actors involved will collide. This will create – in fact it has already –a more pressing need for putting in place some more specific set of principles, norms and rules to govern expectations of behaviour over potentially contentious issues (Masson-Zwaan & Sundahl, 2021; Salmeri, 2021). The current governance structures are notoriously insufficient and agreement would be needed provide solutions to what Stein called dilemmas of common interest or aversion, i.e., situations in which actors need to eschew unrestrained decision making to achieve outcomes that are not individually accessible (Stein, 1982).

Absent some developments regarding international governance of lunar activities, the risk of conflict is inevitably bound to increase, especially in those areas where disagreement is already patent (Salmeri, 2021). There are multiple issue-areas where future strategic interaction on the Moon can be expected to confront the actors with problems of coordination and cooperation (dilemmas of commons aversion/interests) or precipitate *tout court* in a zero-sum conflict. These are more specifically the ones pertaining to safety, security and sustainability of the lunar environment, all objectives that cannot be reached through unilateral action by the actors involved and where without a converge in behaviour, everyone could be worse off.

8.3.1 Lunar Safety

The growth in human and robotic activities by an increasing number of actors, often operating in the same area given the specific topography of the Moon, can be expected to create a situation in which the activities of one actor can inadvertently hamper the safety or directly threaten the security of other actors. There can be multiple sources of unintentional harm, ranging from radiofrequency transmissions to the dust blast produced by landing craft and the possible explosion of hazardous materials.

Absent some general agreement on how to minimize these risks of interferences, there easily could be conflict. As also stressed by Gilbert "unless lunar actors are able to successfully exchange information to enable proximity operations, the proliferation of space activities could increase the risks of conflict and endanger spacecraft and crews. Successful operations of NewSpace activities on the Moon requires that missions and crews are safe from interference by activities of other entities. Some deconfliction tool may be needed" (Gilbert, 2022).

Anticipating these risks, with the Artemis Accords the United States has sought to create a community of like-minded countries to establish "safety zones" around landing sites. Specifically, Section 9 of the Accords commit the signatories to provide notification of their activities and coordinate with any relevant actor to avoid harmful interference. The Accords more specifically state that:

> The area wherein this notification and coordination will be implemented to avoid harmful interference is referred to as a 'safety zone'. A safety zone should be the area in which nominal operations of a relevant activity or an anomalous event could reasonably cause harmful interference. The Signatories intend to observe the following principles related to safety zones:
>
> a) The size and scope of the safety zone, as well as the notice and coordination, should reflect the nature of the operations being conducted and the environment that such operations are conducted in;
> b) The size and scope of the safety zone should be determined in a reasonable manner leveraging commonly accepted scientific and engineering principles;
> c) The nature and existence of safety zones is expected to change over time reflecting the status of the relevant operation. If the nature of an operation changes, the operating Signatory should alter the size and scope of the corresponding safety zone as appropriate. Safety zones will ultimately be temporary, ending when the relevant operation ceases; and
> d) The Signatories should promptly notify each other as well as the Secretary-General of the United Nations of the establishment, alteration, or end of any safety zone, consistent with Article XI of the Outer Space Treaty (NASA, 2020).

Whilst the primary objective of safety zones is to enable actors to minimize risks to space missions operating nearby, their unilateral creation could be easily interpreted as *de facto* occupation or even ownership of areas of the lunar surface, which is outlawed by the OST. As Vazhapully (2020) contends, should safety zones prevent access to areas in the lunar surface to any actor, they would violate provisions of the OST.

Similar considerations may hold true for the increasingly debated protection of historical sites on the Moon. The importance of these sites has been acknowledged by many in the space community (these sites are truly the cradle of our extraterrestrial civilization) and there is a debate on whether these sites should be considered human heritage and hence be protected from unintentional or intentional impairments (Hanlon, 2021). However, the creation of protection instruments remains politically challenging. As also recognised by the White House Office for

Science and Technology Policy in a 2018 report on the matter, "some states might see a US-led attempt to protect space artifacts as a subterfuge for securing indefinite rights over lunar territory, and perhaps even creating a mechanism "to plant the flag" and claim additional territory in the future under the guide of the protection and preservation of lunar site and artefacts." (OSTP, 2018).

Given the possible fallouts associated with the creation of what in the final analysis are exclusion zones, it is not surprising that soon after the announcement of the signature of the Artemis Accords by the first eight partners, the then head of Roscosmos accused the US of trying to bypass core provisions of the OST with the accords (Clark, 2020). A similar concern was voiced by Chinese stakeholders (Lan, 2020; Zhen, 2020).

With one such disquiet already in place, the risks for misunderstanding, miscalculations and even mishaps are all but bound to increase when the astronauts of the two main undertakings start operating on the Moon, likely not too far away from one another. Questions do abound. For instance, would China and Russia accept the size and scope of the safety zone defined by the US for its Base Camp should it overlap with a future ISLR landing site? Who should then have preference and who should decide? Would a first-come-first-served approach be the best to determine who has the right to establish a safety zone? Should the size of a safety zone expand over time and result in a permanent occupation, would a non-signatory of the Artemis Accords be able to access its perimeter and conduct activities therein? Would it be liable for damage should its spacecraft interfere with the activities happening in such a unilaterally declared zone?

All these are outstanding questions that cannot be solved through unilateral actions or minilateral settings. They at least require all relevant actors to coordinate behaviours in order to avoid interference risks, facilitate safe lunar operations (landings, take-offs, transfers, etc.) and ideally establish standards promoting interoperability. The creation of an ICAO-like coordination mechanism has been for instance advanced to insure such coordination (Garretson, 2022).

However, while all actors may be better off with some rules in place that minimize safety risks, they are not and cannot be indifferent to the specific set of rules that should be put in place. Agreement, as the very signature of the Artemis Accords demonstrates, may be easier among like-minded partners. But is less so among political rivals that nurture mistrust in each other's activities. It is hence maintained that the unfolding polarisation of exploration efforts will make the pursuit of such agreement less likely.

8.3.2 Lunar Security

Even more likely sources of conflict are those bound to emerge regarding future lunar security. There remains much scope for ambiguity and cherry-picking within the current international regime dealing with security matters.

On the one hand, article IV of the OST creates an obligation to use the Moon and other celestial bodies for "exclusively peaceful purposes", with peaceful generally understood as non-aggressive, rather than non-military. The article also clearly maintains that "the establishment of military bases, installations and fortifications, the testing of any type of weapons and the conduct of military manoeuvres on celestial bodies shall be forbidden" (OST, 1967).

On the other hand, the article allows "the use of military personnel for scientific research or for any other peaceful purposes", thus allowing future astronauts, cosmonauts and taikonauts to be military officers.[3] The provision additionally maintains that "the use of any equipment or facility necessary for peaceful exploration of the moon and other celestial bodies shall also not be prohibited" (OST, 1967).

The latent tension and potential scope for diverging interpretations has always been visible (Schrogl & Neuman, 2009), but the lack of human missions to the Moon over the past 50 years contributed to silencing the issue. The upcoming return of humans on the Moon, however, is now sparking a new debate over what would qualify as compliance and what might be a violation.

Drawing a line between a peaceful and non-peaceful use will likely become harder. For instance, would a Moon installation operated by Chinese or Russian military personnel qualify as a violation of the space treaty? This is unlikely. Would it be perceived as non-threatening? This is also unlikely. On a similar vein, would a technology demonstration activity undertaken by military personnel qualify as a non-peaceful activity under current international law? This is hardly so. At the same time, would it heighten threat perceptions in other countries? This seems very likely.

Given the dual-use nature of most space technologies, determining intent is often impossible, an occurrence that generates worst-case assessments and security dilemmas. With these dilemmas spiralling upwards, the risks of a progressive militarisation of human lunar activities may be all but inevitable.

Even though all actors may in principle share an interest in avoiding a costly and dangerous militarisation by agreeing on a set of behavioural norms and rules, mutual mistrust would also require the creation of verification and enforcement mechanisms. Like much of current space security debates, upholding security and strategic stability on the Moon will raise key issues related to compliance and policing, in addition to norm- and rule-setting. Simply agreeing what constitutes compliance and what on the contrary represent irresponsible actions or activities would not per se suffice to dispel threat perceptions. Only an institutionalised regime of cooperation, with clearly defined rules that all actors agree and proper enforcement mechanisms that define, monitor and make cheating unaffordable, can properly manage expectations of behaviours and ensure that future lunar activities will pursue peaceful purposes only.

Such elaborated governance structures may be arguably less needed among partners sharing both a programmatic and normative agenda. But within a polarised

---

[3] A 2020 memo between NASA and the Space Force in 2020 already alluded to one such development by highlighting the importance of a closer NASA-Space Force collaboration for operating safely and securely on these distant frontiers (NASA, & USSF, 2020).

community the creation of such a regime will simultaneously become more needed and more difficult to agree upon.

8.3.3 Lunar Sustainability

Long term human presence on the Moon will also raise questions related to the environmental impact that lunar missions will have on the lunar environment and its long-term sustainability. Beyond the applicability of the UN Long-Term Sustainability Guidelines to future Moon missions, what comes under growing scrutiny are the issues related to production, storage, logistics and disposal of lunar resources.

There is wide consensus that in order to operate on the Moon in a cost-effective and sustainable manner, future astronauts will need to significantly reduce their reliance upon Earth-sourced resources. However, operations in shared environments, be they common goods or common pool, often raise concerns related to the overexploitation of their natural resources. On the Moon these concerns are amplified by the fact the lunar environment does not have regeneration systems that allow it to recover from anthropogenic consumptions.

Equally important, the exploitation of lunar resources remains another issue characterised by disagreement about basic principles and norms, and for which the position of the space powers is bound to clash, especially in light of the international community's rejection of the Moon Treaty. The very definition of space resources and utilisation thereof is problematic, as it can either refer to an in-situ resource utilisation, which is considered a lawful activity pursuant article I of the OST, or the much more debatable commercial exploitation of those resources. What is in particular contentious and subject to different interpretations (de Zwart, 2022; Kyriakopulos, 2018; Su, 2017) is the conformity of a commercial exploitation with article II of the OST and general customary international law, which envisage a general prohibition of appropriation by any means.

Against these uncertainties, the United States has enacted a national legal and regulatory framework which provides that private companies may be entitled to exploit space resources and retain ownership rights over them (US House of Representatives, 2015). In April 2020, the Trump administration also issued an executive order that called for a rejection of the 1979 *Moon Agreement* and the notion that space is a global commons (The White House, 2020). It also urged the US government to lead substantial diplomatic efforts with a view to establish, with a community of like-minded partners, the necessary norms and rules for making exploiting space resources on the Moon and elsewhere possible. As reported by Sheldon (2020), Trump's order "sparked a fierce international debate and it is an indication that the current diplomatic and legal arrangements governing commercial space activities relating to space resource extraction, as well as the status of the Moon and other celestial bodies, might yet be disrupted". The US government, however, clarified that it is not claiming sovereignty over celestial bodies and that the Act will be interpreted and applied in accordance with US obligations under international law. In the Artemis Accords, it further re-affirmed that: "the extraction of space resources does not inherently constitute national appropriation under Article II of the Outer Space Treaty, and that contracts and other legal instruments relating to space resources should be consistent with that Treaty" (NASA, 2020).

This position and interpretation of the OST has been questioned by several nations, including European ones (UNOOSA, 2018). The most vocal opposition, though, has been expressed by Russia. Since the enactment of US legislation in 2015, Russian delegates have voiced concerns at UNCOPUOS, deeming illegitimate the unilateral adoption of space legislation governing space resources. According to Russian statements at UNCOPUOS, resources are celestial bodies and therefore subject to the prohibition expressed in Article II of the OST.

Albeit in a more discrete fashion, China has also expressed some reservations (Shen, 2021; He, 2019). As more broadly reported by Weeden (2015): "On the topic of sovereignty in space and utilization of space resources, China has consistently echoed the perspective of developing countries that space is the *common heritage of all humankind*, and any extraction and use of space resources should be done in an equitable manner and consistent with an international framework".

An international framework like the one put in place by United Nations Convention on the Law of the Sea (UNCLOS) was the solution the *Moon Agreement* envisaged to ensure that the exploitation of the Moon and its resources would be carried out in a way that takes into account the interests of less advanced actors and benefits all countries. But none of the major players has been supportive of the approach, thus exacerbating disagreement and the potential for conflict.

Like for other areas where the interests of the developed countries clashed with the ones of developing states, power and prime mover advantage will determine outcomes. Specifically, should powerful actors be able to secure their preferred outcome by acting unilaterally, there will be no basis for building a regime, and an interpretation of international law will be offered to ensure that commercial exploitation falls within the remit of freedom of use principle. Already at the 2021 UNCOPUOS Legal Subcommittee, the head of US delegation made it plain that: "at this stage, the United States sees neither a need nor a practical basis to create such a regime" (UNCOPUOS, 2021).

Aggrieved actors will then be left with few margins of manoeuvre. Would for instance a state be willing to attack the operations of a firm operating under US law on the lunar surface? Absent some more general conflict, this seems unlikely. Would another state be willing to bring suit against minerals or products produced by such a firm if these minerals or products came under its jurisdiction? This seems more likely. And irrespective of how these disputes will be solved, would the lack of agreement intensify competition for the exploitation of resource-rich areas (Goswami & Garretson, 2020)? Would unrestrained individual exploitation eventually lead to a scramble for resources and end-up in a tragedy of the commons? These seem equally plausible fallouts in the longer term.

As in the case of lunar security, actors will be confronted with a dilemma of common interest. The literature on international regimes (Krasner, 1982; Stein, 1982) shows that such dilemmas can be properly solved only through the establishment of an institutionally entrenched cooperation regime; a regime that a polarised space community would unfortunately make very hard to build.

8.4 Conclusions

Activities in outer space, human spaceflight undertakings in particular, continue to maintain a very symbolic value, alternatively serving as an emblem of international cooperation and conflict. In the past, the world has experienced both the space race between the Soviet Union and the US and their "handshake in space" when a Soyuz capsule docked with an Apollo spacecraft. Today, the growing geopolitical tensions here on Earth seem to steer the international space community towards a new contest scenario.

Irrespective of whether the unfolding dynamics fit the defining parameters of the original space race, the progressive polarisation of the international lunar exploration efforts is bound to generate far-reaching spillover effects that will impact international relations not only here on Earth but also on the Moon itself.

The way humans will go back to the Moon will inevitably reverberate on the way they will interact once they reach the Moon. The looming polarisation and competition dynamics between the US-led and China/Russia-led Moon endeavours will more specifically confront the major powers with a more challenging interaction and likely signal the passage from what Sheldon calls *Lunapolitics* into *Lunapolitik*, a scenario where "rival countries adopt a zero-sum approach to their competition with each other, occupying and reoccupying instead of sharing strategic or economically valuable locations on and around the Moon" (Sheldon, 2020).

Such an occurrence can be in turn expected to significantly enhance the risks for misunderstanding, miscalculations and mishaps, ultimately affecting the safety, security and long-term sustainability of the lunar environment.

The possible fallouts of the current competitive dynamics drawn in this chapter are of course not a predetermined dead end, but they most strongly stem from being a self-fulling prophecy.

References

Aliberti, M. (2015). *When China goes to the moon….* Springer.

Aliberti, M., & Krasner, S. D. (2016). Governance in Space. In C. Al-Ekabi et al. (Eds.), *Yearbook on Space policy 2014*. Springer.

Bowen, B. E. (2020). *War in space: Strategy, spacepower, geopolitics*. Edinburgh University Press.

China National Space Administration. (2021). International Lunar Research Station (ILRS) v.1. http://www.cnsa.gov.cn/english/n6465645/n6465648/c6812150/content.html

Clark, S. (2020). Nasa proposals to allow establishment of lunar "safety zones". *The Guardian*. https://www.theguardian.com/science/2020/may/20/nasa-new-space-treaty-artemis-accords-moon-mission-lunar-safety-zones de Zwart, M. (2022). The impact of the Artemis accords on resource extraction. In V. Hessel et al. (Eds.), *In-space manufacturing and resources: Earth and planetary exploration applications*. WILEY-VCH GmbH.

de Zwart, M., & Stephens, D. (2019). The Space (innovation) race: The inevitable relationship between military technology and innovation. *Melbourne Journal of International Law, 20*(1), 1–28.

ESPI (European Space Policy Institute). (2019). *China is one step closer to the moon... and Europe?* (ESPI Executive Brief n.28). https://www.espi.or.at/briefs/china-is-one-step-closer-to-the-moon-and-europe/

ESPI (European Space Policy Institute). (2020). *Artemis accords: What implications for Europe?* (ESPI Executive Brief n.46). https://www.espi.or.at/briefs/artemis-accords-what-implications-for-europe/

Foust, J. (2020). Russia skeptical about participating in lunar gateway. *SpaceNews*. https://spacenews.com/russia-skeptical-about-participating-in-lunar-gateway/

Foust, J. (2022). ESA ends cooperation with Russia on lunar missions. *SpaceNews*. https://spacenews.com/esa-ends-cooperation-with-russia-on-lunar-missions/

Garretson, P. (2022). An ICAO for the moon: It's time for an international civil lunar organization. *The Space Review*.

Gilbert, A. Q. (2022). *Safety zones for lunar activities under the Artemis accords*. Open Lunar Foundation.

Goswami, N. (2022). *The second Space race. Democratic outcomes for the future of Space*. Georgetown Journal of International Affairs. https://gjia.georgetown.edu/2022/01/25/the-second-space-race-democratic-outcomes-for-the-future-of-space/

Goswami, N., & Garretson, P. A. (2020). *Scramble for the skies: The great power competition to control the resources of outer Space*. Lexington Books.

Hanlon, M. (2021). "Due Regard" for commercial space must start with historic preservation. *The Global Business Law Review, 9*(1), 130–156.

Harrison, T., & Johnson, K. (2017). *Back to the moon? Understanding Trump's Space policy directive 1*. Center for Strategic and International Studies. https://www.csis.org/analysis/back-moon-understanding-trumps-space-policy-directive-1

He, Q. (2019). 新一轮月球竞赛与太空治理的前景 [A new round of the moon race and the prospects of space governance]. 外交评论 *[Diplomatic Review], 3*(1), 120–154.

Hunter, C. (2019). The forgotten first iteration of the 'Chinese Space threat' to US National Security. *Space Policy, 47*(1), 158–165.

Johnson, K. (2022). *Fly me to the moon: Worldwide Cislunar and Lunar missions*. Center for Strategic and International Studies.

Jones, A. (2021). China, Russia open moon base project to international partners, early details emerge. *SpaceNews*. https://spacenews.com/china-russia-open-moon-base-project-to-international-partners-early-details-emerge/

Krasner, S. D. (1982). Structural causes and regime consequences: Regimes as intervening variables. *International Organization, 36*(2), 185–205.

Kulacki, G. (2011). US and China need contact, not cold war. *Nature, 474*(7352), 444–445. https://doi.org/10.1038/474444a

Kyriakopulos, G. (2018). *Legal regimes for a sustainable Space resource utilization*.

Lan, S. (2020). 警惕美在月球上演'圈地运动' [Watching the 'enclosures movement' that the US is staging on the Moon]. 解放军报 *[People's Liberation Army Daily]* 4 (April 14).

Masson-Zwaan, T., & Sundahl, M. J. (2021). The lunar legal landscape: Challenges and opportunities. *Air and Space Law, 46*(1), 29–56.

NASA, & USSF (National Aeronautics and Space Administration). (2020). *Memorandum of understanding between the national aeronautics and space administration and the United States space force*. https://www.nasa.gov/sites/default/files/atoms/files/nasa_ussf_mou_21_sep_20.pdf

NASA (National Aeronautics and Space Administration). (2020). *The Artemis Accords*. https://www.nasa.gov/specials/artemis-accords/index.html

NASA (National Aeronautics and Space Administration). (2021). Artemis Partners. Artemis Program. https://www.nasa.gov/content/artemis-partners

OST (Outer Space Treaty). (1967). Article IV In Treaty on Principles Governing the Activities of States in the Exploration and Use of Outer Space, including the Moon and Other Celestial Bodies (1967, January 27). 18 U.S.T. 2410, 610 U.N.T.S. 205 (entered into force 10 October 1967).

OSTP (Office of Science and Technology Policy). (2018). *Protecting & preserving Apollo program lunar landing sites & artifacts*. https://www.whitehouse.gov/wp-content/uploads/2018/03/Protecting-and-Preserving-Apollo-Program-Lunar-Landing-Sites-and-Artifacts-2.pdf

Rajagopalan, R. P. (2018). Opinion | The global space race, 2.0. *The Washington Post*. https://www.washingtonpost.com/news/theworldpost/wp/2018/02/13/space-race/

Russian News Agency. (2022). From international to national: Russia to leave ISS project after 2024. *Tass*. https://tass.com/

Salmeri, A. (2021). *Effective and adaptive governance for a lunar ecosystem*. Space Generation Advisory Council. https://spacegeneration.org/wp-content/uploads/2021/12/EAGLE-Report.pdf

Schrogl, K., & Neuman, J. (2009). Article VI. In Hobe et al. (Eds.), *Cologne commentary on Space Law, Vol. I: Outer space treaty* (pp. 70–93). Carl Heymans.

Seedhouse, E. (2010). *The new Space rage – China vs. the United States*. Springer.

Sheldon, J. B. (2020). #SpaceWatchGL opinion: Lunapolitics or Lunapolitik? *The Choice Is Ours*. https://spacewatch.global/2020/05/spacewatch-gl-opinion-lunapolitics-or-lunapolitik-the-choice-is-ours/

Shen, P. (2021). 论美国对《月球协定》及外空资源开发的政策演变" [On the evolution of the US policy towards the "Moon agreement" and the development of outer space resources]. 太平洋学报 [*Pacific Journal*] 29 (4): 15–26.

Stein, A. A. (1982). Coordination and collaboration: Regimes in an anarchic world. *International Regimes, 36*(2), 299–324.

Su, J. (2017). Legality of unilateral exploitation of space resources under international law. *International and Comparative Law Quarterly, 66*(4), 991–1008.

Suzuki, K. (2013). The contest for leadership in East Asia: Japanese and Chinese approaches to outer space. *Space Policy, 29*(2), 99–106.

The White House. (2020). *Executive order on encouraging international support for the recovery and use of Space resources*. Infrastructure & Technology – Executive Orders. https://trumpwhitehouse.archives.gov/presidential-actions/executive-order-encouraging-international-support-recovery-use-space-resources/

UNCOPUOS (United Nations Committee on the Peaceful Uses of Outer Space). (2017). *Thematic priority 1. Global partnership in space exploration and innovation* (pp. 432–633). International Organization.

UNCOPUOS (United Nations Committee on the Peaceful Uses of Outer Space). (2021). *Agenda item 14 – General exchange of views on potential legal models for activities in the exploration, exploitation and utilization of space resources*. Legal Subcommittee.

UNOOSA (United Nations Office for Outer Space Affairs). (2017). *International Space Law: United Nations Instruments*. https://www.unoosa.org/oosa/en/ourwork/spacelaw/treaties.html

UNOOSA (United Nations Office for Outer Space Affairs). (2018). *Committee on the peaceful uses of outer space: Legal Subcommittee, 57th session*. https://www.unoosa.org/oosa/audio/v3/index-staging.jspx

US Congress. (2011). *Department of Defense and Full-Year Continuing Appropriations Act. Congressional Records*. https://www.congress.gov/112/plaws/publ10/PLAW-112publ10.htm

US House of Representatives. (2015). *Space Resource Exploration and Utilization Act of 2015*. https://www.govinfo.gov/content/pkg/CRPT-114hrpt153/pdf/CRPT-114hrpt153.pdf

US Subcommittee on Space, Committee on Science. (2017). *Are we losing the Space race to China?* US Government Printing Office.

Vazhapully, K. M. (2020). *Space law at the crossroads: Contextualizing the Artemis Accords and the Space resources executive order*. Opinio Juris. http://opiniojuris.org/2020/07/22/space-law-at-the-crossroads-contextualizing-the-artemis-accords-and-the-space-resources-executive-order/

Weeden, B. (2015). *Hearing on China in Space: A strategic competition?* US-China Economic and Security Review Commission.

West, J. (2021). Outer Space. *First Committee Monitor, 19*(5), 27–29.

Zhang, Y. (2013). The eagle eyes the dragon in space-A critique. *Space Policy, 29*(2), 113–120.

Zhen, L. (2020). China, US space rivalry may heat up after Nasa's Artemis Accords signed, analysts say. *South China Morning Post*. https://www.scmp.com/news/china/diplomacy/article/3105722/china-us-space-rivalry-may-heat-after-nasas-artemis-accords?module=perpetual_scroll_0&pgtype=article&campaign=3105722

Milton Keynes UK
Ingram Content Group UK Ltd.
UKHW031659310124
437030UK00006BA/229